in
Central New York

Hikes and Backpacking Trips from the Western Adirondacks to the Finger Lakes

WILLIAM P. EHLING

Photographs by the author

Second Edition

BACK COUNTRY

Backcountry Guides
Woodstock, Vermont

An Invitation to the Reader

Over time trails can be rerouted and signs and landmarks altered. If you find that changes have occurred on the routes described in this book, please let us know so that corrections may be made in future editions. The author and publisher also welcome other comments and suggestions. Address all correspondence to:

Editor
50 Hikes Series™
Backcountry Guides
PO Box 748
Woodstock, VT 05091

Library of Congress Cataloging-in-Publication Data
Ehling, William P. (William Philip), 1920–
    50 hikes in central New York: hikes and backpacking trips from the western Adirondacks to the Finger Lakes / William P. Ehling;
    photographs by the author. — 2nd ed.
        p.   cm.
    Includes bibliographical references.
    ISBN 0-88150-329-0
    1. Hiking—New York (State)—Guidebooks. 2. Backpacking—New York (State)—Guidebooks. 3. Cross-country skiing—New York (State) 4. Snowshoes and snowshoeing—New York (State)—Guidebooks. 5. New York (State)—Guidebooks. I. Title. II. Title: Fifty hikes in central New York.
GV199.42.N65E37   1995   94–47506
796.5'09747—dc20   CIP

Published by Backcountry Guides,
a division of The Countryman Press,
PO Box 748, Woodstock, VT 05091.

Distributed by W.W. Norton & Company, Inc.,
500 Fifth Avenue, New York, NY 10110.

Cover photograph by Peter Finger
Series design by Glenn Suokko
Cover design by Glenn Suokko
Map overlays by Richard Widhu, © 1995 The Countryman Press
Text Formatting by Nathaniel Stout

Printed in the United States of America
10 9

DEDICATION

To my children, Teresa, James, and Clare. May the accounts herein add
to their love of green hills and forest glens and to their joy of hiking their
own part of the world.

ACKNOWLEDGMENTS

A book like this is made possible by others, those with the foresight and dedication
to preserve the land, plant the seedlings that have become today's forests, and con-
struct the footpaths that allow us to walk the hills, glens, and ravines of this region.
To all those—the individual trailbuilder, the concerned environmentalist, the official in charge of our public lands—my sincerest thanks. There are many others to
whom I am indebted, those who many years ago introduced me to some of the trails
covered in this book and those many friends with whom I have hiked throughout
Central New York. I thank Olga, with whom I have hiked many of these trails and
who shared with me the demands of this book, the frequent discomforts of pesky in-
sects along the trail, but in the final analysis the excitement of still another hike in a
new place. Finally, my thanks to the people who made possible what is today the Finger Lakes Trail, one of the most atractive trail systems in New York State, to my
friends of the Onondaga Chapter of the Adirondack Mountain Club, and to all the
people in the New York State Department of Environmental Conservation who provide vital information and great personal assistance.

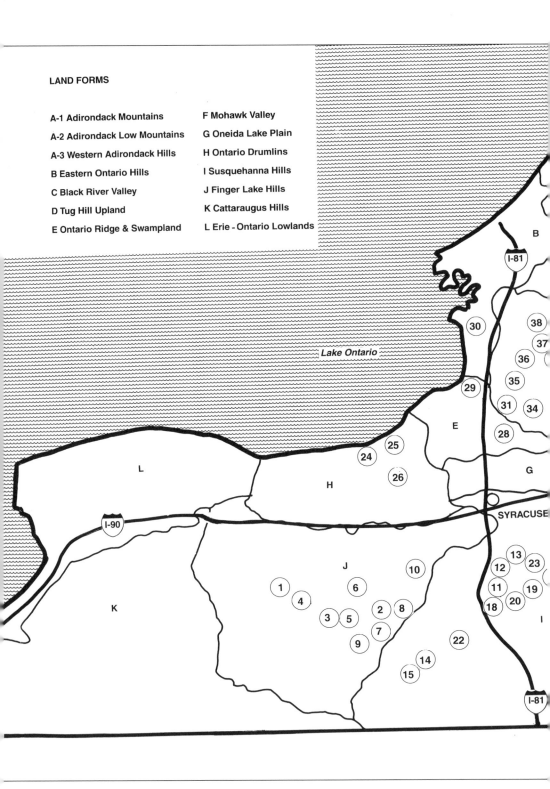

LAND FORMS

A-1 Adirondack Mountains
A-2 Adirondack Low Mountains
A-3 Western Adirondack Hills
B Eastern Ontario Hills
C Black River Valley
D Tug Hill Upland
E Ontario Ridge & Swampland

F Mohawk Valley
G Oneida Lake Plain
H Ontario Drumlins
I Susquehanna Hills
J Finger Lake Hills
K Cattaraugus Hills
L Erie - Ontario Lowlands

Lake Ontario

CONTENTS

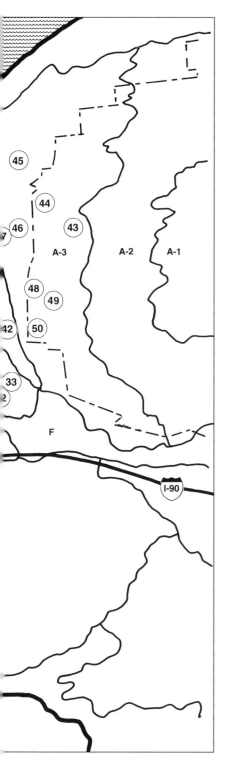

INTRODUCTION

FINGER LAKES HILLS

SUSQUEHANNA HILLS

ONTARIO DRUMLINS AND HILLS

TUG HILL

WESTERN ADIRONDACK HILLS

Map Symbols	
——	main trail
- - -	side trail
℗	parking
⋔⋔	view
⨯	picnic tables
⋔	shelter
|||	waterfall
△	campsite

INTRODUCTION

In Central New York, you need never go far to find a marked trail or public land on which to hike. Foot travel in this part of New York is always an adventure, a trek into new places, and hence always a pleasure.

As you hike the many trails of this region, you are struck not only by the area's attractiveness but also by its diversity. While other regions in New York State and throughout the Northeast, of course, can make the same claim, it is perhaps the richness of the diversity and the sharp contrasts amid it that somehow set Central New York apart.

There is the varied landscape that ranges from the low, rolling forested hills of the Western Adirondacks in the northeast to wide, sandy beaches found along the east shore of Lake Ontario, and extends from the deep blue waters of the Finger Lakes in the west to the deep, wide valleys in the southeast where the Tioughnioga, Otselic, Chenango, Unadilla, and Susquehanna Rivers flow.

It is a region of prosperous-looking farms and attractive villages, as well as narrow urban corridors running from Herkimer in the east to Rochester in the west in the region's midsection and from Binghamton in the east to Bath in the west in the region's Southern Tier. It is a place of vineyards and forested hilltops, summer theaters and religious pageants, boat cruises and canoe races, beach resorts and ski centers.

Yet amid all these signs of civilization you find vast tracts of public lands, thick forests, and miles of foot trails, a quite rural setting that shades into the more rugged grandeur of the backcountry regions where unbroken forests run for miles. Even in a single region, the landscape can prove surprisingly varied. In the flat plain region between Rochester and Syracuse are hundreds of hillocks that mark the presence of hundreds of glacier-produced drumlins, and in the rolling hill country north and south of Syracuse you suddenly encounter breathtakingly deep gorges.

Central New York has a natural richness that you will enjoy in silence and solitude during a day's walk or a weekend outing.

Area and Location. While for those living in the region, Central New York is a well established geographic entity, the reality may be that Central New York is in part a state of mind. The configuration of the state, which almost resembles a boot, doesn't help matters, nor does the designation of local regions by their own names. Lacking the rectangular shape of, say, Pennsylvania or Massachusetts, New York doesn't allow you easily to mark off an area that can be delimited as "central."

Generally, the land surrounding Syracuse is treated as central, but just how far outward this central region goes is not clear. No matter. For the purposes of this book, the eastern boundary of the territory in which the 50 hiking areas are located can be specified by drawing a line from Potsdam in the north through Herkimer in the Mohawk Valley past the western tip of the Catskill Forest

Author standing beside state forest sign

Preserve; this is approximately the same as the 75° longitude line. The boundary on the west is at the 77° 33' longitude mark running south a little to the east of Rochester and through Cohocton in the central area.

In between are the Finger Lakes Region, the elusive central region, the Tug Hill Region, and the Western Adirondack Region—and some of the most scenic landscape in upstate New York.

To put the matter even more simply, all the hiking trails described in this book lie within a 75-mile radius of Syracuse, making it possible to reach every trailhead in about 1½ hours of driving time from there. The region covers 19,000 square miles, including urban and rural areas, farmlands and forestlands, lowlands with elevations of only 260 feet above sea level, and highlands with hilltops exceeding 2000 feet, some of the highest spots west of the high peaks region of the Adirondack Mountains.

Topography and Geology. The topography of this region is shaped by the underlying bedrock and the scouring and erosional action of several continental glaciers that overrode New York State during the Pleistocene period more than 12,000 years ago. It was the glaciers in their forward movement that rounded off the top of hills and mountains and deepened the valleys to give them their unique U-shapes, and it was during deglaciation that glacial meltwaters produced the varied landforms that include gorges, cross-channels, kettle lakes, eskers, kames, plunge pools, valley-head moraines, and outwash plains.

Geologically, four classes of bedrock can be found in this region. In the Western Adirondacks are found igneous and metamorphic rocks, in the Tug Hill Re-

gion sandstone overlaying shale and shaly sandstone, and in the central area and the Finger Lakes Region limestone.

Included in this territory are 10 different landform regions. South of present-day I-90 (New York State Thruway) are two large regions, roughly divided by I-81 and NY 13 to make up the Susquehanna Hills Region in the east and the Finger Lakes Hills Region in the west. These two regions constitute better than half of the state's Appalachian Uplands—a highland region where hills reach almost 2000 feet.

North of the Thruway between Rochester and Syracuse is the Ontario Drumlins Region with its countless small hills that look like overturned tea cups or sometimes like loaves of pumpernickel bread.

Immediately east of this region are the Ontario Ridge Swampland Region (encompassing most of Oswego County) and the Oneida Lake Plain Region surrounding Oneida Lake. North of Oneida Lake is the Tug Hill Region, rising ever so steadily from Lake Ontario eastward until it overlooks the Black River Valley from an elevation of 2200 feet, highest spot west of the Adirondack high peaks. Northwest of Tug Hill is the Eastern Ontario Hills Region, while east of the Black River Valley is the Western Adirondack Hills Region.

These landforms provide a varied landscape that includes a land of low relief bordering Lake Ontario, the sometimes rugged-appearing hill country in the Appalachian highlands, and the dense wildernesslike areas in the central Tug Hill Region and the Western Adirondacks.

Weather and Climate. Central New York's weather can be described as moderate, with warm and usually sunny summers and cold winters marked by predominantly overcast skies. You can expect summer temperatures in the 70s and 80s, while in the winter temperatures will be in the 20s and below. In January and February, cold fronts can send the temperature down to 20 degrees below zero or lower. In general, the mean temperature in January is 20 degrees; lowland areas average a few degrees higher, while highland areas such as Tug Hill average 15 degrees.

The mean temperature for July is a comfortable 67 degrees. Especially in late July and early August, however, temperatures can rise into the low 90s. When the thermometer begins to soar, head for the woods in the highland regions. Hiking forest trails, even on a hot day, can prove surprisingly cool and comfortable.

Average precipitation throughout Central New York is quite uniform, with 2.5 to 3.5 inches falling in every month in most places. Total annual snowfall in and around Syracuse averages in excess of 110 inches for most winters. Because of the "lake effect," that is, conditions produced by air passing over Lake Ontario, the Tug Hill Region is the wettest and snowiest in upstate New York; the average snowfall can exceed 250 inches, making this an ideal spot for snowshoeing and cross-country skiing.

Weekend Backpacking and Camping. Virtually all the hiking areas covered in this book lend themselves to weekend backpacking and camping. While most allow camping without advance permits, a few, such as the Connecticut Hill Wildlife Management Area, require advance permits. These permits can be obtained via telephone or letter from the regional office of the Department of Environmental Conservation (DEC). All such camping-by-permit areas have been noted in the book. In areas where no permit is specified, you may camp for a period of 3 days. If you plan to stay longer than that, a permit is required.

In a number of areas, especially along the Finger Lakes Trail (FLT), Adirondack-type lean-tos can accommodate hikers and backpackers planning overnight stays. The locations of any lean-tos on the 50 hikes are reported in the book.

Trailheads and Trails. Many of the trailheads of the 50 hikes, while easy to find, have no signs or markers to tell you where the trail begins. Nonetheless, careful reading of the information under the "access" section for each hike should allow you to reach a trailhead without difficulty.

Of the 50 hikes, 27 are on trails that are groomed, marked, and maintained by state, county, or federal government agencies or by the Finger Lakes Trail Conference (FLTC). The FLTC, in turn, depends on local hiking groups or individuals to mark and maintain sections of the Finger Lakes Trail, which runs from Allegany State Park in the far southwestern corner of the state across the southern part of the Finger Lakes region to the Catskill Forest Preserve in the east.

The remaining 23 hikes, while they are on public lands, use a trail system that is unmarked; here you walk usually on a combination of dirt roads, truck trails, lanes, and jeep trails. The distinction among these man-made routes is not a sharp one, but there are differences. All truck trails, for example, are dirt roads, but not all dirt roads are truck trails.

Truck trail is a technical designation used by the Department of Environmental Conservation to refer to dirt roads built by the state as access routes to its own land holdings. These are excellent roads, well drained and rarely rutted. They usually are a lane-and-a-half wide (sometimes two) to allow heavy-duty vehicles such as logging trucks to drive into state forests.

Dirt roads off state-owned land are usually county maintained. Lanes, on the other hand, are single-lane roads that, while used by vehicles, are not as a general rule maintained by highway departments; some may be maintained by individual landowners.

The distinction between lane and jeep trail is not sharp. Generally, any road on public lands not publicly maintained is designated as a jeep trail on USGS maps. This refers to a single-lane road, frequently rutted, that can be negotiated only by a four-wheel-drive vehicle.

Hiking and Biking. The sites or areas designated in this book have been selected because they provide fine hiking routes or are especially attractive to hikers. Some of these routes are ones constructed and blazed specifically for hiking purposes, such as those found in many state parks and on the Finger Lakes and Interlocken Trails. Other routes take advantage of the state-maintained road system found in all state forest or wildlife management areas; these routes are variously designated as service roads or truck trails.

Many of these routes lend themselves to biking and are used by mountain bikers. In general, hiking and biking are compatible activities, but a word of caution is in order. Not every hiking trail is a good biking route. Some of them entail steep climbs, pass through boulder-filled ravines, or come close to cliff edges. Be sure to consult a USGS topo map

before deciding to bike any of the hiking routes described in this book. Also keep in mind that biking on footpaths during seasonal wet periods or over trails that have soggy sections can be, and usually is, destructive to trails, promoting unnecessary erosion or washouts during rainy and runoff periods.

Although most roads and trails in state forests may be used for biking, some state parks restrict the use of bikes to designated routes or prohibit bikes entirely. Before attempting to bike in a state park be sure to check at the entrance booth for bike-use restrictions.

In the description of hiking areas it will be noted whether mountain biking is allowed or prohibited.

Ski Touring and Snowshoeing. The hiking areas were picked with an eye to how they lend themselves to such winter activities as ski touring and snowshoeing. With enough snow on the ground, all the trail systems covered in this book can be used by the Nordic skier or snowshoer. Some of them, however, can prove challenging to the ski tourer, demanding the ability of an intermediate or advanced skier. In most cases, though, a novice skier can negotiate the designated trails without too much difficulty.

Some of the hikes in the book are on trail systems especially designed for use by cross-country skiers. This is true of Highland Forest, Chateaugay State Forest, Tug Hill State Forest, Selkirk Shores State Park, and the Lesser Wilderness State Forest. All these trails are marked for skiers, and in the case of Selkirk Shores State Park, the tracks are machine set. The other hiking areas are widely advertised as ski-touring areas and attract large numbers of Nordic skiers.

Gear and Clothing. For day hikes in the summer, not much gear is required, but what is, is essential. The most important item is a sturdy day pack so that you can carry a number of other items that should accompany you on all your hikes, no matter how short.

The "10 essentials" are: (1) food (usually lunch), including such extra ingredients as a meat bar, a tin of pemmican, and a bag of trail mix, say, of raisins, peanuts, chocolate drops, and the like; (2) extra clothing, including rain poncho or parka, windbreaker, and/or a wool shirt or sweater; (3) pocket knife with can opener (a Swiss Army knife is a good choice); (4) a plastic bottle with water (don't assume that stream or lake water is safe to drink; it never is); (5) small first-aid kit containing aspirin, bandages, moleskin, and first-aid cream; (6) pocket-sized flashlight; (7) map or maps of the area where you plan to hike; (8) compass; (9) matches in a waterproof container; and (10) firestarters such as candle stubs, fuel tablets, or fire ribbon.

To this list you can add some additional items to make your hiking more enjoyable: insect repellent and sunburn preventive lotion (seasonal), whistle to use if lost, toilet paper, lightweight binoculars, field guides covering items of personal interest such as birds, ferns, flowers, mushrooms, and the like, camera and extra film, sunglasses, and a wide-brimmed hat to keep the sun off your face, ears, and neck.

Good hiking shoes are a must. Today there are many styles and brands of lightweight boots. Some have an upper portion that is a combination of leather and Gore-Tex; while expensive, they are worth the investment. In any event, the hiking boot ought to be sturdy, about 6 inches high, with a good sole to give you traction. When buying boots, be sure to try them with the socks you should wear on the trail—a thin inner sock and a thicker, wool outer sock.

In wintertime, of course, extra clothing is required. Dress in the "layering" manner with several layers of clothing that can be removed easily as you begin to perspire; don't wear a single, bulky down jacket, which will cause you to perspire quickly and dampen your inner garments. Footgear also changes in the winter; insulated boots or half-packs are necessary if you are hiking in snow or snowshoeing.

Safety and Ethics in the Woods. Compared to the risk involved in driving to the trailhead, hiking in the woods is indeed a safe activity. But mishaps and mistakes can occur—from developing blisters to getting lost. In between there can be such misfortunes as a twisted ankle or a fall resulting in broken bones.

The first step in safety precaution is to plan for the unexpected. This entails becoming familiar with basic first aid. Any course offered by the local chapter of the American Red Cross is a good place to begin. Carry your first-aid kit at all times.

Know where you are going. This entails studying your topographical maps covering the area you plan to hike. Always carry a compass, and know how to use map and compass when you reach the trailhead. The best rule to follow is to never walk alone. At the very least, hike with a partner, but the ideal hiking group numbers three people. If anything happens to a group member, one person can search for help, leaving another to stay with the injured and stricken person.

As more people take up hiking and head into the backcountry, hiking ethics become increasingly important. Whatever you pack in, also pack out; this includes plastic containers, tin cans, wrappers, and the like. The outdoors is not a place to drop your litter. Leave the hiking trail cleaner after you leave than when you begin. This means that if you find litter, pick it up and carry it out.

If you plan to spend a weekend tenting, camp at designated areas or in places where your campsite leaves no trace. Pitch your tent away from water, trailsides, and trailheads. For human waste, find a leaf-covered area or one with soft ground where a suitable hole can be dug. Make sure you are at least 200 feet away from water and from a trail or path.

Don't bathe with soap in lakes or streams, and carry your washwater and dishwater away from the shores. If you plan to camp out, bring a good cook stove; don't try to cook on an open fire. Today's hiking ethic calls for as little use of open fires as possible. If you need a fire, use only deadfall and downed branches. Don't chop down trees.

Clean up your campsite. Try to make the area appear as if no one had tented. Don't bury your trash; pack it out. Finally, respect the rights of others, including the property rights of private landowners and the privacy of fellow hikers.

Distance, Walking Time, and Vertical Rise. At the beginning of each hike, you'll find a summary, listing total hiking distance, hiking time, vertical rise, and map(s).

Total hiking distance includes a round trip or circuit unless otherwise indicated, with measurements made on a USGS topo map. Such distance measures are given in miles or in some fraction of a mile. Most people who are in good shape and sound health usually can hike up to 6 miles without experiencing any discomfort either during or after the hike. Most of the hikes in this book fall within this range.

Hiking time is an estimate, which depends on the speed *you* walk on varying terrain. In general, most people walk about 3 miles in 1 hour on level ground. Moderate uphill walking slows you down to about 2 miles per hour, and steep hills to 1 mile per hour or less. If you plan to walk slowly to enjoy the sights, or you stop frequently to examine or photograph flora or fauna, or take long lunch breaks, then expect to add to the stated hiking time.

Vertical rise refers to the total rise in elevation for the hike. If the hike is a steady uphill walk, vertical rise is the difference between the lowest and highest points on your route. In most cases, however, your hike will be an up-and-down affair; the vertical rise is the sum of all the hills you climb during your hike, and may be considerably more than the difference between the lowest and highest points on the terrain.

Map(s) may be one or more United States Geological Survey (USGS) topographic maps. All the USGS maps are in the 7½' series, with the one exception of Gleasmans Falls, where one of the maps is 15'. Where other maps are available (such as park maps), note of these is made in the map summary.

Land Classification. The state uses different classifications for its land in and outside the Forest Preserve (which is part of the larger land area called the Adirondack Park). Within the Forest Preserve, state land has been divided into four categories: intensive use areas, primitive areas, wild forest areas, and wilderness areas. Other than footpaths, there is little that is man-made to be found in the wilderness areas; wild forest areas, on the other hand, may include man-made objects such as roads, fire towers, radio antennas, and the like.

In the rest of New York, state lands fall into one of four categories: state forests, wildlife management areas, marsh units, and unique areas. While all state lands are administered for multiuse, there is considerable variation in primary use from one class of land to another.

State forests, for example, are managed mainly for lumbering and logging, which create revenue for the state. Wildlife management areas are maintained to support a sizable population of wildlife, such as deer, wild turkey, grouse, and various kinds of game birds. Marsh units in the upstate area are found mostly along the shores of Lake Ontario. The state established them to protect and preserve wetlands—the areas used by ducks, geese, and shore birds as resting, feeding, and nesting places.

Finally, the newest classification—unique area—covers land with physical, biological, and/or ecological properties that are unusual, fragile, or endangered and that need special supervision to be preserved and protected.

Hikes in this book will take you to most of these types of state land.

Some Helpful Information. Any well-stocked bookstore will provide you with dozens of books about hiking, camping, cross-country skiing, and snowshoeing. In addition, a number of public and private organizations in New York can give you specific information about public lands, hiking trails, and places to see. Fi-nally, there are books and guides that can provide more detailed information about the history of a local region and about hiking areas within these regions.

ORGANIZATIONS AND CLUBS

Adirondack Mountain Club (ADK)
RR 3, Box 3055
Lake George, NY 12845
518-668-4447
Publishes regional guides and other publications for hikers. Many chapters throughout New York State conduct group outings and day hikes. Membership is currently $35 a year.

Finger Lakes Association
309 Lake Street
Penn Yan, NY 14527
315-536-7488
Issues an annual booklet, "Finger Lakes Regional Travel Guide," with information about motels and places to see.

Finger Lakes State Park and Recreation Commission
Taughannock Falls State Park
RD 3, Park Road
Trumansburg, NY 14886
607-387-7041
Provides information on and maps of state parks in the Finger Lakes Region.

Finger Lakes Trail Conference, Inc.
PO Box 18048
Rochester, NY 14618
716-288-7191
Provides a guide to the map series covering the Finger Lakes Trail system, and information about the conference and member hiking clubs. Current membership is $10 a year.

STATE OR COUNTY OFFICES

Department of Parks and Recreation
Onandaga County
Onandaga Lake Parkway
Liverpool, NY 13088
318-451-7275
Provides brochures, pamphlets, and other literature on the county's forests, parks, and nature center as well as current listings of seasonal activities.

New York State Department of Environmental Conservation
50 Wolf Road
Albany, NY 12233
518-474-2121
Provides brochures of state lands and pamphlets on outdoor subjects, and publishes a magazine, *The Conservationist.*

New York State Division of Tourism
Department of Commerce
1 Commerce Plaza
Albany, NY 12245
1-800-225-5697 (within US) or
518-474-4116
Issues a State highway map, brochures and pamphlets on various regions, and annual state travel guide.

New York State Office of Parks, Recreation and Historic Preservation
Empire State Plaza
Albany, NY 12238
518-474-0456
Issues an annual *Guide to New York State Parks, Recreation & Historic Preservation* containing information about locations, telephone numbers, and facilities at each site. The office also issues a free "Trails Across New York" map.

BOOKS AND GUIDES

Ehling, William P. *Canoeing Central New York.* Woodstock, VT: Backcountry Publications, 1982.

___. *50 Hikes in Western New York.* Woodstock, VT: Backcountry Publications, 1990.

Brenning, Lee M., William P. Ehling, Scott K. Gray III, and Barbara McMartin. *Discover the Southwestern Adirondacks.* Woodstock, VT: Backcountry Publications, 1993.

Guide to Trails of the Finger Lakes Region, 6th ed. Ithaca, NY: Cayuga Trails Club, 1987. Available from Finger Lakes Trail Conference (see above).

Graham, Frank, Jr. *The Adirondack Park: A Political History.* New York: Alfred A. Knopf, 1978.

Jamieson, Paul F., and Donald Morris. *Adirondack Canoe Waters: North Flow,* 3rd ed. Glens Falls, NY: Adirondack Mountain Club, 1988.

Jamieson, Paul F. *Adirondack Reader.* New York: The Macmillan Co., 1964.

McMartin, Barbara. *Fifty Hikes in the Adirondacks,* 2nd ed. Woodstock, VT: Backcountry Publications, 1989.

Samson, Harold E. *Tug Hill Country: Tales from the Big Woods.* Lakemont, NY: North Country Books, 1971.

VanDiver, Bradford B. *Field Guide to Upstate New York.* Dubuque: Kendall/Hunt Publishing Co., 1980.

___. *Rocks and Routes of the North Country New York.* Geneva, NY: W.F. Humphrey Press, Inc., 1976.

Von Engeln, O.D. *The Finger Lakes Region: Its Origin and Nature.* Ithaca: Cornell University Press, 1961.

FINGER LAKES HILLS

1

Gannett Hill

Total distance: 11 miles	
Hiking time: 5 hours	
Vertical rise: 1176 feet	
Map: USGS 7½' Bristol Springs	

This hike takes you through the magnificent mountainous country just west of the southern tip of Canandaigua Lake—an area variously known as the Bristol Hill region, the Gannett Hill section, and New York's Italian Alps.

"Mountainous" may be a bit of an overstatement. These "mountains" are no match for the European Alps, the western Rockies, or even the high peaks of the Adirondacks. Carved by glacial activity during the Pleistocene period, they are technically only hills, as they barely top out at 2200 feet. But when you hike in this region, your senses insist that you are surrounded by mountains. From a distance, rugged, straight-sided, tree-covered forms dominate narrow valleys. And when you are on top of one of these hills, the world drops away at your feet with breathtaking suddenness, revealing spectacular views of the gorgelike valleys below.

Although the hills hereabouts do have an alpine appearance, you might well wonder why they are called "Italian." First, there are the local place names—Naples, Naples Creek, Italy Hill, and Italy Valley. Second, this is fine wine country. Vineyards grace the valleys and lower hill sections surrounding the village of Naples, the site of a major winery and hub of the local wine industry.

The hike starts in Ontario County Park on the top of Gannett Hill, the highest point in this region. Here you are at the northern end of a spur trail of the Finger Lakes Trail (FLT) system, the Bristol Hill Branch Trail. This trail, which is blazed orange, runs south 27 miles to intersect the main east-west Finger Lakes Trail about 2 miles northeast of Prattsburg. The hike described here, however, only uses part of the Bristol Hill Branch Trail, following it along the Gannett Hill ridge and then over Cleveland Hill to a dirt road. There you leave the trail and return to your start in the county park by way of dirt roads that run over Powell Hill and along the eastern edge of Gannett Hill. Because you do some hill climbing, this hike is best classified as moderate to difficult.

Looking north up U-shaped valley from Gannett Hill

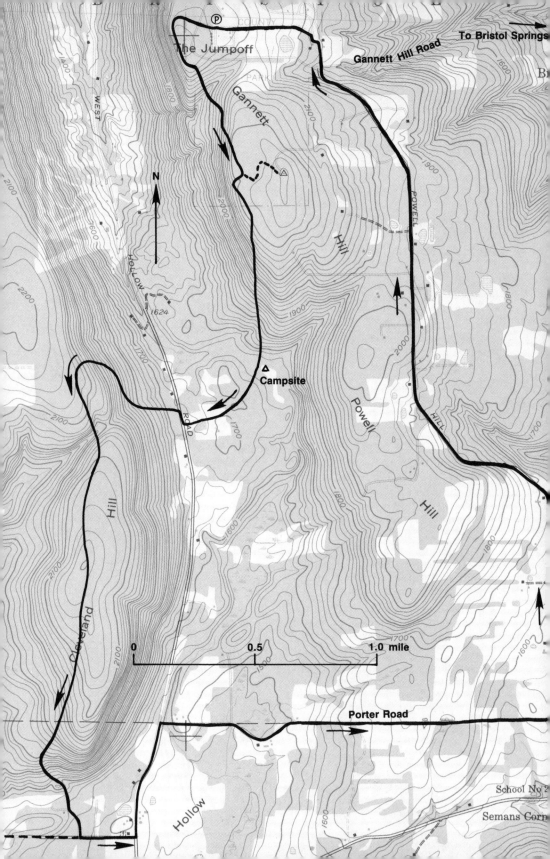

The Jumpoff

Gannett Hill Road

To Bristol Springs

WEST

N

Gannett

Hill

POWELL

Hollow

1624

Campsite

Powell

Hill

HILL

Cleveland

Hill

0   0.5   1.0 mile

Porter Road

Hollow

School No 2

Semans Corn

Access. You can reach Ontario County Park by following NY 21 north out of Naples for 6 miles to Bristol Springs. In this hamlet turn left onto NY 64 and continue 0.5 mile north to Gannett Hill Road. Turn left, and drive 1.5 miles to the park. There is a modest entry fee for your vehicle; a brochure and map of the park are also available at the entrance (or you can obtain them in advance by writing: Division of Human Services, Ontario County, Canandaigua, NY 14424).

Leave your vehicle in the area near the sign pointing to the Jumpoff, and walk the short distance to this overlook. The Jumpoff is aptly named; once you reach the overlook there is nothing but daylight between you and the valley floor 800 feet below.

Trail. Beginning at the Jumpoff, your route follows the FLT spur trail to the left along the edge of the hill for about 100 yards, giving you an excellent view of the valley below, West Hollow to the south, and Berby Hollow to the north. It then swings left, taking you into the woods and onto the flatter land of the Gannett Hill ridge. It soon drops into a gully and then moves uphill for a little more than ¼ mile before leveling out. At this point you are just to the right of Gannett Hill's summit, which at 2256 feet is the highest point in the Bristol Hill region.

After another ¼ mile of relatively level walking, you begin a ½-mile descent into West Hollow. At the base of the hill, on level ground again, you pass an area used for tenting by hikers and soon break out of the woods into an open field. The trail now swings right (west) and in ¼ mile emerges on West Hollow Road (paved).

Cross the highway, turn right, and walk a short distance down the road until you pick up the Cleveland Hill section of the trail on your left, designated by a sign and orange trail markers. Once in the woods, you start uphill; the climb is steep and demanding, requiring you to make a 400-foot ascent in less than ½ mile. As you near the summit of Cleveland Hill, the land flattens considerably, and for almost a mile you walk the relatively level north-south ridge, passing the crest (elevation 2200 feet) at midpoint.

When the trail eventually begins to descend Cleveland Hill's south side, it does so gradually. Over the next ½ mile, however, the slope becomes more pronounced, and the final pitch before the base is quite sharp. When you reach the bottom, the trail leads you across an open field (used by Scouts as a camping area) to a jeep trail that brings you to a dirt road.

Here you leave the Bristol Hill Branch Trail. Turn left (east) and walk the short distance to West Hollow Road. Turn left again and continue north on this road for ½ mile until you come to Porter Road. Turn right onto this dirt road, which runs east through the flatland of West Hollow. Because of the open fields on both sides of the road, you have an excellent view of High Point Hill and Cleveland Hill to the west and Powell Hill to the north.

In 1½ miles you reach Powell Hill Road. Again you turn left and walk north. The first mile is over level ground. Then the road begins to rise as it bends westward, coming gradually up the east side of Powell Hill. Another ½-mile walk brings you to the summit (elevation 2000 feet). To the east you have a grand view of the Naples Creek Valley and Canandaigua Lake beyond. The road now levels out, making the 3-mile walk back to Ontario County Park and your vehicle relatively easy.

The park also boasts numerous well-marked trails that tie into the south-bound Finger Lakes branch trail. It makes a good base for a weekend outing, and several campsites are available for overnight camping.

In winter, snowshoeing along the Bristol Hill Trail can be fun. Once the snow comes, it packs well and stays a long time. Although sections in the flatlands and valleys are ideal for cross-country skiing, generally this is not the place for ski touring; the hill trails are a bit too steep to negotiate with Nordic skis.

2

Taughannock Falls State Park

Total distance: 4¼ miles

Hiking time: 2½ hours

Vertical rise: 559 feet

Map: USGS 7½' Ludlowville

This short 4¼-mile hike takes you around and into an impressively deep gorge to the west of Cayuga Lake where the most striking attraction is Taughannock Falls. Plunging 215 feet into a 30-foot-deep pool, this falls is 55 feet higher than Niagara Falls. In fact, it is one of the highest falls in the eastern United States. In the spring when the waters from melting snow rush into the upper end of the gorge and plunge over the crest, the falls becomes an awesome and breathtaking spectacle. Standing at the base, dwarfed by 400-foot walls that form an immense amphitheater, you will find yourself swept up in the beauty and grandeur.

There are several versions of the origin of the name "Taughannock" (pronounced tau-han-nock). According to

one account, the name originated with the Native American word "Taghkanic," meaning "the great fall in the woods." A more interesting legend ties the name to a Taughannock chieftain of the Delaware tribes, who controlled the lands southeast of the Finger Lakes Region into Pennsylvania. The chieftain, who had been forced to relinquish claim to certain lands, led a band of warriors on a mission of revenge against the Cayugas. The mission was ill fated, the chieftain fell in battle, and his body was hurled into the gorge near the falls, which have born the name Taughannock ever since.

Although it is a bit less dramatic, the geological origin of the falls makes an interesting story, too. The rock layer that forms the base of the gorge and the streambed of Taughannock Creek is Tully limestone, a hard, enduring mineral. The walls of the lower gorge are all black Geneseo shale, which has a crumbly composition. During the postglacial period, the water quickly eroded this rock, washing it downstream to Lake Cayuga to form a large delta that is now the site of the North Point and South Point sections of the state park. Water erosion of the Geneseo shale halted in the lower gorge when the Tully limestone was

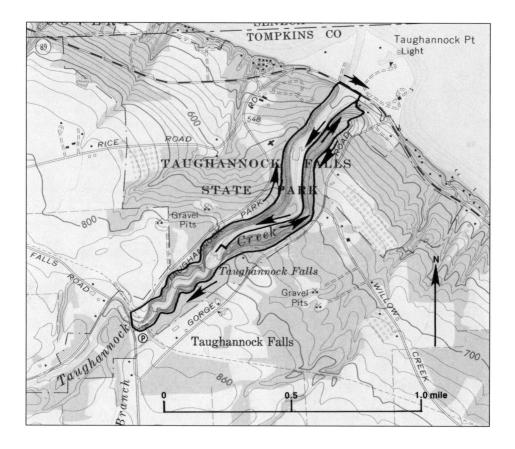

reached and in the middle of the gorge when Sherburne sandstone was exposed. The sections of harder rock that were not eroded eventually stood high above the lower streambed, and Taughannock Falls was born.

There are three trails in the 825-acre Taughannock Falls State Park. The trails that run along both rims of the gorge are known as the North Rim Trail and the South Rim Trail. A third trail, the Gorge Trail, runs from the parking lot at the lower end of the gorge to the foot of Taughannock Falls. There, on the north side of Taughannock Creek, a specially constructed observation area permits you to view the falls head-on.

Access. To reach your starting point at the upper end of the gorge, take NY 96 north from Ithaca or south from Waterloo to the village of Jacksonville. In the center of the village, turn north onto Jacksonville Road, and drive 1.8 miles to the bridge over Taughannock Creek. Park your vehicle in the area on the south side of the bridge.

Trail. Walk across the bridge, and pick up the foot trail on your right. It runs up a small embankment and into a clump of trees. A few feet into the trees you will see a footbridge. (Just before you cross the bridge, you encounter a sign reading "Trail" on your left. It points to a self-guided nature trail that runs along the south side of Taughannock Creek. You can obtain a printed guide to it from the park office at the lower end of the gorge.)

Walk to the middle of the footbridge. To your right (southwest), the water of Taughannock Creek plummets 100 feet down a sloping caprock into a plunge pool. This marks the beginning of the upper gorge system. To your left (northeast), the gorge becomes deeper, with walls that rise 200 feet straight up.

Retrace your steps to the trail and follow it to the right (northeast) alongside Falls Road (paved) for ½ mile to a parking area. To your right, two observation points have been constructed to give you excellent head-on views of Taughannock Falls. The topmost vantage point is level with the parking area; the other is lower and somewhat closer to the falls.

You can now start your hike on the North Rim Trail, which begins at the east end of this parking area and affords you some fine views directly into the gorge. The trail pitches gradually downhill; near the end its slope is more pronounced, until it brings you out of the woods onto NY 89. Across the highway a picnic area on the delta of eroded Geneseo shale fronts on Cayuga Lake.

Turn right onto the highway and walk over the bridge that crosses Taughannock Creek. Look upstream to the wide rock formation that forms a small falls. Continue another 200 feet to a parking area for the lower gorge on your right. You are now ready to follow the ¾-mile-long Gorge Trail. Signs point the way. The gorge is quite wide here, and so is the tree-shaded trail. As you walk toward the falls, you pass through a stand of trees; the base of the gorge first narrows and then widens again. On your left you will notice the piles of crumbly Geneseo shale along the side of the gorge wall.

As you near the falls, the trail turns right and crosses a footbridge, taking you to an observation platform right near the falls and plunge pool.

After you have taken in the spectacular sight, retrace your steps to the parking area on NY 89. Here you can easily find the South Rim Trail for the return route to your vehicle. At first, the trail ascends sharply through the woods to the gorge rim. From here on it is relatively flat. Like the North Rim Trail, it runs along the edge of the gorge, allowing you to look down 400 feet to the floor.

In ¼ mile from the trail's end on Jacksonville Road, you come to a spot where you can look directly down on the falls. The crest is 200 feet below and the plunge pool 251 feet below that. It is an unusual and exciting vantage point.

3

Sugar Hill State Forest

Total distance: 5 miles

Hiking time: 2½ hours

Vertical rise: 750 feet

Maps: USGS 7½' Reading Center;
USGS 7½' Wayne

October is the best time to hike at Sugar Hill. The air is cool, the sky is clear, and the autumn foliage for which the area is famous is at its peak. In fact, to walk Sugar Hill in the fall is to walk through a color explosion, for you are awash in waves of yellow, red, crimson, gold, blue, and purple as the sunlight streams in from all sides through beech, oak, hickory, maple, and ash trees. It is an experience that will sharpen your senses and quicken your spirit.

The design of the trail system here is ideal to allow you to take in the richness of the season. You pass through hardwood stands, down tree-lined lanes, and across deserted farmlands that have now become the territory of saplings and young trees. A network of roads gives easy access to all the trails, and the choices open to the hiker are almost unlimited.

Sugar Hill State Forest covers 9085 acres of hill country between the southern tip of Seneca Lake in the east and Waneta Lake and Lamoka Lake in the west. Atop the area's highest point on the northern edge of the state forest is the Sugar Hill Recreational Area, a state-operated site where you can picnic, camp, and climb a fire tower for a spectacular view of the rugged hill country to the south. There is an archery range nearby, and trails for hikers and horseback riders radiate from the parking lot.

Access. The hike recommended here begins on County Route 21 about 0.6 mile south of Tower Hill Road, at the point where the Finger Lakes Trail (FLT) crosses. This puts you within easy reach of three lean-tos and offers you some fine overlooks facing east toward Seneca Lake.

To reach your starting point, take County Route 28 west out of Watkins Glen (located at the southern tip of Seneca Lake). About a mile out of town, County Route 28 runs into County Route 23; fork left onto County Route 23 and drive about 6 miles until you see a sign on your right directing you to turn left for the Sugar Hill Recreational Area.

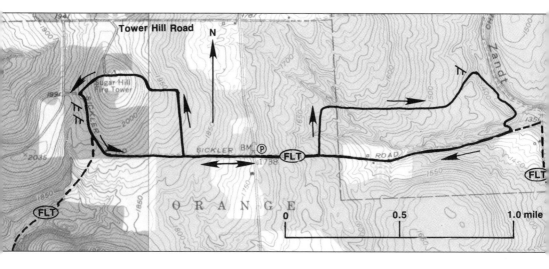

This turn puts you on County Route 21. Drive south for a mile to cross Tower Hill Road. From Tower Hill Road, you continue for 0.6 mile to where an abandoned road crosses County Route 21. Park here, for the abandoned road is a section of the FLT (blazed white) on which you'll begin your hike.

Trail. Start your hike by walking east on the abandoned road, identified on the USGS map as Sickler Road. Although it doubles as a horse trail, no motorized vehicles are allowed.

The road is tree-lined for part of the way, but soon it becomes more open as you pass through fields where saplings and small trees have just begun to take over. After about ¼ mile, a trail marker points to your left (north). Turn here and follow the FLT as it crosses another abandoned field, dips into a gully, and passes through a wooded area. The trail soon turns right (east) and crosses aspen stands, wooded areas, and more abandoned fields until it brings you to the first of the three lean-tos.

There is an old, unused wagon road behind the lean-to; it swings north and offers an alternative route by which you can return to County Route 21. Your hike, however, continues on the FLT, which passes in front of the lean-to, taking you southeast through some open areas and back into the forest on some high ground. Watch on your left for the deep cut formed by Glen Creek—the creek that eventually flows into the deep Watkins Glen Gorge, some 3 miles to the east. In this area the cut is known as Van Zandt Hollow.

The FLT follows the western edge of the hollow until it encounters a feeder stream. Here it turns right (west) for a short distance, crosses the stream at a low spot, and heads back in an easterly direction to Sickler Road.

At this point, the FLT turns left (east) toward Watkins Glen. Your route, however, follows Sickler Road to the right (west), heading uphill through a wooded area. You soon cross an open stretch and pass the point where you earlier turned off Sickler Road. A short walk brings you back to your vehicle.

Author pausing to rest along the trail

You may stop now, but the recommended hike continues west on Sickler Road (which is also the FLT here) for ¼ mile through a heavily wooded area.

Remain on the FLT until you encounter an intersecting trail on your right. This is a blue-blazed spur loop. Turn onto this trail and walk north for ¼ mile where the trail turns west; another ¼ mile brings you to a large open area on your right. This is the heart of the Sugar Hill Recreation Area and the highest spot (elevation 2080 feet) in the region. It's a fine place to take a break and have lunch. Here you will find a fire tower open to the public, several cabins, hitching rails for horses, and an archery range. During the summer the area is a popular site for horseback riding.

The fire tower on top of Sugar Hill offers striking vistas of the surrounding landscape, especially to the west and east. Back on the ground, return to the blue-marked spur trail and continue walking west in a downhill direction. The trail soon turns southward and then intersects the FLT coming from the south. Turn onto the FLT and follow it as it turns east on what quickly becomes the abandoned Sickler Road. From here it is ¾ mile back to County Route 21 and your parked vehicle.

This area is actively used during the winter months by snowmobilers and ski tourers. The hiking trail is particularly suited for ski touring, for it crosses varied terrain, adding zest and challenge to a fine day's skiing. The snow is plentiful here, and it packs well in the forest area and on the trails, providing excellent ski conditions during January, February, and March.

4

Hi Tor Wildlife Management Area

Total distance: 7 miles

Hiking time: 4 hours

Vertical rise: 1010 feet

Maps: USGS 7½' Naples; USGS 7½' Prattsburg; USGS 7½' Middlesex

Hi Tor has a distinctive sound to it. "Tor" is an Old English word meaning high, craggy place or, perhaps more picturesquely, a high rock or pile of rocks on a hilltop. It probably comes from the Old Welsh "turr" or the Old Celtic "tur." (While the USGS topo maps refer to "High Tor," the state's Department of Environmental Conservation (DEC) uses "Hi Tor" on its signs, so this is the spelling we'll follow here.)

The land on which Hi Tor Wildlife Management Area is located pretty well matches its name. It is made up of highlands and marshlands and includes deep, narrow valleys, cut by the glaciers that overrode New York more than 12,000 years ago, as well as hills and valleys on top of hills. These are steep hills, straight-shouldered and heavily forested. They also are deeply cut and clefted by streams that give the area its gullies, gorges, and eroded cliffs.

Hence, a craggy hilltop is a good description of the area, much of which is quite scenic, and the hiker can see it all, even when walking through the woods along the edge of a gorge.

Hi Tor maintains its English connection by keeping close company with such places as South Bristol, Bristol Springs, Pulteney, and Middlesex, but in the best European tradition it also has the Latin neighbors of Naples, West Italy Hill, and Italy Valley.

Hi Tor Wildlife Management Area is made up of a number of closely situated but separate units, two of which are quite large. The largest is a 3920-acre parcel on the high hills immediately east of the village of Naples. Just north of this hilly section is a 1000-acre marsh in the lowlands bordering the south end of Canandaigua Lake. A third parcel, still farther north, is called South Hill, which, according to legend, was the birthplace of the Seneca Indians, one of the tribes of the Iroquois Confederacy. As they occupied land in the western Finger Lakes region, they were called "keepers of the western door" of the confederacy.

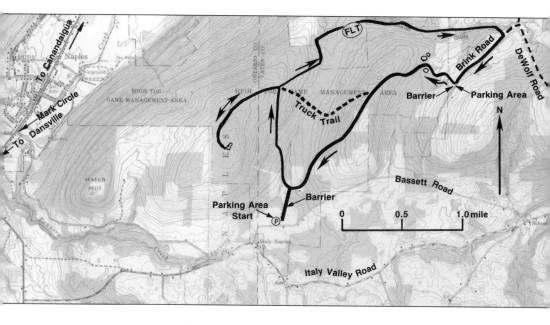

Hi Tor's major attraction for the hiker today is its trail system. Running through the large southern portion of Hi Tor is the Bristol Hill Branch of the Finger Lakes Trail (FLT). This 27-mile-long spur trail begins at Ontario Park on Gannett Hill (see Hike 1) and intersects the FLT trunk trail about 2 miles northeast of Prattsburg.

Access. The trailhead to Hi Tor's hikeable trails can be reached from Naples. To reach Naples take NY 21 from Dansville or Wayland in the west or from Canandaigua or Manchester in the north (Manchester is at exit 43 of I-90). Once in Naples, drive to the southern end of the village where you will reach a fork in the road. NY 21 bears to your right and NY 53 to your left. Take the left leg and drive 1.3 miles; here a road—County Route 20—intersects on your left. Turn and follow the county route uphill for 2.2 miles to

where a dirt road—Bassett Road—intersects on your left; you are now in the Hi Tor Wildlife Management Area. Turn here and drive north 0.4 mile to where a lane or service road intersects on your left. Park here.

Trail. Start your hike on the lane, heading north past a road barrier erected to keep out unauthorized vehicles. Hi Tor is an excellent place to hike, and since it contains several interconnected roads, it is also ideal for biking. In winter, of course, the same routes can be used by Nordic skiers or snowshoers.

As you hike north on the service road, you cross fairly level terrain for ¼ mile where the road forks. Turn onto the left leg (the right leg is the one you will be using on your return). After crossing a small streamlet (the headwaters of Tannery Creek) the road starts uphill and continues its ascent for the next ½ mile, where you intersect another service road running in an east-west direction. Here you encounter the Finger Lakes Trail coming down the road on your left. The FLT markers are white blazes painted on trees.

The vertical rise from the Tannery Creek headwaters to this point is 220 feet. You are now at one of Hi Tor's high spots (elevation 1800 feet). If you turn left here, the east-west route brings you in ¼ mile to a fair-sized pond, constructed by the state's Department of Environmental Conservation to provide water for the area's animals, including migrating waterfowl. You'll find several more of these man-made ponds during your hike. Interestingly, they are located on the highest part of the Wildlife Management Area; in spite of their location, there is enough seepage from the forested surroundings to keep the ponds filled.

Retrace your steps to the intersection. Turn left (north) onto the road displaying the FLT blazes and running in a northeast direction. Follow the trail markers along the road as the trail slowly heads downhill. At the ½-mile mark, the trail turns left off the road and into the woods, taking you to an overlook with a fine view of Canandaigua Lake and South Hill to the north.

The trail swings right and soon crosses the road on which you walked earlier; a little over ¼ mile more and a gradual descent brings you to the edge of an impressively deep gorge (Conklin Gully). The trail stays on the south rim of the gorge as it heads east.

This Conklin Gully trail section is a delight. It is scenic, relatively flat, and cool even on hot days. The gorge becomes less deep and a little wider, until after 1 mile it is quite shallow. The trail now climbs a small hill and swings south

away from the gully. In ½ mile more, you come to a dirt road, Brink Road.

If you want to add 2 more miles to your hike, you can follow the FLT left on Brink Road to DeWolf Road, where either a right or left turn will bring you to overlooks. The more scenic choice is the southern route of the FLT that reaches the top of West Italy Hill with a view across Italy Valley.

Back at the spot where the trail intersected Brink Road, a turn right onto Brink Road takes you in little over ½ mile to a parking area on the north side of the road. Running west from Brink Road is a single-lane truck trail. A barrier at the start prevents unauthorized vehicles from using it, but you can turn right here and follow the dirt road downhill.

In less than ½ mile, you come to an open area and a series of ponds, one on the south side of the road and two on the north side. The trail soon leaves the fieldlike area, enters the woods, and heads gradually uphill. About ½ mile brings you to a fork; take the left leg, and continue in a southwesterly direction.

A short distance from the intersection on your left you pass a knob, 60 feet above the road; this hilltop is Hi Tor's highest spot (elevation 1900 feet). It is not, however, the area's highest elevation; that's found farther east about 1½ miles away on what is called West Italy Hill (elevation 2040 feet), over which the FLT passes in its eastward journey.

The trail now starts downhill, descending 400 feet in a mile. When you reach the bottom of the hill, you will encounter a fork in the road. Turn left onto the route you took at the beginning of your hike. Follow this south back to your parked vehicle on Bassett Road.

5

Watkins Glen State Park

Total distance: 10 miles (2 days)

Hiking time: 5 hours

Vertical rise: 560 feet

Maps: USGS 7½' Beaver Dam; USGS 7½' Reading Center; USGS 7½' Montour Falls; Park Pamphlet and Map

Of all the gorge-shaped glens in the Finger Lakes region, none is more beautifully sculptured by thousands of years of water erosion or more varied in scenic splendor than 3½-mile-long Watkins Glen, after which the state park is named.

The glen's origin dates back thousands of years to the invasion of what is today New York State by a mile-thick continental ice sheet. In its forward advance, this glacier bulldozed out huge depressions that later filled with water to become today's Finger Lakes. However, it was during the postglacial period, when the glacier was melting, that Watkins Glen began to take form. As vast quantities of water were released by the retreating glacier, streamlets turned into rivers,

plunging down slopes and cutting their way through shale rock to form a deepening trench. With that, the gorge of Watkins Glen was born.

This incision in the landscape became the route of Glen Creek, which over the centuries has been cutting its way ever more deeply into the existing rock layers. The fast-flowing waters of Glen Creek created this natural wonder, Watkins Glen, by eroding the weak sedimentary rocks laid down millions of years ago, when a shallow sea covered much of what is now the United States.

What we have today in the lower portion of Watkins Glen State Park is a gorge with high but gracefully sculptured walls, 19 plunging waterfalls, glistening plunge pools, and large water-drilled potholes, all in plain view as you walk the park's Gorge Trail. The park also contains two sizable man-made ponds: Punch Bowl Lake in the glen's middle section and Glen Creek Lake in its upper section.

The state has provided several access roads leading into the park; there are main, upper, and south entrances. The main entrance is located in the village of Watkins Glen. The upper entrance, used by people who prefer to walk down rather than up the Gorge Trail steps, is

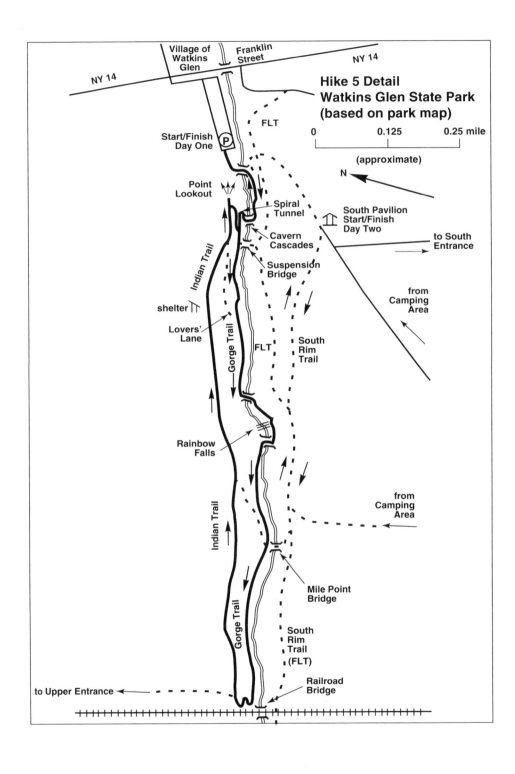

Hike 5 Detail
Watkins Glen State Park
(based on park map)

Village of Watkins Glen

Franklin Street

NY 14

NY 14

0   0.125   0.25 mile

(approximate)

N

FLT

Start/Finish Day One

P

Point Lookout

Spiral Tunnel

South Pavilion Start/Finish Day Two

Cavern Cascades

to South Entrance

Suspension Bridge

from Camping Area

Indian Trail

shelter

Lovers' Lane

Gorge Trail

FLT

South Rim Trail

Rainbow Falls

from Camping Area

Indian Trail

Mile Point Bridge

Gorge Trail

South Rim Trail (FLT)

to Upper Entrance

Railroad Bridge

located above where the Gorge Trail ends. The south entrance takes you to the Six Nation Camping Area, with 305 camping sites grouped into six sections and named after the six nations of the Iroquois Confederacy—Mohawk, Oneida, Onandaga, Cayuga, Seneca, and Tuscarora. One additional access road on the south side takes you into the upper section of the park where the road forks, with one route running east to a turnaround spot south of Punch Bowl Lake and the other running west to a cluster of buildings making up Hidden Valley Group Camp.

In addition to the Gorge Trail, the park features several other walking trails—the Indian Trail and Lovers' Lane on the north side of the gorge and the Rim Trail and the Finger Lakes Trail (FLT) on the south side. The FLT, which enters the park at the west end, uses the Rim Trail in the lower half of the park before splitting off to intersect NY 329 near the park's main entrance.

To complicate matters more, this is also the route of the North Country National Scenic Trail, a federally sponsored trail that makes use of existing trails such as the FLT. When completed, the North Country Trail will run from Crown Point, on the eastern edge of New York, to Minnesota via a section of the Keystone Trail in Pennsylvania, the Buckeye Trail in Ohio, and the trail systems in Michigan and Wisconsin. To keep things simple, we shall speak of the FLT as the trail that runs the full length of the park.

From the start of the Gorge Trail to where it ends in the parking area at the upper entrance the distance is 1½ miles; combining this with a return route via the Indian Trail gives you a trek of 3 miles. Following the Gorge Trail requires you to climb 832 steps. Fortunately, level stretches are found between one set of stairs and the next, making the upward climb less demanding than may at first be supposed. Nonetheless, the vertical rise from start to finish is 560 feet.

Shuttle buses run from the parking area at the main entrance to the upper entrance, permitting people to make a one-way downhill trip on the Gorge Trail.

An overnight stay at the park's camping area is recommended; this will allow you to explore the park's several trail systems. The first day trek would include the Gorge Trail (going up) and the Indian Trail (coming back); the second day's outing would entail a round-trip of 7 miles on the FLT to Glen Creek Lake.

Access. The entrance to the state park is located in the center of the village of Watkins Glen. Drive 2 blocks south of Fourth Street on Franklin Street to the entrance on your right, where you will find a parking area. The park charges an entrance fee. You can reach the village via NY 14 from Geneva, which lies 54 miles to the north, and by the same route, NY 14, from Elmira, located 23 miles to the south.

Trails. If you are staying at the park's camping area, start your first day's outing with a hike through the 1½-mile-long gorge. Drive your vehicle to the main entrance gate in the village and leave it in the park's parking area.

First Day
From the parking area to the upper entrance area and back via the Indian Trail
Distance: 3 miles
Hiking time: 2 hours

The start of the Gorge Trail is found at the west end of the parking area. Here you enter a short tunnel; this, as well as the gorge's other tunnels, was hand-cut during the early 1900s. As soon as you emerge from the tunnel you cross a stone bridge. On the bridge's right side is a rock wall that contains a large hole. The hole was excavated in the mid-1800s and a dam was erected behind it; water passed from the dam through the hole and over the waterwheel of a gristmill located in what is now the parking area.

As you look upstream from the bridge you see the water-eroded rock walls of the lower gorge. Once over the bridge, you turn right and pass a flight of stairs running uphill on your left; these steps lead to the Finger Lakes Trail, the Lily Pond, and the South Pavilion, as well as to the suspension bridge that crosses the gorge farther upstream. A few more steps on the Gorge Trail bring you to where an evening performance called "Timespell" is conducted nightly—a sound and light show that tells the story of Watkins Glen from the beginning of the earth to the present.

Up ahead you will see an attractive falls, which people can walk behind, called Cavern Cascade. Follow the trail as it turns right, takes you behind the falls, and into what is called the Spiral Tunnel. The tunnel steps lead upward to where you emerge on a level section of the trail. This is shortly intersected by a set of steps descending on your right; these lead to a short route called the Cliff Path, which, in turn, takes you to Point Lookout and the Indian Trail. These are the trails you will take on your return.

For now, however, continue on the Gorge Trail for several hundred feet; you will pass beneath the suspension bridge rising 85 feet above the gorge and then through another short tunnel. A set of stairs takes you upward and into a section of the gorge called the Narrows. Unlike the lower gorge which, while rela-tively deep, is open, in the Narrows, as the name implies, the gorge walls are set so close together that this section has its own microclimate—an environment that is shady, cool, and moist. The sides of the rock walls, wet with dripping water, are covered with ferns and mosses.

A few more steps bring you to where the Gorge Trail is intersected by a path that descends a set of stairs to your right. This short path is called Lovers' Lane. However, continue on the Gorge Trail up a staircase and into a large, spacious, sunlit area called the Cathedral section. Here the gorge's high walls are set back to create an almost amphitheaterlike appearance: In contrast to the shady, damp Narrows, the Cathedral area is open, sun-filled, and dry. The vegetation here is similar to that found in desert canyons, with shrubs, wildflowers, and grasses.

Several hundred feet farther and up several sets of stairs you will come to a bridge that crosses to the south side of the gorge. You are now entering a section called the Central Cascade, which contains the gorge's highest waterfalls, plunging 60 feet down into a deep pool. Immediately upstream you encounter the Glen of Pools, containing many of the gorge's awesome plunge pools—potholes drilled by the swirling water carrying sand and gravel.

Next comes Rainbow Falls, plunging down the side of a steep hill. Over time the water has eaten back layers of shale rock near the bottom of the cliff, allowing you to walk behind the falls. Depending on the angle of sunlight, a rainbow may form in the falls' mist. Once past the falls, the trail turns right and crosses a stone arch bridge. From atop the bridge you can see up and down the deeply cut streambed and behold its stunning beauty.

Beyond the bridge you enter another section of the gorge that differs from those gone before. This part is also narrow and shaded, but here the gorge's sides act more like overhanging cliffs where hidden springs release dripping water that falls on the trail like rain. You will pass a series of falls, pinched by narrow walls; these are called Pluto Falls after Pluto, the Greek god of the dark underworld.

You are now slightly past the halfway mark; an additional 100 yards and two more staircases bring you to Mile Point Bridge. Here several trails intersect. One on your right comes downhill from the Indian Trail. Another crosses the bridge over the gorge, coming downhill from the South Rim Trail and the FLT. Stay on the Gorge Trail. The next ½ mile leads over more level terrain and past less dramatic but still scenic landforms.

Just ahead is a railroad trestle crossing the gorge high overhead, but before you pass underneath it, you start an upward climb on a long series of steps. These finally take you past the start of the Indian Trail to the top, where you will find the parking area of the upper entrance, as well as a concession building and a comfort station.

After you have rested, start your return by descending the staircase you used earlier. A short distance down the steps brings you to where the Indian Trail intersects on your left. Turn here and follow the trail eastward. The Indian Trail runs along the side of the hill for ⅝ mile to where a trail intersects on your right; it leads downhill to the Mile Point Bridge.

You, however, continue on the Indian Trail. En route you come to several spots that give a fine overview of the gorge. Before the trail ends you pass a lean-to on your left. At the mile mark you come to an intersection with Lovers' Lane on your right, a path to Point Lookout on your left, and a third route running straight ahead to the suspension bridge over the gorge.

A view of Watkins Glen

Turn left and walk the short distance to Point Lookout which allows you a scenic view to the east. Turn around; a couple of steps will take you to a set of stairs (on your left) leading down to the Gorge Trail. Take it and then turn left to go through the Spiral Tunnel; continue downward on the Gorge Trail to the Entrance Tunnel. A few more steps take you to the parking area and your vehicle.

Second Day
From the camping area to Glen Creek
Lake and back by the FLT
Distance: 7 miles
Hiking time: 3 hours

From the camping area walk northeast to the South Pavilion area where you encounter the South Rim Trail. Turn left (west) onto the South Rim Trail and follow it for ¼ mile to where it becomes part of the FLT. (Since only a part of the FLT runs on the park's South Rim Trail, we will simply refer to this route as the FLT.)

Continue, then, on a westward course on the white-blazed FLT. Soon you come to a path from the camping area intersecting on your left, and a short distance beyond to a set of stairs on your right leading downhill to Mile Point Bridge crossing the Gorge Trail.

Stay on the FLT for ½ mile where it passes beneath the railroad trestle at the trestle's south end. The trail continues an additional ½ mile through a forested area along the rim overlooking the upper gorge. A high concrete dam is located where the land narrows and the gorge begins. Lying behind the dam is an impoundment in the form of an attractive pond called Punch Bowl Lake. On the lake's south side is an open area with a pavilion, a large wood-frame building designed for use by large groups.

A path on your left leads uphill a short distance to a parking area and turnaround point. However, continue to follow the white-blazed FLT into the woods. The FLT starts to make a gradual ascent and in ½ mile emerges from the woods to intersect a park road coming from the turnaround point. The FLT continues westward for ¼ mile on the park road until it intersects another park road coming downhill from NY 329 on your left; on your right the park road travels downhill, across Glen Creek and into Hidden Valley Group Camp, an area containing a dozen buildings where people stay during campout.

The FLT, however, crosses the park road and reenters the forest area, continuing along the side of the hill overlooking Glen Creek. A trek of 1¼ miles brings you to the southern edge of Glen Creek Lake. This is your turnaround point, a fine spot to rest and, perhaps, have lunch.

When you are ready to go, retrace your steps to the park road; cross it and pick up the other park road intersecting on your right. Follow the FLT's white blazes until the FLT leaves the road and turns downhill on your left. Continue on the park road to the turnaround point. Take the path on the north side of this point and follow it a short distance downhill to the south shore of Punch Bowl Lake. Here again you pick up the white-blazed FLT. Follow it back to the state's camping area and to your camping site.

6

Finger Lakes National Forest

Total distance: 9¾ miles (2 days)

Hiking time: 5½ hours

Vertical rise: 1010 feet

Maps: USGS 7½' Burdett; USGS 7½' Lodi; National Forest brochure

The Finger Lakes National Forest occupies the high terrain between two of the largest Finger Lakes—Cayuga Lake (the longest) on the east side and Seneca Lake (the deepest) on the west. It also displays a number of features that set it apart from other forested areas in central New York.

To begin with, it is the only major forestland in the immediate vicinity—and it is attractive, to boot. Once inside, you hike past sparkling ponds and through stands of evergreens, oaks, and maples; the environment reminds you of a wild forest in the Adirondacks. It stands in sharp contrast to the cultivated landscape surrounding it, full of dairy farms, fruit farms, and seemingly endless miles of vineyards—vineyards that have made the Finger Lakes region famous for its white wines.

It is not only unique as a forestland but is also the lone federally owned piece of real estate (13,232 acres) in New York State and the smallest national forest in the United States. Nevertheless, it is the single largest tract of public land found amid the cluster of the five Finger Lakes.

This national forest is also situated on the highest land in the area. It sits astride the spine that runs through three adjoining hills—Burnt Hill (elevation 1850 feet), Hector Backbone (elevation 1840 feet), and Butcher Hill (elevation 1540 feet)—extending from ½ mile north of the hamlet of Bennettsburg (lying east of Seneca Lake) in the south to ½ mile below the hamlet of Lodi in the north.

The forest is linear in shape—12 miles long but only 5 miles at its widest part. Although narrow, it contains a surprising number of trails. The longest is the 10-mile-long Interlocken Trail running the length of the forest on top of the area's ridge. As its name implies, this trail locks together all the other trails to give you 25 miles of interconnected routes; these include a section of the Finger Lakes Trail and the Southslope Trail in the south, the Burnt Hill Trail, Gorge

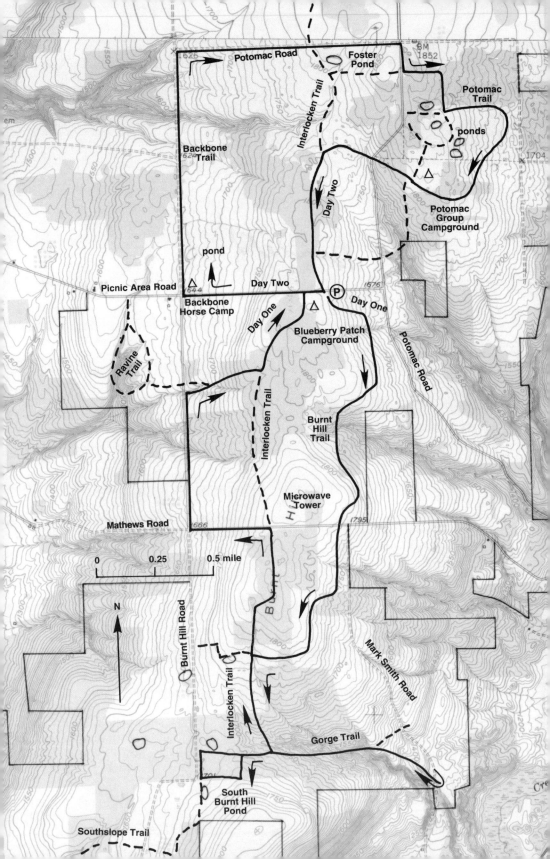

Trail, and Ravine Trail in the central section, and the Backbone Trail and Potomac Trail in the north.

This land provides an ideal habitat for virtually all the large and small game animals found in New York State, including white-tailed deer, wild turkey, and an occasionally reported black bear. The wooded areas are especially attractive to ruffed grouse; it is not unusual for a hiker to be startled by the unexpected roar of a half-dozen birds exploding almost underfoot.

As with all national forests, the Finger Lakes National Forest follows the policy of multiuse. This means that a variety of recreational pursuits is encouraged—birding, hiking, camping, horseback riding, hunting, fishing, and, in winter, cross-country skiing and snowmobiling. In addition, local cattlemen are allowed on a lease arrangement to graze their livestock in the fields and open areas; about a third of the land is grassland.

The forest traces its origin back to the Great Depression of the 1930s, when the federal government bought farms to help their owners relocate to better land or other jobs. Over 100 such farms in this region were so acquired and the land turned over to the federal Soil Conservation Service to be managed as the Hector Land Use Area. In the late 1950s the area was switched to the US Forest Service and in 1985 was renamed the Finger Lakes National Forest, Hector Ranger District.

Access. The main access route is NY 414 running south from Seneca Falls or north from Watkins Glen (located at the south end of Seneca Lake). One mile south of the hamlet of Hector on the left side of NY 414 is the Hector Ranger station, which serves as a visitors' center. Trail information and a trail map can be obtained here. From the visitors' center, backtrack 0.5 mile towards Hector to County Route 2. Turn right here to get to the National Forest.

Once on County Route 2, drive east and uphill for 2.3 miles to a crossroad called Logan. Route 2 now becomes Picnic Area Road; an additional 0.3 mile brings you to a sign indicating that the national forest begins on the left side of the road. Drive 0.35 mile farther; you are now in the national forest.

Continue uphill for 0.9 mile on what is now a two-lane dirt road, past a crossroad and the Backbone Horse Camp on your left, to the top of the hill where you will see Blueberry Patch Campground to your right. A short distance beyond and on your left is a small parking area and the trailhead of Burnt Hill Trail.

The recommended hikes assume that you will spend at least one overnight at one of the campsites in Blueberry Patch Campground. If you prefer a single-day outing, leave your vehicle at the small parking area. Blueberry Patch is not a name lightly bestowed; next to the campground is a 5-acre area managed for blueberry production.

Trail. Three trails—Interlocken, Burnt Hill, and Backbone—are all within easy reach of Blueberry Patch Campground. Incidentally, the campground has a picnic area, nine campsites for tents or self-contained recreational vehicles, a hand-pump well, and vault toilets. A fee is charged for overnight use, which is on a first-come, first-served basis. Free camping elsewhere, however, is allowed throughout the national forest.

If you plan a weekend campout, your hikes may be divided over 2 days.

First Day
From camping area via Burnt Hill Trail and Interlocken Trail
Distance: 5¼ miles
Hiking time: 3 hours

The first day's hike combines Burnt Hill Trail and Interlocken Trail to form a loop that brings you back to Blueberry Patch Campground. At the entrance to the campground, turn right on Picnic Area Road and walk a short distance to the parking area on your right.

The beginning of Burnt Hill Trail is a little to the left of the parking area, where it follows a fence as it heads south. The large field on the other side of the fence is called North Velie Grassland, which, in turn, overlooks the lush farmlands across Hector Falls Creek valley. This grassland is used by local cattlemen to graze their livestock. The field also contains nesting boxes for the American kestrel, which prefers a grassland habitat.

Follow the trail by the fence for little over ¼ mile until you enter a wooded area. From here the trail meanders along the side of the north end of Burnt Hill; at the ¾-mile mark, it dips into a gully through which a streamlet flows—the headwaters of Hector Falls Creek.

The trail, still hugging the side of the hill, now reaches the central portion of Burnt Hill, on the top of which is a large open field, usually used by cattle. (A fence separates you from the cows.) At the 1¼-mile mark, you leave the woods and emerge on a one-lane dirt road, called Mathews Road on the map.

Cross the road and reenter the woods. In about ¼ mile, the trail dips into a small gully; here, too, is the start of a feeder streamlet flowing eastward into Hector Falls Creek. Shortly after this, the trail bends to the right and heads uphill for a brief while before again turning south for almost ¼ mile where it curves in a westward direction. An additional ¼ mile brings you to an intersection with another trail running in a north-south direction; as the sign at the intersection notes, this is the Interlocken Trail, the one on which you will later return. Burnt Hill Trail crosses the Interlocken Trail as

it heads west, and in ¼ mile ends at Burnt Hill Road, a one-lane dirt road.

However, your route is to continue south by turning left onto the Interlocken Trail. A gradual downhill descent for ½ mile brings you to a trail intersection with the Gorge Trail. This ¾-mile trail is worthy of exploring, since it allows you to follow a route that begins as a slight depression, turns into a gully, and then grows into a gorge through which still another stream flows eastward into Hector Falls Creek. The Gorge Trail ends at a dirt road, Mark Smith Road.

Retrace your steps back to the trail intersection and continue walking westward from the intersection for about ⅛ mile to where the Interlocken Trail turns south. A ¼-mile spur trail leads westward to Burnt Hill Road. On the other hand, the south-running Interlocken Trail follows a course for less than ⅛ mile where it turns right and in another ⅛ mile brings you out on an elbow turn of Burnt Hill Road. This is your turnaround point.

From here the Interlocken Trail continues southward for 1 mile where it intersects with the Finger Lakes Trail (FLT); from the junction the FLT runs south through Bennettsburg. En route south, the Interlocken Trail passes two ponds; at the south end of the second pond it is intersected by the ¾-mile Southslope Trail, a spur trail running north from the FLT which comes uphill from Watkins Glen.

But back to the turnaround spot: from here you head north on shaded Burnt Hill Road for ⅛ mile to where you encounter the entrance to the Gorge Trail on your right. Turn here and follow the Gorge Trail for ¼ mile to the intersection with the Interlocken Trail, the spot you passed earlier. Turn north and retrace your footsteps to the intersection with the Burnt Hill Trail.

Now, however, remain on the Inter-

Pond in the Finger Lakes National Forest

locken Trail as it follows a northward course through the forest; a ¼-mile uphill climb brings you to the south crest of Burnt Hill, and an additional ¼ mile takes you to Mathews Road, the road you crossed earlier when you were walking south on Burnt Hill Trail.

The Interlocken Trail crosses the road and passes through a gate into a large open field in which cattle may be grazing; in the center of the area is a microwave tower. If you wish to avoid the cattle, turn left (west) on Mathews Road and walk downhill for ¼ mile to where you intersect Burnt Hill Road. Turn right (north) and continue your hike on Burnt Hill Road for ⅜ mile till you encounter the Ravine Trail, which runs westward and downhill on your left; across the road, a footpath (an extension of the Ravine Trail) runs eastward. Take this latter trail and in ¼ mile you will intersect the Interlocken Trail; turn left (north) here and continue walking northward for ⅝ mile to where you inter-

sect Picnic Area Road. About 200 feet on your right is Blueberry Patch Campground.

Second Day
Loop from camping area via Backbone, Potomac, and Interlocken Trails
Distance: 4½ miles
Hiking time: 3 hours

In this hike you cover a 4½-mile loop involving the Backbone Trail, Potomac Trail, and Interlocken Trail. Starting at Blueberry Patch Campground, turn left (west) onto Picnic Area Road and follow it downhill past the sign reading "Backbone Horse Camp" to the intersection with Burnt Hill Road on your left. Once across Picnic Area Road, this road changes its name as it becomes the route of the Backbone Trail, which runs straight north.

Turn onto this trail and walk past the facilities for the equestrian set; these facilities include parking areas with hitching rails, cooking grills, picnicking and camping areas, and vault toilets. This route, of course, is used extensively by horseback riders, but it is also a fine trail for hikers. As you walk north you will find the terrain to be level for the first ⅝ mile, although the land rises several hundred feet on your right. You next cross several gullies through which waters drain into Sawmill Creek in the west.

At the 1-mile mark, a lane intersects on your right (east). Turn here and start an uphill climb for ½ mile to where you cross the north-south Interlocken Trail. Cross this trail and continue eastward for ⅜ mile on the Backbone Trail and over a small feeder stream until you reach a dirt road, Potomac Road; here you will find a small parking area.

Turn right (south) on Potomac Road, and walk ⅛ mile to a trailhead on your left. Take this trail. In ⅛ mile the trail turns south and in another ⅛ mile intersects an east-west trail, the Potomac Trail. Turn left (east) and follow it gradually downhill for 2½ miles to where the trail turns southwestward for ½ mile. Here it turns northwest, taking you into the Potomac Group Campground.

The campground is designed for groups of 10 to 40 people. Facilities include open picnic areas, cooking grills, a hand-pump well, and vault toilets; a fee is charged for reserved use of camping sites.

Continue on the Potomac Trail for an additional ¼ mile to where it reaches Potomac Road. Cross the road and continue on the trail, which now carries you westward until in ¼ mile you intersect the Interlocken Trail. Turn left (south) on the Interlocken Trail, which climbs to the top of the crest of an unnamed hill (elevation 1800 feet). An additional ⅜ mile along the top of this crest brings you to Picnic Area Road and, in a few steps, to Blueberry Patch Campground.

7

Enfield Glen/Treman State Park

Total distance: 4½ miles

Hiking time: 3 hours

Vertical rise: 600 feet

Maps: USGS 7½' Mecklenburg; USGS 7½' Ithaca West; Park Brochure and Map

Enfield Glen is a deeply cut gorge, over 10,000 years in the making and one of the area's scenic wonders; it serves as the centerpiece of the 1025-acre Robert H. Treman State Park, located 5 miles south of the city of Ithaca.

Through its forested, 2¼-mile length flows Enfield Creek, a lively, fast-moving stream rushing through flumes and chutes and cascading over rocky ledges to produce more than a dozen falls, some small and others impressively large.

There are three spectacularly high falls among the many smaller ones found in the glen. One waterfall, about three stories high, is located at the lower end of the river, at the head of what in summertime is a dammed-up swimming pool. A second large waterfall is found in the glen's midsection, and a third—the highest and most impressive—is situated in the park's upper section, a short distance from the parking area.

The term "glen," of Scottish Gaelic origin, means valley, usually one of gentle expanse. However, the glens found in New York's Finger Lakes region are deeply eroded gorges, cut over millennia into the steep-sided hills surrounding the Ithaca area. Enfield Glen is a prized example of this kind of landform.

These glens are a direct link with the postglacial period of some 10,000 years ago, when the continental ice sheet that had advanced to cover Canada and the northern United States (and virtually all of New York) started its slow retreat. Melting back as the earth's temperature grew warmer, the ice sheet released torrents of water that rushed down hillsides to valleys below and, in the process, cut into the soft shale rock and less resistant limestone. Once the initial cut had been made, local drainage produced streams that continued the work of erosion, eating ever more deeply into the landscape to give us today's gorges.

Geologically, Enfield Glen is a combination of two glens, one very old and the

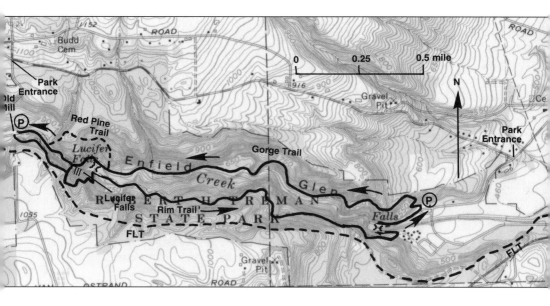

other far more recent. The lower part of today's glen, with its wide, forested sides, is the result of water erosion that occurred between two glacial periods. The upper gorge, on the other hand, was cut after the last ice age; being the younger gorge, it is more rugged in appearance. The two gorges join just below Lucifer Falls.

Like the term "glen," the name "Enfield" serves as a geographical link, not only with Enfield Creek, but also with the hamlet of Enfield, around which the creek passes, and the town (ship) of Enfield, in which it arises.

Culturally, Enfield goes back to the early white settlers of the area. In the upper section of the state park is a two-story building called the Old Mill; it was once a gristmill, powered by the waters of Enfield Creek, where corn and wheat were ground until 1917. The mill was part of a farm community known as Enfield Falls. This community has disappeared, but today the Old Mill serves as a museum piece to familiarize visitors with the past.

In spite of all this, Enfield Glen almost lost its identity when it became part of the newly established park named after Robert H. Treman. In 1920 Treman, with his wife Laura, donated 367 acres in Enfield Glen to the state to create the Enfield Glen Reservation. In 1924 the reservation became part of the Finger Lakes Park Commission, whose first chairman was Mr. Treman. On his death in 1938, the park was named in his memory.

The park has two parking areas, one in the lower and one in the upper section, so you can choose to start your hike at either end. The more popular choice, and the recommended one, is to start at the lower end.

This lower section contains a cabin area, a picnic area, two camping areas, and a beautifully crafted bathhouse built of limestone blocks; the building is located next to Enfield Creek and the lower falls. During summer months the creek is dammed into a swimming pool. Here water erosion has eaten its way back upstream to the present-day falls, producing, in the process, a large amphitheaterlike bowl that partially encircles the swimming pool. This sculptured landform creates an impressive place in which to swim.

The park contains three main hiking trails and one short loop. Running through its length are the Gorge Trail and the Rim Trail, both 2¼ miles long one way. On its southern flank is a section of the Finger Lakes Trail (FLT), which actually runs from Allegany State Park to the Catskills and is, in cooperation with the federal government, also part of the North Country Scenic Trail. The FLT inside the park is 3 miles long. Also in the park's upper half is the Red Pine Trail, which forms a ½-mile loop on the east side of the gorge, running westward from the Gorge Trail uphill to the park's upper section.

Access. The easiest approach to the trailhead is to follow NY 13 south out of Ithaca for 5 miles to the intersection with NY 327, on your right. Turn onto NY 327 and drive west for 0.1 mile to the intersection with the park's entrance road, on your left. You are now entering the park's lower section.

Turn here and drive a short distance to the entrance gate, where you must pay an entrance fee. Continue for another 0.1 mile past the park office to a large parking area. The trailhead to the Gorge Trail is found on the left side of the park office.

Trail. The recommended hiking route includes the Gorge Trail, which takes you uphill from the park's lower section to its upper section, and the Rim Trail, which brings you back along the southern side of the gorge.

As you hike these two trails you will encounter several anomalies. The first part of the Gorge Trail takes you, not into the gorge itself, but up along the hillside and almost to the top of the gorge's northern rim. Only at about the midway point does the Gorge Trail finally descend to the edge of Enfield Creek and into the heart of the gorge itself.

On your return along the Rim Trail, your vertical descent is 600 feet between the upper and lower park areas. Yet en route you appear to be doing more uphill climbing than descending—to be going up to get down. This is because, as you start back, you descend a long flight of stairs to the bottom of the gorge, and then make a long climb to the top before abruptly descending to the park's lower level.

The trailhead of the Gorge Trail is next to the park office. A sign directs you to the trail, which almost immediately takes you uphill and into the wooded area by the parking lot. It carries you upward on a long set of stairs that switchbacks several times before reaching a more level area; here the trail turns left (west) and continues its uphill course.

From here it follows a route cut into the side of a steep hill that pitches down about 20 feet to where Enfield Creek is rushing downstream. At this point the gorge is compressed into a V-shape and includes several flumes and chutes through which the creek must pass. Actually, you hear more of the stream than you can see through the trees. A mixture of beeches, oaks, maples, and hemlocks covers all of the lower two-thirds of the gorge. Hemlock appears to be the dominant species.

For the next mile the trail follows an up-and-down course, more up than down; on at least three occasions you have to climb stairways of 70, 50, and 12 steps, respectively. So far, the Gorge Trail is an uphill trek.

At about the mile mark, the trail dips to cross a wooden bridge over a gully, only to head uphill again. Soon, however, it begins a gradual descent to an unusual landform—a high, narrow, natural earthen causeway leading over a deep ravine; it looks like a misplaced esker. The route is so narrow that wire fencing has been placed on both sides of the trail.

From here it is another gradual descent to some stone steps leading down to the creek's edge, which the trail will follow to the end. You are now finally walking along the bottom of Enfield Glen, with the gorge's hillsides rising sharply on both sides of the creek.

Continuing upstream, you start passing a series of small falls, each about 100 yards apart. These were produced when large slabs of rock in the streambed cracked across the creek to form steps several feet high; these cracks or "joints" occur where tension within the rock strata produces fractures. In this ¼-mile stretch you encounter five such falls before reaching an area where the creek widens.

A little farther on the trail passes between a small stone retaining wall built next to the stream on your left and a high limestone wall, eroded by water over the centuries.

Now you come to the middle waterfall, at 25 feet the highest in this middle section. A short flight of stone steps takes you past the falls and back into the gorge's forested area. After a gradual uphill climb, you come to a sign that reads "Red Pine Trail"; this points to a trail intersecting on your right. Continue, however, on the Gorge Trail for another couple hundred yards to where you encounter a wooden footbridge crossing the stream. The bridge route leads to the intersection of the southside Rim Trail and the adjoining 166-step stairway that brings a hiker down from

Flume in upper gorge at Treman State Park

(or up to) the hilltop overlook. Later you will pass these spots on your return trip.

Once past the bridge, the Gorge Trail starts uphill, taking you out of the wooded area and along the side of limestone rock cliffs. A short stretch of level ground provides the opportunity to stop and admire, to your left, the 115-foot-high Lucifer Falls. This is the park's highest waterfall.

You are now entering the so-called younger gorge, formed after the last great ice age. The high rock walls on both sides of the falls were cut into their present form by water erosion over the last 10,000 years.

An additional 101 stone steps lead upward past another, smaller falls and then past still another, even smaller falls. At last you reach an artfully constructed stone-arch bridge crossing a flume through which Enfield Creek rushes. Upstream the creek cascades over a series of low ledges as it passes through a deep, narrow cut whose rock walls rise straight up on either side.

A short distance farther brings you to a sign that reads "Rim Trail"; this directs you uphill, to your left. Straight ahead is the park's entrance and upper section parking lot. Next to the entrance is the two-story Old Mill building, which you may wish to visit; inside you can obtain a brochure describing the history of the Old Mill and the one-time hamlet of Enfield Falls.

Return to the trailhead of the Rim Trail and follow it for several hundred yards to an overlook spot with a fine head-on view of Lucifer Falls in its entirety. The drop-off in front of the retaining wall is straight down to the bottom of the waterfall—a breathtaking sight. A good time to visit this spot is in the spring or summer after a heavy rain, when Enfield Creek is swollen with runoff water and the surging power of the falls is most impressive.

From the overlook it is only a few steps to the 166-step stairway leading down along the cliff to the creek's edge. Once at the base, the trail intersects another one on your right; this is actually the continuation of the Rim Trail. The straight-ahead trail section leads over the wooden bridge and to the Gorge Trail you walked earlier.

Turn right and follow the Rim Trail as it parallels the creek for a short distance before starting a gradual ascent on the right. The trail soon levels out, but in less than ¼ mile descends to a set of wooden stairs and an adjoining small wooden bridge over a gully.

From here the trail begins a long uphill climb before reaching a more level stretch near the top of the hill. You are finally on the rim of the gorge. To your left the side of the hill is extremely steep, pitching downward at about a 70-degree angle; this has prompted the erection of wire fencing along the trail to prevent mishaps. The hillside to your right is a gentle slope leading quickly to the top.

At about the mile mark, the trail begins a gradual downward route; its pitch is hardly noticeable until you reach a fork. A Rim Trail directional sign points to the route on your left; once on this trail, the pitch is most pronounced. This steep downward course continues for about ¼ mile until it reaches the base.

At the park's cabin colony, pass two cabins and turn left. Follow the path that takes you, in several hundred yards, to the park's swimming-pool area and the lower falls.

This path leads over the dam structure to the bathhouse. A right turn at the bathhouse brings you to the picnic area and, just beyond, to the parking area and your waiting vehicle.

8

Buttermilk Falls State Park

Total distance: 4 miles

Hiking time: 3½ hours

Vertical rise: 650 feet

Maps: USGS 7½' West Ithaca; USGS 7½' East Ithaca; USGS 7½' Willseyville; Park Pamphlet and Map

In the spring, when the land is still wet from the winter's snows and the April rains, Buttermilk Falls puts on its most spectacular performance. It is then that the swollen Buttermilk Creek rushes down a narrow gorge, cut deeply over the centuries, and then races over a wide rock face to cascade, white and foaming, into a pool at the base.

Unlike most falls which flow over a rock ledge and plunge straight down, Buttermilk Falls is formed by a long, steep incline about the width of a two-lane road. In their descent, the waters dance over the washboardlike rock face and take on a whitish, buttermilklike appearance. A head-on look at this water display from the base of the falls is breathtaking.

A path takes you across the pool's outlet and to its south side, where you are almost within touching distance of the falls as you make your ascent beside the rushing waters. All this is found a stone's throw away from NY 13 and the entrance to the 751-acre Buttermilk Falls State Park.

Upstream from Buttermilk Falls itself lie some other impressive falls. All told, 10 falls are located in Buttermilk Glen, the gorge portion of the lower park; these, each one more spectacular than the last, are 30 or more feet high. Between the falls are flumes, narrow raceways, and huge potholes drilled by the plunging waters over the centuries.

Once you see the water power on display in the gorge section it is easy to understand why early settlers constructed dams and mills along this portion of Buttermilk Creek. In the early 1800s a mill was built at the foot of the falls, and in 1872 Van Orman's Dam was built in the gorge itself, becoming the source of water for the city of Ithaca until 1903. A gristmill dam, called Scott's Dam, was built in the upper park in 1875. These dams no longer exist.

Before the arrival of white settlers, Native Americans lived near Buttermilk Falls in a village called Coreorgonel; it

Buttermilk Falls

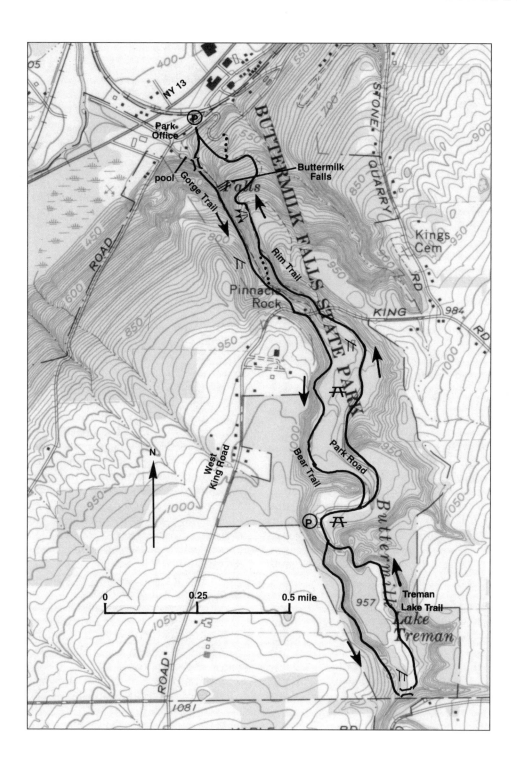

contained 25 log cabins surrounded by cultivated fields and apple and plum orchards. During the revolutionary war, a contingent of General John Sullivan's Continental Army drove the Native Americans from Coreorgonel and burned the village on September 4, 1779.

Access. The state park comes in two parts—the 1.07-mile-long main park and a smaller, 0.6-mile-long parcel—separated by 4 miles of private land. The former, site of Buttermilk Falls, contains a large picnic and camping area as well as several hiking trails; the latter, better known only to local residents, contains a small picnic grove and a sizable swimming pool adjacent to a large pond.

The main park is located 1.5 miles south of the city of Ithaca; it can be reached by NY 13. The park entrance at the foot of Buttermilk Falls is on the south side of the highway. The park's smaller parcel is situated a short distance southwest of the hamlet of Danby on NY 96B which, too, runs south out of Ithaca. Once in Danby, turn right (southwest) onto Hill Road; 0.7 mile brings you to the entrance (on your left) of the small park surrounding Jennings Pond (elevation 1278 feet).

Joining the two parks is Buttermilk Creek, which starts at Jennings Pond and flows northward and gradually downhill for 4 miles, where it enters the upper end of the main park. From here it is 0.5 mile to where the creek empties into the man-made, 0.5-mile-long Treman Lake (elevation 957 feet). The lake's outflow is control-released into Buttermilk Gorge. From the pool (elevation 410 feet) at the base of Buttermilk Falls, the water flows into Cayuga Inlet on the west side of NY 13 and then north into Cayuga Lake.

Trails. The park contains several walking trails. Two are in the lower park the Gorge Trail, which takes you upstream through Buttermilk Glen on the south side of the creek, and the Rim Trail, which runs high above the gorge along a steep hillside on its north side; both are ¾ mile long. In the upper park are the ⅝-mile-long Bear Trail and the 1½-mile-long Treman Lake Trail.

The recommended hiking route, to start, is the Gorge Trail; the return route is the Rim Trail. The beginning of the Gorge Trail is found on the south side of Buttermilk Falls, where the falls meets the pool at the base. From the park office walk past the pool area and cross a wooden bridge spanning the outlet stream.

Once over the footbridge, you start an upward climb by mounting a flight of stone stairs; the whole ¾-mile-long Gorge Trail is a continuous set of stairs, with only a few short stretches of level terrain. After an upward climb of 500 feet the trail curves to the right, bringing you to a nice view of the Cayuga Creek valley and the hills beyond. From here the trail curves again, this time to your left, leading you past a high falls tumbling over rock ledges on your immediate left.

The trail continues for another 1000 feet past another waterfall. Immediately behind it is a doorlike cut in the face of a wall; behind this opening is, first, a flume, then, a falls—all squeezed into a deep, narrow gorge. An additional ¼ mile brings you to where a short set of stairs leads to a lean-to. From here it is 500 feet to a wooden bridge spanning the creek and leading to an uphill path that intersects the Rim Trail.

Continue uphill on the Gorge Trail; in 400 feet you will come to the Pinnacle. This steeplelike rock formation was carved by water thousands of years ago as the gorge was slowly being cut. As the waters ate their way through the shale rock, two routes were eventually formed; as the waters kept cutting deeper, they left a central section of rock exposed until, after a long period of time, the spiral-shaped Pinnacle emerged.

An additional 500 feet brings you past the last falls and to a more level stretch of Buttermilk Creek; then to the last set of steps, as you finally emerge by a highway bridge arching gracefully over the creek. Crossing the bridge is West King Road; this is where the Gorge Trail ends.

Directly across the highway, however, is a footpath entering the woods; this is the start of the Bear Trail, which runs southeast along the west side of Buttermilk Creek for ¾ mile, ending when it intersects the upper park road. Once you reach this intersection, turn right onto the park road and follow it for 500 feet to a parking area.

Another footpath starts here and takes you south up a slight rise to where Treman Lake is dammed on your left. The footpath bears to the right and enters a wooded area on the hillside overlooking Treman Lake, to your left. The trail follows an up-and-down course for ¾ mile, passing a lean-to as it makes a descent to a stone bridge crossing Buttermilk Creek, which, at this point, feeds into Treman Lake.

Once across the bridge, the trail turns northward to follow the lake's shoreline for a short while and then starts an uphill climb. However, since the side of the hill pitches into the lake, the trail's course is largely an uphill journey; your hike entails climbing one set of stairs after another until you reach the top of the hill. A short distance farther brings you to a left turn. Here you descend by a flight of stairs to the top of the stone dam. Cross the dam's top and then climb a short flight of stairs to intersect the foot trail you took earlier to walk around the lake.

Retrace your steps to the parking area. Now, however, stay on the park road as it crosses Buttermilk Creek (actually the creek flows over the road) and then turns left to take you north through a wooded picnic area to the upper park's entrance and West King Road. Across the intersection you will find the trailhead of the Rim Trail.

At first the Rim Trail is level, following what was once a dirt road; soon, however, it narrows to a pavement-width foot trail. After a few hundred feet and a fenced-in overlook, the trail follows a route cut into the side of a steep hill, pitching down sharply into the gorge on your left.

At the ¼-mile mark, a trail intersects on your left, coming up from the gorge via the wooden bridge you passed earlier when walking the Gorge Trail. The Rim Trail now starts a gradual descent, which becomes steeper as you proceed downhill; here the trail is black-topped to reduce erosion brought on by water rushing downhill after rainstorms.

At the ½-mile mark is a second overlook, from which you can see several falls within the gorge to your left. Continue downhill on what is now a steep trail until you come to the concession building across the road from the park office. This ends your hike.

9

Connecticut Hill Wildlife Management Area

Total distance: 15 miles (2 days)

Hiking time: 7 hours

Vertical rise: 2010 feet

Maps: USGS 7½' Alpine; USGS 7½' Mecklenburg

As a landform, Connecticut Hill resembles a fat finger pointing south. On the east and west sides as well as at the fingertip, the forested land drops off precipitously, sometimes over 700 feet to the narrow valley floor that partly encircles the southern half of the hill.

Across the top of the hill is a large tract of state land known officially as the Connecticut Hill Wildlife Management Area. Five miles wide and seven miles long, it sits astride two counties, Schuyler County on the west and Tompkins County on the east. At 11,654 acres, the wildlife management area is the largest in New York.

Topographically, the hill is composed of a series of ridges, knobby or peaked hills, and valleys, many deeply dissected by small streams to form impressive gullies and gorges. The southern half of the hill, clefted and cut in all directions, is best described as craggy and rugged. The central section is a bit more level, but the landscape is still rolling. It is the nearest thing to an alpine area that this region has, which is what must have inspired the founders of the two hamlets at the southern tip of the hill—Alpine and Alpine Junction (site of the old Lehigh Valley railroad station). Local people just call the area the "Hill."

Why the name "Connecticut" in the middle of New York State? The reason is that the state of Connecticut acquired the land in 1800 and held it for 50 years before selling to private owners. One of the later owners was R.H. Treman, after whom Treman State Park, located a short distance southwest of Ithaca, is named.

The height of the hill is much the same as that of other hills in the landform region called the Finger Lakes Hills, which is at the northern edge of the Appalachian Plateau. The highest spot (elevation 2099 feet) is a knob with a radio tower and several antenna dishes at the northern edge of the state forest. Other high spots are Rowell Hill (elevation 1840 feet) in the east, VanLone Hill (elevation 1730 feet) in the west, and

Swan Hill (elevation 1700 feet) in the southwest. In between, there are over a dozen unnamed hilltops that range from 1830 to 2010 feet.

Ecologically, the hill is unique, with probably as diversified a mixture of trees, shrubs, and plants as can be found in this part of New York. It is rich in evergreens (pines, hemlocks, and cedars) and hardwoods (ranging from cockspur hawthorne to sugar maple).

The hill was settled by the late 1700s, and by the mid-19th century much of it had been cleared for cultivation and pasture. The number of farms had peaked by 1880 when, as in the case of many hilltop farms across the state's southern tier, farmers found that the poorly drained, low fertility clay soil could no longer support competitive agriculture. By 1926, only 20 of the original 109 farms were still operating; the rest stood idle or abandoned. During the Great Depression, New York acquired the farmland through the Federal Resettlement Administration, which helped farmers relocate by purchasing their land.

In the 1950s, the state initiated serious silvicultural practices to improve both timber quality and deer browse. For the professional conservationists, the state land became a giant outdoor laboratory in methods to arrest woodland succession. Potholes were blasted for waterfowl; mowing and burning kept fields open, while clear-cutting and selective cutting were used to create openings in mature forest. Maintenance of habitat diversity has become the identifying mark of the wildlife area.

As a result, the land supports a sizable deer herd, large numbers of ruffed grouse, and large flocks of wild turkey, among other sorts of wildlife that probably you will see while on your hike. Connecticut Hill is also a great place for birding; you'll spot dozens of species ranging from the Eastern wood pewee and brown thrasher to the vireos and warblers. Woodland flowers range from pink azaleas to the pointed blue-eyed grasses and pink lady's slippers.

To get a feel for this unusual land and to enjoy its many picturesque vistas, you have to spend several days on the hill, or at least camp for a weekend. Camping is allowed only by permit, which you can obtain by writing or calling the Regional Wildlife Manager, PO Box 1169, Cortland, NY 13045 (607-753-3095).

Access. The top of the hill can be reached from all sides. The commonly used routes, however, are Black Oak Road in the north, Connecticut Hill Road and Carter Creek Road in the southeast, and Swan Hill Road (which runs out of Alpine) in the southwest. We suggest using the Connecticut Hill Road, which can be reached via NY 13—14 miles south of Ithaca in Pony Hollow, or 14.6 miles north of Horseheads. Turn west onto the Connecticut Hill Road (a dirt road), and drive uphill 2.6 miles where you will see two white blazes on a tree, marking the spot where the Finger Lakes Trail intersects the road. Park here.

Trail. The 15-mile trail system suggested here is for those who plan to camp overnight. If you wish, you can pitch your tent in the open area next to the road where you parked your car, or you can backpack to some other spot along the trail. Spots that are ideal for tenting include the open area at the corner of Boyland and Hulford Roads, ½ mile south on Hulford Road, and off the road south of Swan Hill. But there are many other places you may find to your liking in the woods themselves.

First Day

Connecticut Hill Road and back via Finger Lakes Trail and Hulford Road
Distance: 8¾ miles
Hiking time: 4½ hours

For the first day's loop, follow the white blazes of the Finger Lakes Trail (FLT) from your parking spot north along Connecticut Hill Road for ¼ mile, where the FLT turns right off the road and enters a stand of large red pine. A short distance into the forest, the trail turns left and heads straight north for just a little over a mile, where it begins to turn to the right. A short distance farther brings you to Boyland Road; follow this road for less than ¼ mile where the trail turns left onto a lane. A little way down the lane, the FLT leaves the lane and turns right as it heads downhill into the forest.

This downhill stretch takes you in a little over ½ mile to Connecticut Hill Road. The trail exits onto the road, follows it for about 100 yards, and then turns left up an embankment into the forest. The trail dips down a bit at first but then starts to slope upward for a little over ½ mile where it makes a 90-degree turn to the left onto an abandoned farm road. A ¼ mile more brings you to the corner of Black Oak Road; continue west a short distance on this dirt road to where you see Tower Road intersecting on your right. Follow Tower Road north past the radio tower and antenna dishes for almost ½ mile to a picnic area with several tables and fireplaces.

This part of the state land is man-

Old tree root next to trail

aged by the Park Commission rather than by the Department of Environmental Conservation (DEC). No camping is permitted here, but with its picnic tables it is an ideal spot for a lunch break or a rest. If you follow the FLT blazes from the picnic area a short distance to Cayutaville Road, you'll come to an open area with a fine view of the hill country in the west.

Retrace your steps southward for 2½ miles to the Boyland-Hulford Road intersection. Turn onto Hulford Road, and follow it southward for a little less than ½ mile. On both sides of the road are fields maintained by the DEC. You are also at one of the area's high spots, which gives you a nice overlook to the south toward the hilltops of Newfield State Forest 4 miles away.

The walk for the next mile is all downhill through the forest with a couple of fields en route. As you near the bottom, the road turns left and then follows the west edge of a deep ravine through which flows Carter Creek. A ¼ mile farther, the road crosses a bridge over a small brook and then heads uphill and westward through a fairly large open area. Soon you are back in the forest with the trees shading the road as you climb upward for a little over a mile, eventually reaching Connecticut Hill Road. Turn left (south) here; a short distance brings you back to your vehicle and to your tent if you're camping here.

Second Day
Connecticut Hill Road and back via Swan Hill and Finger Lakes Trail
Distance: 3⅝ miles
Hiking time: 2 hours

For the second loop, follow Connecticut Hill Road from your vehicle south for about ½ mile; here the road turns left, while another unnamed dirt road turns right. Turn right (west) on that road. It pitches downward for just over ½ mile, passes Swan Hill Road, crosses a small brook, and then starts to rise.

About ¼ mile from Swan Hill Road, the dirt road turns 90 degrees and heads north. Continuing due west, or straight ahead, however, is a lane. If you stay on this lane for ¼ mile, you will find excellent views to the west and to the south from an open area on Swan Hill.

Retrace your steps to the intersection. Turn left (north) here, and follow the road due north for about ½ mile. About the halfway point, you get another view, this time to the north; from here the road slopes downward until it reaches a narrow valley with a small brook. Just before you reach the bridge crossing this brook, you will spot the white blazes of the FLT, which enters the forest on your right.

Turn right onto the FLT, and follow it due east. It will take you mostly uphill, leveling out as you near the trail's intersection with Connecticut Hill Road and the spot where you parked your vehicle.

10

Fillmore Glen State Park

Total distance: 3¾ miles

Hiking time: 2½ hours

Vertical rise: 349 feet

Maps: USGS 7½' Sempronius; USGS 7½' Moravia; Park Brochure and Map

Fillmore Glen State Park is narrow, deep, and linear in shape. The word "glen," in this part of upstate New York, is used to denote a gorge of impressive dimensions and is a label bestowed on only a few of the gorges found in the Finger Lakes region—Watkins Glen (see Hike 5), Enfield Glen (see Hike 7), and Buttermilk Glen (see Hike 8).

The park extends southeastward and uphill from its base until it reaches high land (elevation 1720 feet) overlooking a broad U-shaped valley running northward to eventually encompass the blue waters of Owasco Lake, one of the five Finger Lakes.

Near the park's upper end you are surrounded by more state land, Summer Hill State Forest. Between the park and the forest, you get the best of two worlds—a deep, botanically rich gorge and a high, level, sprawling forest. While the park (938 acres) is administered by the state's Office of Parks, Recreation and Historic Preservation, the state forest (4345 acres) is managed by the Department of Environmental Conservation.

The recommended hike takes place in Fillmore Glen State Park; it follows the gorge uphill to the upper dam, returning by a route that follows the gorge's south rim. Summer Hill State Forest, on the other hand, is high but flat and contains a network of dirt roads open to hiking. Biking these roads, however, may prove the better choice, since you can cover virtually all of them in half a day.

Although these parcels of state land are connected at the top of Summer Hill, no hiking trail joins the two. If you like exploring and bushwhacking, however, you can hike from the park's upper dam to the state forest by following a stream as it flows downhill into the pond; the one-way distance is only 1¾ miles. An easier way to get from the state park to the forest is to drive, using Toll Gate Road and Erron Hill Road as your access routes.

Fillmore Glen State Park contains three hiking trails and one snowmobile trail (which serves as a biking or hiking

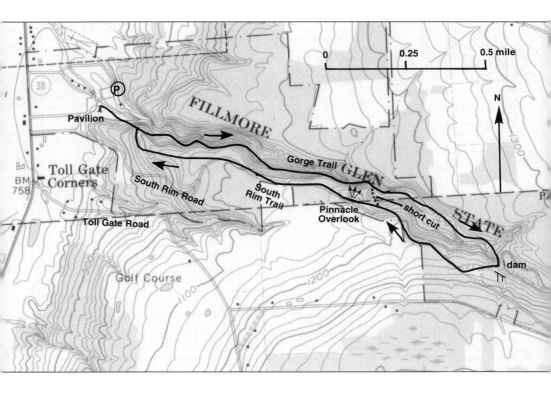

trail during the summer months). Each of the hiking trails—the North Rim Trail, the South Rim Trail, and the Gorge Trail—is 1⅞ miles in length. All the trails begin at the Pavilion area near the park entrance and end at the dam in the upper reaches. The snowmobile trail also starts near the park's entrance and runs southeast along the top of the hill overlooking the gorge, eventually dipping downward to cross Dry Creek and emerge at the intersection of Clover Leaf Road on the southern edge of the park.

From the park's entrance (elevation 751 feet) to the end of the hiking trails at the dam (elevation 1100 feet), the vertical rise is 349 feet. From the park's entrance to the top of Summer Hill (elevation 1720 feet), the vertical rise is 969 feet.

Walking the various trails in the state park allows you to become more familiar with the area's geological, botanical, and political histories as well as its natural beauty.

Geologically, the flatness of Summer Hill was produced when an ice sheet called the Wisconsin Glacier bulldozed its way across New York in its southward advance more than 15,000 years ago. Fillmore Glen Gorge, on the other hand, was formed during the postglacial meltback. Vast quantities of water released by the retreating glacier on Summer Hill poured down the steep slopes into what is today's Owasco Inlet valley. In the process, the torrent of water cut its way into the shale rock and later, more slowly, into the underlying sandstone and limestone beds to give us today's gorge.

Fillmore Glen, being cool and damp

during the summer months, is especially suited for a variety of abundant plant life. This plant diversity was of special interest to Dr. Charles Atwood, a local physician and keen amateur botanist who devoted much of his energy to the successful establishment of a public park in the 1920s. A plaque dedicated to his efforts can be found in the park at the far end of the Pavilion Area. Trails were opened in 1921 and, in 1925, a 39-acre site was transferred to the state as Fillmore Glen State Park.

The park's name honors Millard Fillmore, who became America's 13th president after Zachary Taylor died in office in 1850. Fillmore, born in 1800, was a New Yorker, and the state remembered its native son by naming the park for him. The site of his birthplace is located just outside Summer Hill State Forest, about 5 miles northeast of the state park; it can be reached by Fillmore Road. A replica of the log cabin in which he was born stands inside the park entrance.

Access. Fillmore Glen State Park can be reached via NY 38, running south from Auburn on the west side of Owasco Lake, or NY 38A, also from Auburn, running south on the east side of Owasco Lake. Both routes meet in the center of the village of Moravia. From here, continue driving south on NY 38 for 1 mile until you reach the entrance of the state park, on your left. An admission fee is charged at the entrance gate.

Trail. Running through Fillmore Glen is the misnamed Dry Creek. This stream has its source in a low drainage area on top of Summer Hill; a dam 1⅞ miles upstream holds back its waters in a fair-sized pond. The water in the pond is control-released, allowing it to flow downhill through the gorge to the park's picnic area, where it is dammed for the

second time to allow swimming during the summer.

Along the gorge's water route you will find rock layers forming "joints," which give rise to impressive waterfalls; five are found between the park's Pavilion and the upper dam.

The recommended hiking trail begins on the east side of the Pavilion. From the Pavilion building it is a short walk past the lower picnic area on your right and the swimming area on your left to a set of stone steps that takes you to the upper picnic area. Just beyond, the Gorge Trail begins.

Before mounting the stairs, turn left and cross an attractive stone bridge arching over Dry Creek. A short trail takes you to what is called the "Cowsheds," a deep recess cut by postglacial waters. Next to this amphitheaterlike recess is the almost three-story-high Lower Falls. Several legends account for the origin of "Cowsheds." It has been said that years ago, before the area became a park, cattle from a nearby farm came here to escape the summer heat. A more fanciful account holds that some local cattle rustlers hid their stolen cattle here.

Retrace your steps over the bridge to the stone stairs and climb to the upper picnic area. Follow the path past several stone picnic tables and up a slight incline; the path then takes you down a set of stone steps to an overlook and a view from on top of the Lower Falls.

From the overlook continue your hike on what is now the Gorge Trail. Follow the path on the right side of Dry Creek until you reach a wooden bridge, the first of eight such bridges you will meet while hiking upstream. As you walk along the edge of the stream, notice the gorge's coolness—a welcome change on a hot summer's day—as well as the abundant plant life alongside the path.

After crossing several bridges, you begin a fairly long walk on the stream's right side. Soon you come to a fine view of a streamlet plunging down an almost perpendicular hill on the gorge's north side; this is most spectacular in the spring, when the runoff is at its best. Before long you cross still another bridge. Here the gorge's walls rise straight up; on your left, they ascend to form a peak called the Pinnacle. (On your return trip via the South Rim Trail you will have a chance to stop at Pinnacle Overlook for a fine view of the gorge from on top.)

A short distance farther brings you to the seventh bridge, which leads to a lean-to on the right side of the stream. Here you will find a path heading uphill; should you decide to shorten your hike, this trail takes you to the South Rim Trail and the Pinnacle Overlook.

If you plan to continue upstream to the dam, stay on the path on the left side of the stream. You will shortly see the fifth waterfall, Upper Falls. From the Gorge Trail a path leads a short distance downhill to a good spot for a head-on view of the three-story-high falls.

Back on the Gorge Trail, the path takes you across the last bridge and up a long set of steps to the dammed pond. This is a good spot to stop, rest, enjoy the view, and even have lunch. You have now completed 1⅞ miles of the Gorge Trail, with a vertical rise of 349 feet.

The trail continues around the lower side of the dam, over the concrete dam

Stream running through gorge

itself, and uphill past another lean-to to a turnaround area for vehicles. Follow the hardtop road downhill until you come to a sign on your right directing you to the Pinnacle Overlook. Here you will also encounter a footpath running through the trees along the edge of the gorge's south rim and paralleling the hardtop road; this is the start of the South Rim Trail.

Follow the footpath downhill through a wooded area until you reach the upper picnic area. From here take the stairs down to the lower picnic area and the Pavilion area where your vehicle is parked.

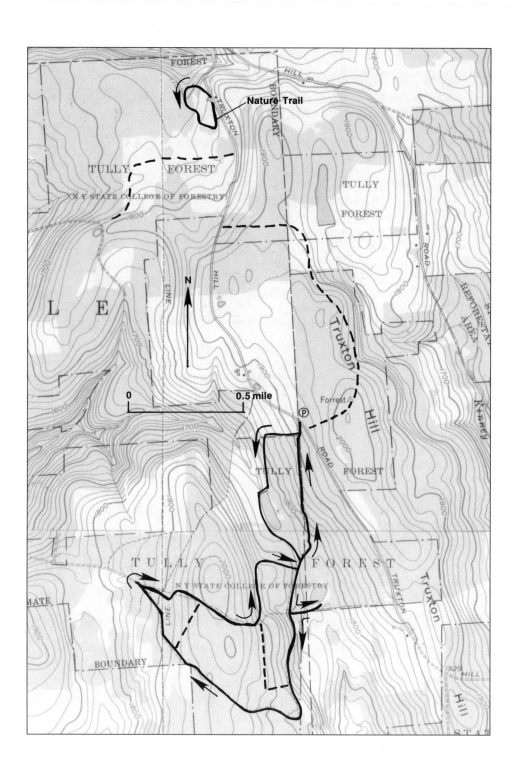

Nature Trail

N

0   0.5 mile

11

Heiberg Memorial Forest

Total distance: 5 miles

Hiking time: 2½ hours

Vertical rise: 1932 feet

Maps: USGS 7½' Tully; USGS 7½' Truxton

"Variety" is probably the best single word to describe the Heiberg Forest area, for here you will find a diverse network of trails, fire lanes, and dirt roads to hike, as well as many vistas, overlooks, and an assortment of ponds that hold numerous species of game fish. You will also find a self-guided nature trail that is a delight to walk, and a series of trails that lead you through large stands of hardwoods and into the territory of several herds of white-tailed deer. From here you may emerge into an area of thick overgrowth, the ideal habitat of the ruffed grouse for which this forest is well known.

The 3780-acre Heiberg Memorial Forest is located atop Truxton Hill (elevation 2020 feet), a wide, flat ridge that overlooks the towns of Tully to the north and Truxton to the southwest. At first glance, it looks like many other state reforestation areas—but a bit tidier, perhaps. The difference is in its use, for this is an outdoor classroom and experimental station used by the State University of New York College of Environmental Science and Forestry. Officially, it is designated as the "Tully Campus, Heiberg Memorial Forest." Still, the touches of civilization here are few, in the forms of the resident forest manager's home and adjacent truck garage.

Hiking in Heiberg Forest, you are walking through biological time and succession as the land returns to its natural state. First settled by pioneers in the late 1700s, the area developed from virgin forest into farmland. However, the soil proved to be highly acidic and poorly drained, and by the 1840s the farmers had turned to lumbering to supplement their incomes and supply the railroad's growing demand for fuel. This only added to the region's economic difficulties, as quality timber soon became scarce and fast water runoff on the naked land made farming more and more unfeasible. Between 1870 and 1925, two-thirds of the population left the area, and the fields that had been so painfully cleared began to revert to hardwoods.

Conifers were planted later when the state began to purchase land in the 1930s.

As you walk, look about for evidence of the succession from wilderness to farmland to wilderness. You may find old stone fences running through the forest, traces of old wagon roads, barbed wire embedded in old trees, and mature forest in areas where crops once grew.

Access. Heiberg Forest and Truxton Hill can be reached from Tully, south of Syracuse and just off I-81. From the center of Tully drive east on NY 80 for a mile, and turn right onto Railroad Street. At the end of the block, bear left and then right across the railroad tracks onto Grove Street, which at the village edge changes to West Hill Road. Continue uphill on West Hill Road for 1.8 miles. When you reach the hilltop, look back. You have a fine vista of Tully village, the wide, north-south Tully valley, and the Tully Lakes, a cluster of large and small "kettle lakes" formed by the retreating glacier thousands of years ago.

Just ahead where the road flattens there is a sign on your right. It reads: Heiberg Memorial Forest, State University College of Environmental Science and Forestry. An arrow points to a dirt road intersecting on your right. This is Maple Ridge Road (Truxton Road on the USGS map) and it takes you into Heiberg Forest.

In ¼ mile you come to another sign on your right by a parking area. This one directs you to a well-maintained nature trail that begins here, travels in a loop, and returns to the parking area. It is short, so you can choose to walk it now or on your way back.

From the nature trail parking area it is ⅜ mile to where a lane (actually a service road) intersects on your left; this is

Heiberg Memorial Forest

blocked by a metal barrier to prevent use by unauthorized vehicles, including all-terrain vehicles. The ½-mile-long lane, which takes you through the woods to Pond 1, may be walked.

Continue, however, on the main road. The wooded area on your left has been posted as a nontrespassing experimental area. An additional ⅜ mile brings you past several parcels of privately owned property with homes on your right, then past several structures, including the "North and South Classroom Buildings," the college's garage and maintenance buildings, and the forest manager's home. From here it is ⅜ mile to another dirt road intersecting on your right. Park here off the road.

Trail. Start your hike by taking the road on your right at the intersection. Follow it for 100 feet to a barricade (which is usually open). At this point turn right off the dirt road and follow a little-used lane downhill past a large stand of evergreens on your left. This route brings you to Pond 3. At the base of the hill, the trail turns left, running along the forest edge for ¼ mile. On your right are open fields; ahead you can see Pond 3, which is stocked with rainbow trout. You may fish here, but you must obtain a permit from the forest manager, because the pond is a research site. You will find the rainbows big and sassy whether you fly fish or spin cast.

It used to be possible to continue south on the abandoned road running along the east side of the pond. This is no longer the case; the path is blocked by deadfall. The evergreens along this route rotted in the soggy soil and fell into each other, making foot travel impossible.

However, you can follow another route that entails a bit of easy bush-whacking. At the north end of the pond, cross the earthen dam to the west side and then turn left (south), following the edge of the pond until you enter the woods. Continue south through the forested area for ¼ mile where you intersect a dirt road.

Turn right and follow the dirt road for about ½ mile past a stand of tamaracks to where a firebreak lane intersects on your left. It is barricaded against unauthorized vehicles; however, a short walk down this lane brings you to an attractive impoundment, Pond 2, an ideal place to take a lunch break. This pond, like the others in Heiberg Forest, is used by white-tailed deer as a watering hole and by ducks and geese as a resting and feeding site during fall and spring migrations. It may also be fished if you have secured a permit from the forest manager.

Return to the dirt road and continue walking south and uphill; ¼ mile brings you to another firebreak lane intersecting on your right (designated by a dashed line on this book's map). If you wish to shorten your hike, take this lane west and uphill a short distance to where it is intersected on your right by another firebreak lane; if you turn right here and follow the lane north, it will bring you back to the dirt road you walked earlier. On the other hand, if you wish to continue on the longer route, follow the dirt road south and uphill for a short distance to where the road turns sharply to your right; from here the road runs in a northwesterly direction over flattened terrain. A mile farther on the lane starts to pitch downward. Here you will find a small parking area and an unmarked firebreak lane on your right. Bear right onto the fire lane, which runs straight in a southeast direction for ¼ mile, turns left and then right, and again heads in a straight line downhill. Halfway down it intersects another fire lane. Turn left here and follow the fire lane. In ½ mile it turns and heads downhill to intersect the road you walked earlier. The walk through this section of Heiberg is most pleasant. The fire lanes are broad, clean, and canopied by tall trees. When you reach the dirt road, turn left and walk back to your vehicle. On both sides of the road are stately cedars that give a special charm to this last stretch. The road ascends gradually and then flattens out as you near your vehicle.

This also is great ski-touring country. The terrain is varied, with small hills and level stretches—just the kind of landscape ski tourers love—and the snow comes early, packs well, and stays deep. The forest is laced with ski-touring trails, and there are miles of woodland trails for the snowshoer to walk. Maple Ridge Road is plowed as far as the forest manager's house, giving you easy access to all the key trails.

12

Highland Forest

Total distance: 4½ miles	
Hiking time: 2½ hours	
Vertical rise: 1160 feet	
Maps: USGS 7½' DeRuyter; Park Map	

This 2700-acre county park sits astride Arab Hill (elevation 1940 feet) in the high land south of Syracuse. As you enter the park, and just before reaching the parking lot, you are treated to a vista of rolling hills, woodlands, and farmlands, for Highland Forest is the high point of the region, overlooking the lower lands to the north.

With its almost Adirondack-like appearance and its network of walking trails, fire lanes, and truck trails, Highland Forest is ideal for the hiker. As it is popular for horseback riding, the county maintains riding trails and provides a corral. Near the parking lot there are facilities for picnicking and a softball diamond. During the winter months the forest is a mecca for cross-country skiers, for it offers some of the finest maintained public trails in central New York.

The Onandaga County Parks and Recreation Department has developed an excellent system of hiking trails in this large forest tract. Highland boasts four hiking trails that begin and end at the parking lot at the northern end of the forest. The "A" loop is just short of a mile long and takes only 30 minutes to walk. The "B" loop runs just over a mile and takes 40 minutes; the "C" loop, at 2¾ miles, takes 1½ hours, and the Main Trail, at 8¼ miles, takes 4 to 5 hours. The forest also has a number of interconnected jeep trails, truck trails, and fire lanes so the enterprising day hiker can make up an endless variety of hikes to suit particular interests and timetables.

The county also encourages mountain bikers to use all the area's interior roads and fire lanes as well as ski trails during the summer months. A map is provided at the park office, showing all possible routes. Biking season runs from May 1 to November 15, daily from dawn to dusk. However, hiking trails (marked with a yellow pine-tree symbol) are closed to bike traffic.

The route presented here travels for some distance on each of the four maintained hiking trails and on some of the many jeep and truck trails. This is a day-use area, so don't plan on camping out. Overnight camping is restricted to organized groups, such as the Scouts, and only then by reservation. If you alter the route described here, be sure to return to your car before dark.

Access. Highland Forest is located south of Syracuse and east of Tully, just off NY 80. From the village of Fabius, travel east on NY 80 for 2.2 miles until you see a Highland Forest sign on your left that directs you to your right onto the paved Highland Park Road. After making the turn, drive uphill for 1.1 miles to the parking area on your right, opposite a cluster of buildings: the Community House (in winter a warming hut for cross-country skiers), the park office, and the Pioneer Museum, housing a collection of farm implements, home furnishings, books, and other items of rural life in Onandaga County in the 1800s and early 1900s.

Trail. The trailhead is on the far side of the parking area, next to an information booth and map board. At the park office, you can obtain both a mimeographed guide to the "A" loop, which doubles as a nature trail, and a scaled contour map, showing all the trails, roads, and fire lanes. The trail system is well marked; look for the stylized yellow pine-tree design painted on trees.

Starting at the information booth, you enter the woods on the "A" loop and cross a footbridge over one of the several small brooks you come to on your hike; together these streams make up the headwaters of the Tioughnioga River, which flows south through Cortland and Binghamton to the Susquehanna River.

Beyond the bridge, the trail winds through hardwood trees for ¼ mile and enters an evergreen stand. This is a good place to test your skill at tree identification, so bring your field guide. Many of

the trees throughout the forest are human-planted, and the variety is most impressive. Among the evergreens are red, white, Ponderosa, pitch, jack, sugar, and lodgepole pine; white, Norway, Engleman, and blue spruce; Douglas and balsam fir; and white cedar. Among the hardwoods are American basswood, quaking aspen, white ash, black cherry, yellow birch, American beech, paper birch, sugar maple, northern red oak, and red maple.

A short distance into the evergreens, you reach a set of signs; two point left for the Nature Trail and Picnic Area, and one points right for the Main Trail. The "A" loop returns to the parking area by way of the Nature Trail.

You continue on the Main Trail. In about 400 feet a sign points left to the "B" loop, which also returns directly to the parking area. Stay on the Main Trail. A few hundred feet farther, you cross a dirt road and enter a stand of white and red pines, which soon gives way to hardwoods.

The trail now runs due south, parallel to a gully on your left, which becomes deeper as you walk south. After a mile, the trail begins to descend more steeply, finally turning left into the gully at a point where two brooks merge. After swinging back and forth across the water three times on footbridges, the trail winds up a slight incline to intersect a truck trail.

Bear left on the truck trail, still heading uphill. By now you have passed over an area that 50 years ago was farmland. In 1930 the county acquired its first parcel of land from two farmers, and with that purchase Highland Forest was founded. During the next 3 years of the Great Depression, the county obtained nine more farms, and by 1935 it had acquired two additional parcels to make up 90 percent of what is now the forest.

View from Highland Forest

You soon reach a sign marking the place where the "C" loop and the Main Trail diverge. The "C" loop continues on the truck road, but the Main Trail, which is still your route, heads to the right and downhill into a gully. The small brook at the bottom drops into a much deeper ravine on your right.

Here a sign points right to Easy Street and left to Goat Trail. Unless you like hard climbing, stay on Easy Street, which swings right out of the gully and makes a sharp left up a moderate ¼-mile incline. At the top, the trail takes you out of the woods, across a power-line right-of-way, and back into the forest again. The trail levels out 1000 feet beyond the right-of-way, and a sign informs you that you have reached the highest point in the forest, 1940 feet.

You soon begin a gradual descent. The trail, here a truck road, bends left (east) and shortly encounters a jeep trail with a marker on the right-hand corner. (The jeep and truck trails are numbered, not named.) The corner marker has two numbers: 27, which is the road you have been walking, and 25, which runs in front of you. An arrow also points left to the park office. Following the arrow, keep left on Road 25 for 1500 feet until it intersects Road 29. Turn left and head uphill; in ¼ mile it brings you back to the power-line right-of-way. Cross it and reenter the woods, where you will see another sign to the Goat Trail. Take this trail, which leads downhill to the brook you crossed earlier. Retrace your route to the truck road, turn right, and walk about 50 feet to the power-line cut. You are now back on the "C" loop.

The hike continues, however, to the right up the truck trail. When you come to the Arab Hill Camp, go around a road barrier, and head uphill for ¼ mile, where you intersect another stretch of the Main Trail, which has been running north on Road 5. At this point, the Main Trail turns off Road 5 to follow the power line for about 1000 feet before bearing left into the forest again. Stay on the Main Trail, which now runs north for ½ mile and then loops back, running southwest for ¼ mile and then due west for another ¼ mile, bringing you back to the park office and your start.

This area is a ski tourer's delight. There are four groomed and maintained trails designed for novice through advanced, and the snows come early and stay late—usually into the end of March.

13

Morgan Hill State Forest

Total distance: 9½ miles

Hiking time: 5 hours

Vertical rise: 1988 feet

Map: USGS 7½' Tully

Like the persons for whom they were named, Fellows Hill, Jones Hill, and Morgan Hill are next-door neighbors. Spread over these three hills, all about 2000 feet in elevation, are 5508 acres of state land, making a varied hiking terrain. Officially, this area is called Morgan Hill State Forest, although locally it is known variously as Fabius Forest, Morgan Hill, or Shackham Woods.

Through this state land and over some adjoining private land runs the Onandaga Trail. Designed, marked, and maintained by members of the Onandaga Chapter of the Adirondack Mountain Club, it is one of the spur trails to the Finger Lakes Trail (FLT) system. The trail is well groomed and marked with orange blazes painted on trees.

The several dirt roads (officially called truck trails) make ideal mountain-biking routes. They are hard packed and well maintained by the state, making cycling a pleasant experience as you climb moderate hills and speed along the level stretches of Shackham Road and Morgan Hill Road.

The entire Morgan Hill State Forest area is covered with trees, with about 70 percent in pine and spruce plantations and the other 30 percent natural hardwoods. In the middle of the forest there is even a section of virgin timber several hundred years old. You will find some fine overlooks here, as well as magnificent Tinker Falls, a pond stocked with brook trout, a lean-to, a rushing wilderness brook, and a series of hills, gullies, and ravines to add variety to your hike. The area in and around Morgan Hill State Forest also displays a variety of landmarks produced by the several ice sheets that once covered New York—a kettle lake, a through valley, a hanging falls, and outwash hummocks. In short, the Morgan Hill area is a hiker's delight.

Access. You begin your hike on the Onandaga Trail at Spruce Pond, a small impoundment just 0.2 mile southwest of Fellows Hill. (The pond is not shown on

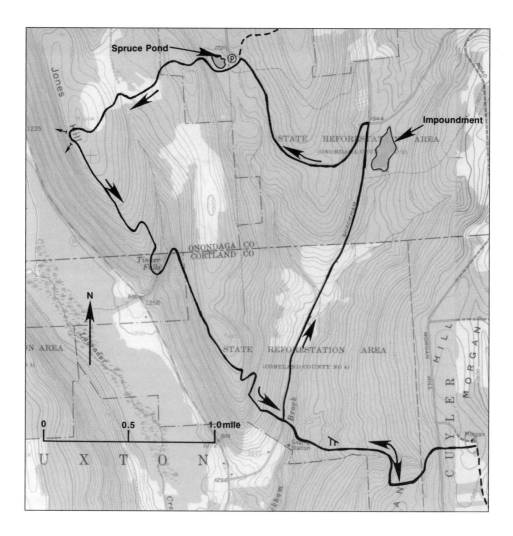

the USGS map as it was created after the map was last updated.)

Spruce Pond, in turn, can be reached from I-81 by exiting at Tully (about halfway between Syracuse and Cortland) and then heading east on NY 80. Just beyond the hamlet of Apulia, look for Herlihy Road, a hard-packed, two-lane dirt road. Turn right onto it; in 1.2 miles you reach Morgan Hill State Forest, marked by the end of farm fields and the beginning of woods.

From this point another 0.7 mile brings you to a fork. Take the one-lane dirt road to your right and drive 0.1 mile past a stand of evergreens to a parking area by the dam at the south end of Spruce Pond. Leave your car here.

You will notice that this area is used for picnicking and camping. If your interests include fishing, you can try the pond for the beautiful red-spotted brook trout stocked by the state.

Trail. On a tree near the parking area is painted the word "Hike" and an arrow pointing across the dam. On the other side, a second sign indicates the beginning of the trail. Follow the trail halfway around the pond and then to your left up a relatively short but steep hill.

Where the orange-marked trail reaches the crest it flattens out and heads west. In about 5 minutes you start a gradual descent that brings you to a large stand of smooth-barked beeches. Beyond this point the trees become smaller and gradually thin out as you enter what was once a field, now taken over by saplings and evergreens. From here you are hiking on private land for the next mile.

You soon leave the field and enter a stand of trees that shades an unused wagon trail and a small brook that flows southward to Tinker Falls. After crossing the brook, you pass through another abandoned field before reentering the woods. The trail wanders a bit here and then brings you to the summit of Jones Hill (elevation 1964 feet).

Your path now descends sharply for about 100 feet. To your immediate right an opening through the trees offers you the first vista—a grand view of Labrador Hollow. The hollow is an excellent example of what geologists call a "through valley"—a valley gouged out by advancing glaciers which overran New York State several times during the Pleistocene epoch, with the last period of glaciation climaxing about 12,000 years ago. Also notice the distinctive U-shape of the valley, another sign of the work done by the advancing glaciers.

The drop-off at the overlook is an abrupt and breathtaking 700 feet. Below you lies the half-mile-long Labrador Pond, a "kettle" lake left behind by the retreating glacier. It is tucked in a narrow valley between Jones and Labrador Hills. A little to your right, Labrador Hollow fans out to the north around and beyond the hamlet of Apulia Station. Still farther north, you see a series of smaller hills covered with crop fields and pastureland.

The trail continues for ½ mile along the crest of Jones Hill to an open area with a fine overlook, once used by hang-gliders for their flight down to the fields on the north side of Labrador Pond. It is a nice spot to stop for lunch while enjoying the sights of Labrador Hollow. In the next ½ mile you follow an abandoned lane before turning left on the hiking trail as it heads downhill, eventually leading to a brook. In early spring this brook is high, but by midsummer it may be nothing more than a trickle. Turn right and follow the path to Tinker Falls, where the water plunges some 20 feet off a limestone ledge. This is a "hanging falls," created when the glaciers produced and then deepened the through valley that is now Labrador Hollow. Tinker Falls is a pleasant sight at all times, but most impressive in spring when the brook is running heavy with meltwater.

From Tinker Falls continue south along the ridge for another ½ mile. You now begin a descent, with the trail switching back and forth until it emerges on Shackham Road, a well-maintained, two-lane dirt road 470 feet below the ridge crest. The trail crosses this road and drops sharply for 80 feet to Shackham Brook, a picture-book scene in spring and early summer when its water flows over rocks and boulders, forming riffles and small pools en route through the ravine past large stands of pines and hardwoods. Cross the brook, and follow the trail along the edge of the ravine on your right. You climb fairly steeply for a little better than ½ mile, at which point you come to a lean-to and a stone fireplace. This is an ideal place to stop for a breather. If you are planning a camping trip, the lean-to can be your overnight shelter.

Continue uphill for another ¼ mile to Morgan Hill Road, a one-lane hard-packed dirt road. Follow the trail markers across the road. A 10-minute walk brings you to an open area, once the site of a fire tower which was removed in the mid-1980s. There also is a dirt road leading from Morgan Hill Road to the old fire tower site; it parallels the hiking trail a short distance to the north.

You are now at the summit of Morgan Hill (elevation 2000 feet). This is a good place to camp if you are a weekend hiker or a through-hiker looking for an alternative site to the lean-to you passed earlier. On the southeast edge of the clearing, the orange trail continues south along an abandoned road that now serves as a foot trail. If you follow this route, it brings you downhill to a cluster of farm buildings, then via a blacktop road to the hamlet of Cuyler, and later to Cuyler State Forest (see Hike 20).

Retrace your steps across Morgan Hill Road and downhill past the lean-to to Shackham Road. Turn right and continue north for 2 miles to the first intersection.

Here Herlihy Road crosses Shackham Road. Through the trees on your right, you see a small pond, a man-made impoundment that is large enough to bring canoeists here for an afternoon of paddling. Turn left onto Herlihy Road and head uphill. After a gentle climb of ¼ mile, the road flattens out, and it is an easy 1½-mile hike back to Spruce Pond and your car.

SUSQUEHANNA HILLS

14

Shindagin Hollow State Forest

Total distance: 3½ miles

Hiking time: 2 hours

Vertical rise: 510 feet

Map: USGS 7½' Speedsville

Shindagin Hollow is a long north-south valley, almost gorgelike in its narrowness, located 10 miles southeast of Ithaca and Cayuga Lake. It was once the route of a well-used Native American trail that ran northeast from the main Cayuga-Owego trail to what is now the village of Caroline, where it met another heavily traveled Native American route, the Onandaga-Owego trail. Today this valley sits in the heart of the large parcel of state land called Shindagin Hollow State Forest.

Running in an east-west direction through the forest and across the hollow is the well-marked Caroline section of the main Finger Lakes Trail (FLT), maintained by the Cayuga Trails Club. Using portions of this trail and taking advantage of the network of dirt roads

that laces the state forest and adjoining lands, it is possible to devise several delightful loops that will take you through wildernesslike stretches of forest, into deep ravines and narrow valleys, and over open high spots where you can see miles of the surrounding countryside. The entire area is situated on a high tableland averaging about 1500 feet above sea level. The scenic variety found in the forest makes this one of the most attractive sections of the FLT.

While the hiking loop recommended here is relatively short (3½ miles), it gives you a good sample of the region's charm, covering some open highland with views to the north and east, a part of the narrow Shindagin Hollow, and a deep ravine that the FLT follows along its eastern rim to the Shindagin Hollow lean-to.

The lean-to is a good place to spend the night if you would like to cover more territory and explore other sections of the FLT. A ½ mile south of the starting point for this hike, on South Road, the FLT continues east through Potato Hill State Forest. Continuing northward, you arrive at the region's highest point at Padlock Lookout Tower (elevation 1900 feet), where you can see 20 to 30 miles in all directions. You can also follow the

Group of hikers in Shindagin

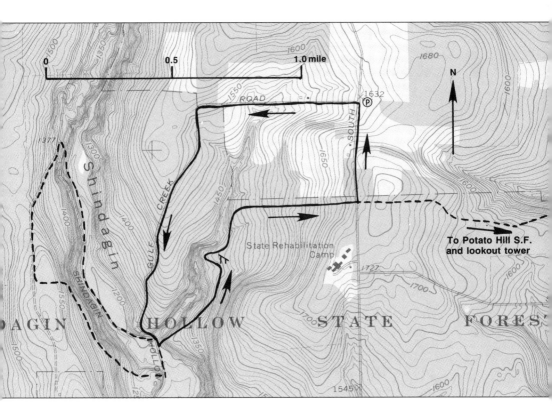

FLT to the west out of Shindagin Hollow, across Willseyville Creek in the adjoining valley, and into another unusually attractive region where you will enter Danby State Forest (see Hike 15).

Whatever your preference, you are walking in one of the most heavily forested areas in Central New York. With its rolling hills and lush valleys, it is a delight to the eye and a treat for the hiker.

Access. To reach the trailhead from Ithaca, drive east on NY 79 for 5 miles to NY 330, which forks to your right. Continue on NY 330 another 5 miles until you intersect Old Seventysix Road at the junction called Guide Board Corners. Turn left onto this road, and drive 2.4 miles to the hamlet of Caroline Center.

If you are approaching from I-81, exit at Whitney Point, and follow NY 79 west 21 miles. Look for Old Seventysix Road on your left just beyond the village of Slaterville Springs; once you are on Old Seventysix Road, drive to Caroline Center.

In Caroline Center, turn south onto South Road, a two-lane, hard-packed dirt road. Drive 1.2 miles to Gulf Creek Road on your right. Park your vehicle at the intersection.

Trail. Start your hike by walking west on Gulf Creek Road, which runs through open fields, giving you a good view of the countryside to the north and west. For the next ½ mile the road descends gradually, crossing a trickle of a brook (in spring), and then begins a short ascent to the forest edge. You are now entering the northern section of Shindagin Hollow State Forest at one of the high spots of the region (elevation 1550 feet).

A short distance into the forest, the road turns sharply left and heads south. Within several hundred feet it begins the descent into Shindagin Hollow. It is a 4-mile walk from the road's turn to the bottom of the hollow; about halfway down the road pitches downward more sharply, with the slope becoming more pronounced as you near the bottom. The trees along the road provide cool shade during the summer.

At the bottom, Gulf Creek Road intersects Shindagin Hollow Road. You are now in a narrow ravine with forested sides that rise sharply almost 350 feet. Flowing through the hollow is Shindagin Hollow Creek.

Turn left onto Shindagin Hollow Road and follow it south for about 100 feet. To your left you will see a cut into the side of the hill. It is the outlet of a deep, narrow gorge; the FLT follows its eastern rim. During the early spring as the snow waters roar down the mile-long gorge, you are treated to an impressive sight here. At the outlet, just before the spot where the waters pour into the Shindagin Hollow Creek, there is a narrow cut in the shale rock. As the waters rush through this cut each spring, they form a raging cataract. Shindagin is a corruption of the Native American word Shandaken, meaning "rapid water." It may have been here during the spring runoffs that the Native Americans watched the torrential waters of the gorge meeting those of Shindagin Hollow Creek and spoke of the place as Shandaken.

A few feet south of this point on Shindagin Hollow Road, a white FLT marker directs you across a creek (during the summer and fall it is a dry streambed) to an abandoned road. Follow this road uphill. The initial climb of several hundred feet is quite steep, but soon the road levels out. After a gentle ½-mile climb, the trail turns sharply to your left and begins a gradual downward pitch. Within a short distance the trail flattens.

To your left is a 30-foot drop into a ravine; ahead and a little to your right is the Shindagin Hollow lean-to. The hemlocks surrounding it make this a most inviting place to stop for a break or to stay overnight.

Follow the white blazes of the FLT as they take you north past the lean-to. The trail snakes through the forest along the ravine's edge for about ¼ mile, and then it turns right taking you up for ½ mile on a straight easterly course to South Road. Once on South Road, turn north. In less than ½ mile, you are back at your vehicle.

The FLT crosses South Road, and, if you like, you can add a few more miles to your hike by continuing eastward. The trail takes you through a hardwood forest for 1½ miles and eventually across Boyer Creek to the paved highway, Old Seventysix Road. If you stay on the FLT, another mile brings you to the Potato Hill State Forest. The walk through this forest is 2¼ miles long, and another mile to the north brings you to the Padlock Lookout Tower.

Another loop that you may wish to add to the recommended hike follows Shindagin Hollow Road north for a mile. Here a jeep trail forks to your left and runs south, almost paralleling Shindagin Hollow Road. If you follow this jeep trail, you will intersect the east-west FLT. You can then turn left (east) on the FLT and follow it downhill to the hollow and back onto Shindagin Hollow Road.

These hills hold the snow well. Most of the dirt roads in the area are plowed, giving you direct access to the FLT. This section is ideal for cross-country ski enthusiasts as the terrain is just varied enough to make ski touring challenging and interesting.

15

Danby State Forest

Total distance: 9 miles

Hiking time: 4½ hours

Vertical rise: 1472 feet

Map: USGS 7½' Willseyville

Danby State Forest is a large land tract (7086 acres) situated 14 miles south of Ithaca. It occupies the highland region just south of NY 96B, a highway that runs southeast from Ithaca to Owego, passing through the hamlet of Danby, from which the state forest derives its name. This high area is tableland, a rolling, wooded landscape mixed with open fields. It is uncommonly picturesque, especially in late spring or early summer when the valleys are carpeted in deep green and the hilltops are still dressed in softer yellow-green.

Essayist and naturalist Hal Borland wrote that "half the benefit, and even more of the satisfaction, of walking comes from the leisurely change of scene." In Danby, there is always a leisurely change of scene. Here you find long fields as well as deep woods, tree-lined lanes as well as meandering foot trails passing through

forest glens and sun-washed glades, and with each new turn comes a change in mood. You can walk for literally miles without seeing any houses, farms, or people, and yet this sense of remoteness is complemented by a feeling of openness that results from the many overlooks where the surrounding hilltops and valleys spread out before you.

Danby State Forest is a long swath of land bounded on the west by Michigan Hollow, on the north by Danby Creek Valley, and on the east by Willseyville Valley. The distinctive geological characteristic of the region is its sharply pointed hilltops with steep sides and narrow valleys, which make the landscape look more rugged and mountainous than it actually is. Most of the hills barely rise over 1600 feet, yet they seem much higher.

Through the area, this run of 8 miles of Finger Lakes Trail (FLT) was built and is currently maintained by the Cayuga Trails Club, one of the several sponsoring groups of the Finger Lakes Trail Conference.

Michigan Hollow takes its name from early settlers who started for Michigan but decided to stay here instead, giving the area the name of their once-hoped-for destination. Geologically, the hollow straddles a divide, where water flows from one pond northward to form Buttermilk Creek, which eventually empties into Cayuga Lake, and from another pond southward to form Michigan Creek, which flows to the Susquehanna River.

Willseyville Valley and nearby Danby Creek Valley are what geologists call "through valleys," carved by glaciers that deepened the valleys and steepened the hillsides. The east side of Eastman Hill is a good example of such oversteepening, with a drop of 700 feet into Willseyville Valley at about a 35-degree angle.

Willseyville Valley is also known as the "Warrior's Trail." This was the main Native American trail from Cayuga Lake to the Susquehanna River, and the route taken by the Native Americans and Tories in 1779 during the revolutionary war to harass troops of the Continental Army seeking to join the Sullivan Expedition. The first settlers who came to Ithaca from Owego in 1789 used this trail, widening it for their ox carts.

The hike recommended here runs eastward over the highest point of the region, downhill, and up again to the top of Eastman Hill. With several substantial climbs it is a moderate-to-difficult hike, but the effort is worth it.

Access. The trailhead can be reached by taking NY 96B south from Ithaca 6.4 miles to Danby. Continue through Danby another 2.6 miles to paved South Danby Road on your right. This road can also be reached from the south by taking NY 96B; then drive north through Willseyville for 4.5 miles to South Danby Road, on your left.

Once on South Danby Road, drive south 1.5 miles, and watch for white blazes on both sides of the road that indicate where the FLT crosses. The first blaze is on the right. Drive beyond it over a small brook (Miller Creek) for 225 feet. Another FLT marker can now be seen on your left. Park here.

Trail. Follow the FLT uphill to the east; in several hundred feet you reach an abandoned road that runs due east. The FLT, marked by white blazes, follows this road steadily uphill for almost a mile through thick woods, mostly pine and hemlock. As you near the top of the hill, the ascent becomes more moderate, and the trail finally levels out as you pass through a stand of pines just before reaching Travor Road.

Turn left and follow this dirt lane northward for about ¼ mile until it bends to your left. Here the FLT leaves Travor Road and continues north along an old farm road past a cellar hole. Shortly the trail takes you into a stand of larches, where it bends to the right, moving through a small clearing, and then turns left (north) into another larch plantation. For the last ¼ mile you have been making a moderate ascent. You now are almost at the highest point in the region (elevation 1758 feet); this unnamed hilltop is in the woods just off to your left. A little farther along, a spur trail bears off to the right about 100 feet to the Tamarack lean-to, a delightful place to spend the night.

Just beyond the spur trail, the main trail pitches downward. The hill here is quite steep; in less than ¾ mile you descend 584 feet. En route you pass a second spur trail that goes south about 100 feet to a spring. Continue downhill through the woods until you emerge in an open area; turn left for a short distance and continue until you reach a small stream (Danby Creek) at the base of the hill. Just ahead is NY 96B, and across Danby Creek Valley you see a cluster of hilltops: Durfee Hill, Roundtop, and Eastman Hill.

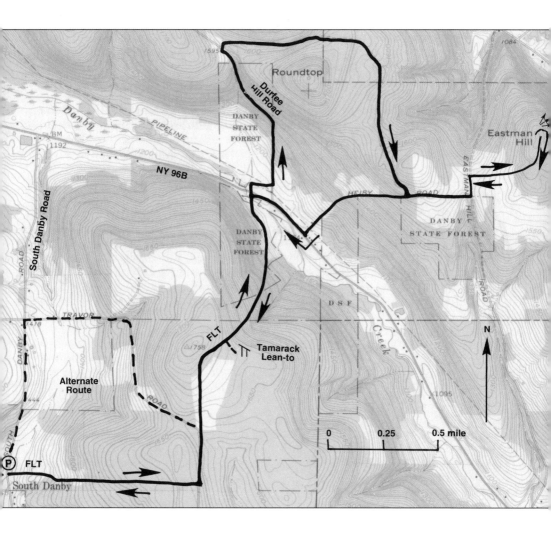

Follow the creek a short distance to a culvert and NY 96B. Cross the highway and follow the trail on the other side as it cuts to your right at an angle to reach, in a few hundred feet, a dirt road, Durfee Hill Road. Turn left (north) onto this road. In less than ⅛ mile the road starts up a steep hill; at the ¼-mile mark it bends slightly to your left and continues its upward climb until it is intersected on your right by an old wood lane at the ¾-mile mark.

Follow the white blazes into the lane and head east through the forest, following the marked trail along the north side of the peaked hill called Roundtop (elevation 1800 feet). The lane runs east for ⅝ mile and then curves slowly to your right as it heads south downhill for ¾ mile. Here it intersects Heisy Road, a dirt road that runs along the northern edge of another parcel of Danby State Forest.

Turn left (east) on Heisy Road and

follow it for ½ mile to where it intersects another dirt road, Eastman Hill Road. Turn left (north) onto Eastman Hill Road and walk about ⅛ mile to where the trail leaves the road and enters the woods. An uphill climb of ¼ mile brings you to the crest of Eastman Hill (elevation 1690 feet). If you continue a few hundred yards along the ridge, you should be able to see eastward through the trees to catch a glimpse of Willseyville Valley, 595 feet below.

Now retrace your steps to Eastman Hill Road. Turn left (south), and in a short distance you come to Heisy Road. Turn right (west), and follow Heisy Road downhill to NY 96B where you turn right and walk ¼ mile north to pick up the FLT. You can now retrace your route on the FLT uphill past the lean-to, across Travor Road, and then downhill to your vehicle.

An alternate route back to your vehicle takes you right (northwest) on Travor Road and then west to the intersection with South Danby Road. Turn left (south) here and walk ¾ mile back to your vehicle. This route takes you over a hill and through some fields, offering you delightful views to the north, east, and south. You may lengthen your hike during a weekend outing by following the FLT west from the spot where you parked your vehicle. A 3-mile walk brings you to Michigan Hollow, where the FLT crosses Michigan Creek.

16

Beaver Creek State Forest

Total distance: 7½ miles

Hiking time: 4 hours

Vertical rise: 1060 feet

Map: USGS 7½' Brookfield

Beaver Creek State Forest extends from Mount Hunger on the west to Witter Hill on the east. Beaver Creek, an attractive and productive small trout stream that gives its name to the state forest, flows south through the long valley that makes up the middle section of the 3346-acre tract of state land.

The state forest lies 18 miles due south of Utica. A mile from its southern boundary is the village of Brookfield, and 4 miles from its northern boundary is US 20. You will be hiking in the Susquehanna Hills, which rise out of the Mohawk Valley in the north and level off in the south at an elevation between 1800 and 2000 feet.

The highest spot in the area is Witter Hill, at an elevation of 1900 feet. From the trailhead to the summit, the rise is 500 feet. Topographically, this is high rolling country where, as on Witter Hill, you find hills and valleys on top of the hills themselves. You'll be walking through woods of heavy-boughed conifers and thick-trunked hardwoods that make this a pleasant region for hikers.

Access. The trailhead in the state forest is reached via US 20 in the north. From Sangerfield at the junction of US 20 and NY 12, drive east 0.6 mile to a road that intersects from the south. A sign here calls it Brookfield Road (elsewhere it is called Beaver Creek Road). Turn right here, and drive 4.5 miles south past Mount Hunger on your right to an intersection with Bliven Road. Turn left on Bliven Road, and drive 0.5 mile to its intersection with the north-south Fairground Road, where you turn right. Drive south another 0.8 mile to a parking area on your left. Park here. On the area's north side are hitching rails to accommodate about 20 horses, a reminder that this is equestrian land. It also is biking territory. A sign here informs you that you have arrived at the trailhead of the 3430-acre Beaver Creek State Forest; it also tells you that the "off-trails" are closed to horses and mountain bikes from October 31 to May 1.

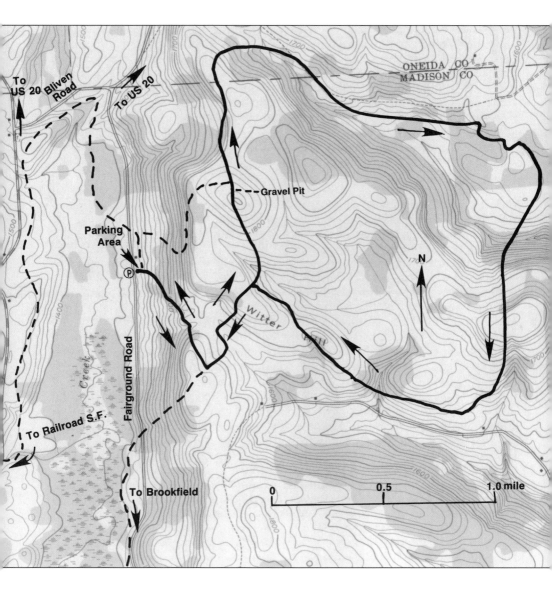

Trail. Your hiking trail consists of several miles of truck roads and horse trails. While the trail system is not marked for hiking, round yellow signs with a horsehead silhouette indicate the route of the bridle paths that you can follow. Beaver Creek is linked to its close neighbor, Baker Memorial Forest (see Hike 17), by horse trails on which you can walk miles from one state forest to the other.

These groomed and maintained trails start on the west side of Beaver Creek and loop north and then east, taking you over open terrain, across hilltops and into valleys, and then down along the east side of Beaver Creek Valley to the fairground just outside the village of Brookfield.

At the starting point in the trailhead parking area, look for a yellow-marked trail the width of a narrow lane. Take this route and head uphill in a southeasterly direction. It is straight and steep for the first ¾ mile until you intersect a dirt road about 300 feet above your starting point.

Once you turn left on the dirt road, hiking becomes a little easier, even though you are still moving uphill. Just about ½ mile brings you to a lane that forks to your right with a yellow arrow pointing down the path. This will be your exit when you complete the loop in a clockwise fashion, but for now continue north on the dirt road.

From the exit road, it is just short of a mile to the north-south ridge of Witter Hill; another ¼ mile brings you to the knob of the hill with a narrow dirt lane intersecting on your right; a few hundred feet on this lane brings you to a gravel pit. Back on the main road, continue in a northerly direction past an intersection with a horse trail on your left and then past a large clear-cut area on your right; then to an S-turn. You now start a series of short descents and ascents as the road dips and rises in the rolling, forested terrain. In the next ½ mile, you encounter two dips that drop you to an elevation of 1700 feet before you climb back to 1800 feet.

As you reach the northern edge of the state forest, the road swings to your right and heads east. For the next 1½ miles it is relatively level. As you hike through the hardwoods, the trees on your right begin to thin out. Suddenly, you look down into a narrow, forested valley about 100 feet below.

Farther down the road, an arrow directs you onto a narrower horse trail on your right heading south. The first ½ mile is fairly flat; the trail begins then to descend, slowly at first and now more steeply as you near the bottom. Your ver-tical drop is 160 feet in less than ¼ mile.

Next you start an upward climb, a steep ascent of 340 feet. After a brief level stretch on the top, you begin your second—and steeper—descent, which takes you through a stand of spruce trees and down 200 feet. At the bottom, you move through a stand of hardwood and then break out into a large, ½-mile-wide bowl-like valley. This would be a most attractive spot on any trail, but after hiking through miles of forested landscape, you will be especially surprised by the pleasant openness of this hilltop meadow.

The horse trail, mowed during the summer, takes you around a makeshift road barrier (a large pile of rocks to block motorized vehicles) to a gravel road. The land on your left is private and posted; on your right is state land. Turn right onto the gravel road and head uphill and eastward past the meadow and back into the forest. You are now walking on the backbone of Witter Hill; the high point in this southern section is 1740 feet. Another ½ mile brings you to the intersection with the dirt road you hiked earlier. Turn left, and retrace your steps to your vehicle at the picnic area.

You can call it a day. On another day, though, you might follow the yellow-marked bridle path from the picnic area north as it runs parallel with Fairground Road. Soon the trail crosses the road and continues northward on the west side of the road, passing alternately through open stretches and wooded areas.

The trail soon meets Bliven Road and swings west over a small hill, across Beaver Creek, and then over another hill as it enters more open and attractive terrain on its southward journey. You can follow this trail south for several miles and then east for another 1½ miles to enter a second state forest, an 850-acre tract with the odd name of Railroad State Forest. Here you will find a bridle-path loop about 3½ miles long.

17

Baker Memorial Forest

Total distance: 15 miles (2 days)

Hiking time: 8 hours

Vertical rise: 960 feet

Maps: USGS 7½' Brookfield; USGS 7½' Hubbardsville; USGS 7½' Sherburne

This is equestrian country. From a hiker's viewpoint, that's all to the good, for horse trails make excellent hiking trails. If you add the dirt roads, lanes, and snowmobile trails to the 130-mile horse trail system in the area, you have well over 150 miles of walking trails. That should keep even the most eager and able hiker occupied for a week or more should he or she have a mind to go the whole distance.

This is also picturesque hill country. Topographically, the hills are much more peaked than those farther west, a feature that marks them as Susquehanna Hills in contrast to the rounder and flatter Finger Lakes Hills. You will find the skyline angular and irregular and the landscape cleft and rugged looking—aspects that give this region a special charm.

Officially, this vast state forest (8070 acres) is named in memory of Charles E. Baker, a regional state forester who was responsible for foresting and developing it into the present multiuse recreation area, but you wouldn't know that from the signs. They read that the land is managed by the state's Department of Environmental Conservation as the "Brookfield Horse Trails: 130 Mile Trail System," one of the largest such systems in the state.

The horse trails not only loop and circle throughout Baker Forest but also connect with those in nearby Railroad State Forest and Beaver Creek State Forest (see Hike 16). They include forested hilltops, open valleys, large ponds, and high ground overlooking Beaver Creek swamp—actually a lush green valley filled with evergreens.

Another of the forest's big assets is the camping area—actually two adjoining areas with picnic tables under shelter and dozens and dozens of well-designed spots for camping and tenting. And it's all free.

Baker Forest merits more than just a day hike. Plan on 4 or 5 days, and if you can't manage that, try for at least a long weekend. You can use the camping area as your base while you try the various trails, or you might consider backpacking to the fire tower and tenting there,

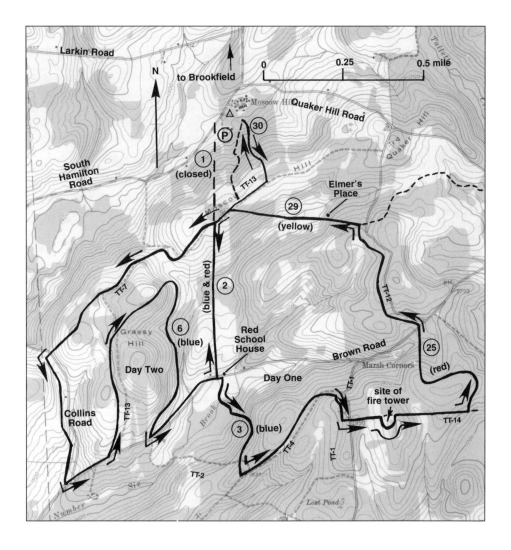

where there is an ideal spot among the evergreens. You'll even find a fireplace for cooking. However, if you plan to stay more than 3 consecutive days, you must obtain a camping permit. To get such a permit, contact the New York State Department of Environmental Conservation, Sherburne, NY (607-674-2611).

All horse trails in Baker Forest are color-coded with red, blue, and yellow disks with a horse head silhouette,

so you'll have no difficulty following them. Each main loop is about 33 miles long, and all begin at and return to one Assembly Area. The best way to master the color-coded trail system is to study the map in a free booklet, "Horse Trails in New York State," which you can obtain from the Regional Office, Department of Environmental Conservation, Sherburne, NY 13460.

The marked trails radiate in various

directions over Baker's many hills. The extensive forest has three designated high places as well as a number of un-named high spots. Along the forest's northern boundary are, from east to west, ½-mile-long Quaker Hill (elevation 1860 feet), mile-long Moscow Hill with a knob at the west rising to 1740 feet, and Grassy Hill, with two knobs each rising to 1820 feet.

These are fair-sized hills for this region. Vertical rise from the Assembly Area to the top of Moscow Hill is 300 feet, which gives you a nice steady climb over a half mile.

Access. From the east, Baker Forest can be approached via Skaneateles Turnpike, which begins at NY 8 (running south out of Bridgewater on US 20) and heads west 9 miles through Brookfield to West Brookfield, where you drive south for a mile on South Hamilton Road to the Assembly Area and the trailhead. Or from the west, take NY 12, which runs south out of Utica, crossing US 20 at Sangerfield. From Sangerfield, follow NY 12 south 9.3 miles to East Hamilton. A state sign on your right directs you to "Brookfield Horse Trails." Turn left here onto Larkin Road, and drive 1 mile to where Crumb Road intersects on your right. Turn south on Crumb Road, and drive 1.4 miles to its intersection with South Hamilton Road. Turn left (east) onto South Hamilton Road, and drive 2.2 miles, where you will see a sign on your right to the Assembly Area. Park here.

Trail. At the Assembly Area you will find hitching rails for horses, picnic tables, a large display board showing the map of the state forest, and a plaque mounted on a huge boulder. The plaque is in memory of Charles E. Baker, who served as district forester from 1930 to 1967 and

after whom the state forest is named. At the south end of the Assembly Area is the trailhead, and the beginning of Trail 30. It is marked with several different-colored disks—yellow, red, and blue horse trail markers; a white marker designating a carriage route; and an orange snowmobile marker. A short distance to your right is Trail 1, which has been closed to prevent further overuse.

If you are tenting in the camping area next to the Assembly Area, your starting point each day is at the beginning of Trail 30 in the Assembly Area.

First Day
Assembly Area to Fire Tower and back
Distance: 6½ miles
Hiking time: 3 hours

At the Assembly Area, turn right onto Trail 30, and head south uphill to the top of Moscow Hill, where you intersect the east-west dirt road, TT-13 (TT stands for truck trail). Here the yellow-coded horse trail turns left onto TT-13. Follow the yellow markers for ½ mile southwest past Trail 45 (intersecting on your right) and Trail 29 (on your left) to where a narrow horse trail marked by red and blue disks crosses the road. This is Trail 2. Turn left and take Trail 2 south into the woods.

This narrow trail runs straight south, heading downhill for ¼ mile to where Trail 46 intersects on your right. Stay on Trail 2. Just beyond the ½-mile mark the trail rises a bit before starting a downhill descent. Here Trail 55 intersects on your left. Continue south on the red-blue Trail 2 for a little over ¼ mile. As you approach the valley, the trail crosses a small brook (which eventually feeds into Number Six Brook) before it turns right and comes out on Brown Road.

Horse trail in Baker Memorial Forest

The trail jogs here. Follow the trail markers by turning left on the road; a short distance up the road, a marker directs you to your right and back into the woods. Just beyond where you turn off the road, you will see on the north side of the road a red building on a small parcel of private land, marked as the Red School House.

Once into the woods, a small sign tells you that this is Trail 3. Soon you cross what is the beginning of Number Six Brook and then start a fairly stiff climb, rising 220 feet in less than ¼ mile before you finally reach a level area. Soon the blue trail comes out on a dirt road; from Brown Road to this one (TT-2 on the map) the distance is just short of a mile.

Continue straight ahead on TT-2 for a short distance to an intersection with TT-4; the blue trail turns right and follows TT-4 southwest. You, however, turn left on TT-4 and follow it uphill for about ¼ mile, where another blue horse trail comes out of the woods and heads northeast on TT-4. Follow the blue markers. A half mile farther brings you to the intersection with TT-1.

Turn right, and follow TT-1 a short distance to the top of the hill, where an arrow with a red marker directs you to turn left onto another dirt road (TT-14). A ¼-mile hike on this red-marked trail brings you to a fork; follow the right leg, which takes you into an evergreen stand and then to a parking area, the highest point in Baker Forest (elevation 1900 feet).

On your left is an open area, once the site of a fire tower that was removed in the late 1980s. Now this site is used for picnicking and tenting.

The road on which you came to this site is actually a loop, so follow it back to the red-trail road. Turn right, and continue east on TT-14 and downhill for almost ½ mile, where an arrow directs you to turn left off the road and into the woods. The red-marked trail (Trail 25) now climbs to the top of the hill, levels off for a brief stretch, and then heads downhill, covering a mile before intersecting with Brown Road and TT-12. Follow TT-12 north.

For almost a mile, this shaded road is relatively flat, but then it begins to go downhill where Trail 56 intersects on your left. As you near the bottom, a horse trail marked with yellow disks crosses the road (Trail 29). Turn left onto this yellow-marked trail. As you do, you will see a sign on a tree that reads "Elmer's Place."

You are now traveling west. The trail becomes more rocky as it heads downhill, finally crossing a narrow wooden bridge over a small brook. Here you see Elmer's Place, an unoccupied one-room house, on your right. The trail now begins a modest climb until it makes a sharp right-hand turn onto a dirt road (TT-13). Turn right and follow TT-13 for

¼ mile past Trail 45 (intersecting on your left) to Trail 30 on your left; turn here and follow Trail 30 downhill to the Assembly Area.

Second Day
Assembly Area to Grassy Hill and back
Distance: 8½ miles
Hiking time: 5 hours

As before, leave the Assembly Area and head to the top of Moscow Hill and the dirt road, TT-13. Turn right onto TT-13. Follow the blue markers that take you southwest on TT-13 for a little less than a mile to an intersection with another dirt road, forking to your right. Here the blue-coded horse trail and TT-7 (and your route) leave the road and head into the woods in a southwesterly direction.

This trail stays in the woods for the next mile as it follows the northwest ridge of Grassy Hill; then it starts to slope downward, descending 100 feet to intersect a dirt road, Collins Road. At this point, the blue-marked trail turns left and follows Collins Road for almost a mile, where it turns right into the woods. You, however, continue on Collins Road a short distance to the intersection with Brown Road.

Turn left, and follow Brown Road uphill for almost ½ mile to an intersection with TT-13, forking to your left. Take TT-13, and start an uphill climb for a little over ½ mile (an ascent of 160 feet). A southern knob of Grassy Hill lies nearby on your right. A little way farther, the blue-marked trail swings back into the woods and climbs a short distance to the northern and second knob of Grassy Hill.

After a short level stretch, the terrain slopes down sharply. The blue-marked trail, which has become Trail 6 after leaving TT-13, turns right to lead you along the side of the hill in a southerly direction past Trail 46. For the next mile, you follow a level trail, before you make a short descent to exit onto Brown Road.

Turn left, and follow the red-coded Brown Road, which heads downhill, crosses a brook, and levels out; just short of the mile mark, Brown Road intersects with the north-south blue-red horse trail that you walked the day before. Turn left onto this blue-red trail, and head into the woods. Go north uphill and across the brook, and a mile brings you to the top of Moscow Hill and TT-13. Turn right on TT-13 and follow this route for almost ½ mile to Trail 30 (on your left) which takes you back to the Assembly Area.

18

Taylor Valley State Forest

Total distance: 12 miles (2 days)

Hiking time: 6 hours

Vertical rise: 2120 feet

Maps: USGS 7½' Cuyler; USGS 7½' Cincinnatus

For many a hiker, Taylor Valley is the prettiest valley in this general region. The glacier of some 12,000 years ago shaped it; more recently human beings have groomed it, especially in the central section where the valley has been reforested. The glacier-cut of the 12-mile-long valley is what gives it its eye-appeal—a rounded valley floor with steep, almost vertical hillsides.

The central section of the valley is state land and virtually empty of signs of civilization. Nor do you find much by way of farms or hamlets in the southern end. You only begin to see farms when you reach the small hamlet of Cheningo. For the most part, you are surrounded by steep forested hillsides rising 800 feet on both sides of the north-flowing Cheningo Creek.

Taylor Valley State Forest occupies most of the hilltop territory as well. The 4650-acre state forest spreads from Mount Roderick (elevation 1900 feet) in the southwest to Allen Hill (elevation 1980 feet) in the east and Seacord (elevation 1910 feet) in the northeast.

Through all this state land runs the groomed Finger Lakes Trail (FLT), marked by white blazes on trees. The trail runs 6 miles from Telephone Road in the south across Taylor Valley Road to end at Cheningo-Solon Pond Road in the north.

The state forest recommends itself as a place for a weekend campout. You have several choices: you may backpack to one of the bivouac areas (Morrell Brook in the south or Sum Gay Gulf in the north), or stay at the convenient camping area right off the main paved road, Taylor Valley Road. The FLT passes through this area, where there are picnic tables, fireplaces, and several dozen campsites. A camping permit is required here. To obtain one, call or write: Regional Wildlife Manager, PO Box 1169, Cortland, NY 13045 (607-753-3095).

Access. The camping area at Taylor Valley Road can be reached via NY 91 out of Truxton to Cheningo; NY 91 now becomes Taylor Valley Road, and 2 miles

View of Tassel Hill (background) across Chittning Pond

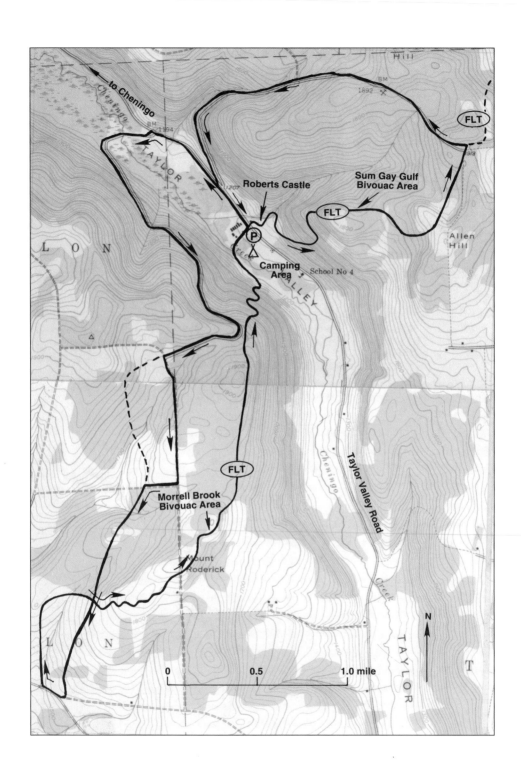

to Cheningo

FLT

Roberts Castle

Sum Gay Gulf
Bivouac Area

FLT

Camping
Area

School No 4

Allen
Hill

FLT

Morrell Brook
Bivouac Area

Mount
Roderick

N

0   0.5   1.0 mile

from Cheningo you see the camping area on both sides of the road. Truxton can be reached from Cortland via NY 13 or from Syracuse via NY 91.

Trail. You can combine the FLT with a number of hard-surfaced dirt roads, truck trails, and lanes to form loops in both the southern and northern portions of the state forest.

First Day
Taylor Valley Road to Telephone Road and back
Distance: 8 miles
Hiking time: 4 hours

We'll assume you have decided to stay at Taylor Valley Road, so try the southern loop first. Start by walking north on Taylor Valley Road from the campsite for almost a mile, where an unnamed dirt road intersects on your left. This road takes you into a small wooded area where soon the trees give way to a marshy spot through which Cheningo Creek flows. The marsh with its several small ponds and waterholes is a good place for waterfowl. If you're lucky, you may see some mallards in the water or taking off as you approach. The area also is home to quite a few large snapping turtles.

The road crosses Cheningo Creek, turns left, and heads uphill now under a canopy of trees. A mile brings you to the top of the hill for a vertical rise of 600 feet. Here the road loops to your right, and in ½ mile farther comes to an intersection. Take the lane forking off on your left. The lane runs due south for almost a mile, where a road comes in from your right. Turn west onto this road, and a short walk brings you to another intersection.

Turn left here, and follow this dirt road south. It soon crosses what in the spring is a small brook, rises gradually for a while, and then starts descending until it reaches the intersection with Mount Roderick Road and Telephone Road. Turn right onto the highway (Telephone Road), and walk a short distance downhill until you see the white blazes on a tree on your right that indicate the beginning of the FLT.

Turn right onto the trail, which runs due north for a little over ½ mile, and then turns right and uphill. Follow the trail as it runs east. The uphill climb is steady (past a gravel pit) until you reach the summit of Mount Roderick; this area, called Aspen Ridge, is open, with some fine views to the east. In a little over ¼ mile you pass Morrell Brook bivouac area.

The terrain is now fairly level. A half mile more on the trail brings you back into the hardwood forest, where the trail now begins to pitch downward, with a drop so gradual you are hardly aware of it. A mile farther brings you to a small hilltop pond on the western edge of the trail, which might be a nice place for lunch.

Just beyond the pond, the trail begins a steep descent, switching back and forth as it drops 600 feet in just over ¼ mile. As it nears the bottom, it begins to level out, passing a beaver pond on your right. Look closely through the trees, and you'll see the beaver dam.

The trail now crosses a log footbridge over Cheningo Creek, and in another few minutes you are back at your campsite.

Second Day
Taylor Valley Road via truck trail and back
Distance: 4 miles
Hiking time: 2 hours

Follow the FLT markers on the north side of Taylor Valley Road in an area called Roberts Castle. The FLT follows a lane for a short distance, and then turns sharply right to head up a steep hill.

It is a steady climb for the next ½ mile. The white-blazed FLT takes you first in a southeasterly direction and then in a northwesterly direction until it reaches a flattened area that is the crest of an unnamed hilltop (elevation 1800 feet).

The trail now takes you straight in an easterly direction; after walking for ⅜ mile on fairly level terrain, you start to climb again as the trail takes a circular route along the northwestern slope of Allen Hill.

From here it is ⅜ mile to where the trail crosses a lane and climbs a small hill; from the lane it is ¼ mile to where the FLT intersects yet another lane, serving as a short extension on the end of a truck trail. The FLT turns right and follows this lane a short distance before turning off to descend a hill and cross the Cheningo-Solon Road en route to Cuyler Hill State Forest (see Hike 20).

You, however, turn left, leaving the FLT. Follow the blue-blazed lane for ⅛ mile to where you encounter the terminus of a hard-surfaced truck trail; follow it in a westerly direction. At first the road is level, but soon it slopes downward for almost ¼ mile before heading uphill. In ¼ mile more you come to a gravel pit on your right and the height-of-land. The crest of Seacord Hill is off on your right.

Continue on the dirt road as it heads downhill. The vista ahead to the west is an attractive one. Soon you come to another dirt road intersecting on your right. Continue past this road on your downward trek. The descent becomes more pronounced now. Soon the road turns left and pitches down even more sharply. It is ½ mile more to Taylor Valley Road. Turn left onto the highway, and follow it back to your camping area.

19

Bucks Brook State Forest

Total distance: 8 miles

Hiking time: 4 hours

Vertical rise: 760 feet

Map: USGS 7½' South Otselic

The charm of this place is its unpretentiousness. A tract of state land east of Cortland, it is known officially as Bucks Brook State Forest, just a forested hilltop where you can hike quietly along a section of the Finger Lakes Trail (FLT).

Yet as the poet Ezra Pound noted, "Learn of the green world what can be thy place." Perhaps you will find this small hilltop such a green world, for the pleasure of walking is somehow heightened here. In spring, when the trees put on the season's first yellow-green dress, the hilltop becomes a delight of renewal. In summer, it turns into a cathedral of green coolness. In autumn, amid the fall foliage of yellows and reds, it evokes a wistful memory of summer gone.

Here, as with some other areas along the FLT, there are problems of map names and other official designations. The state Lands and Forests Division uses a departmental name: Chenango 20. A later and less technical label given this same area by the state is Bucks Brook State Forest, after the stream running through it, although no one around here seems to use this title. The map published by the Finger Lakes Trail Conference calls the hilltop over which the FLT runs McDermott Hill, making this the popular name. However, if you are using a recent USGS quadrangle map you will find no McDermott Hill listed, nor will you find any indication that this is even state land. Finally, although most state forests have special name signs posted along the roadways through them, you will find no such signs here. To the average person passing through this forest, it is simply a quiet wooded place.

The suggested loop, which follows a completed section of the FLT out and dirt roads back, is a good day's hike. It takes you through an inviting stand of hardwoods and evergreens, over quietly flowing, sun-flecked brooks, through a small gorge, and to a hilltop from which you can see the surrounding countryside stretching away in all directions. And should you wish to spend the night, there is an ideal campsite in a partial

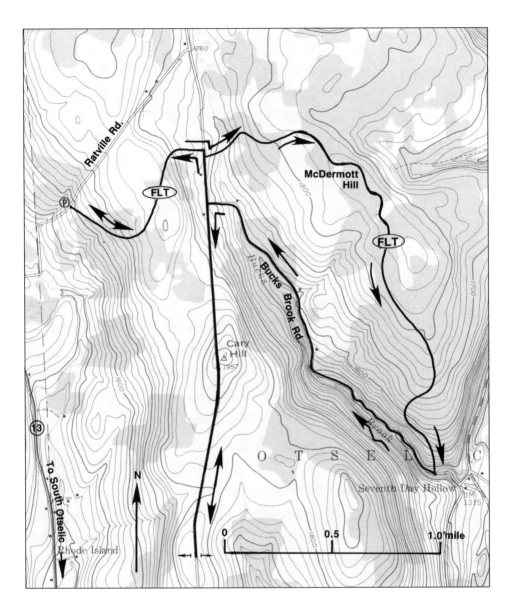

clearing near McDermott Hill. During the day this fern swale is warmed by shafts of sunlight, and during the night it collects and holds the soft talk of the night peepers.

When you walk, do so slowly; this wooded area is host to a great number of mushrooms, and if you look carefully along the path's edges, you may see, as I did, an impressive variety on a day's walk. Watch for the various amanitas, collybias, galerinas, pholiotas, russalas, and polypores, especially *Polyporus versicolor,* or "turkey tails." Bring along your mushroom field guide; it makes identification easier and more fun.

Access. This state forest lies between DeRuyter and South Otselic. From DeRuyter on NY 13, take the DeRuyter Turnpike south 3 miles to the top of the hill where Ridge Road (dirt) cuts off on your right. Follow Ridge Road 1.5 miles to Ratville Road, another dirt road, where you turn right. Past the second house (and barn), Ratville Road narrows to a single lane. One mile from that point, you encounter trail markers— hand-lettered words painted on trees on both sides of the road—for the McDermott Hill section of the FLT. Park in the small area off the road just beyond.

Trail. Turn left (southeast) onto the FLT. It leads you uphill through the woods for ½ mile, and then, on more level terrain, gradually loops to the left (north). After ¼ mile, it turns right (east) and a short distance beyond brings you to Ridge Road. Walk along the road to your right (south) for about 25 yards to pick up the trail on the other side. Soon after you reenter the woods, you slant downhill and cross a small stream. This is Bucks Brook, which flows south and eventually empties into the Otselic River just below the hamlet of Seventh Day Hollow.

From here the trail moves uphill through evergreens that soon give way to maple and beech. At the crest the land flattens, indicating that you are now walking a ridge. Soon you enter a stand of tall, well-spaced red spruce, one of the several attractive areas in this forest.

The trail now swings gradually to your right and heads south. Soon it pitches downward, taking you into a small gully

where in spring a brook flows eastward. In summer the gully is usually dry. The trail leads up the other side to another level. On your right is one of the area's highest points (elevation 1860 feet), designated as McDermott Hill on the FLT map.

You soon come to a partial clearing filled with ferns. If you are planning to camp overnight, this may be the place you will want to stay.

Continuing south ½ mile, you begin a gradual descent. Within the next ½ mile the slope steepens, and as you near the trail's end the downward pitch becomes quite pronounced. The FLT terminates on Bucks Brook Road (dirt) in a modest-sized gorge called Seventh Day Hollow. The gorge's vertical sides are exposed shale, and its bottom is just wide enough to accommodate the road and Bucks Brook. The creek bed and exposed sites by the roadside are good places to search for fossils.

Now turn right on Bucks Brook Road and head north. Following the twists and turns of the brook, the road ascends gradually, rising out of the gorge into a ravine and then into a wider-bottomed hollow. One mile from the trail's end, you emerge from the woods; fields spread off to your right along the lower side of McDermott Hill. You soon reenter another wooded section from which you emerge in ¼ mile. A short climb up a small, open hill brings you to Ridge Road. If you wish to shorten your hike, you can turn right (north) now and head back toward your vehicle.

The full hike, however, continues south on Ridge Road to a fine overlook. You reach the summit of Cary Hill (elevation 1957 feet) in ¾ mile. The wooded areas on both sides prevent you from enjoying any vistas, though, so walk another mile to the ridge's next high point. Here fields on both sides of the road allow you find views of rolling hills to the east and west.

When ready, turn around and walk back along Ridge Road, past the intersection of Bucks Brook Road and, ¼ mile beyond, to the FLT crossing. Turn left here. Another ½ mile brings you to your vehicle on Ratville Road.

This is good ski-touring and snowshoeing country. The snows come often and stay on the ground long, especially in the forest. Ridge Road is plowed in winter, allowing you access to the FLT, the northern end of which is ideal for ski touring. The southern section from McDermott Hill to Bucks Brook Road is too steep to negotiate on skis.

20

Cuyler Hill State Forest

Total distance: 7¾ miles

Hiking time: 4½ hours

Vertical rise: 1364 feet

Maps: USGS 7½' Cuyler; FLT Map "Randall Hill"

It is not always easy to put a name to a hike. This one could be called the Randall Hill hike, as it takes you over Randall Hill, a 7-mile-long ridge northeast of Cortland. I prefer to call it Cuyler Hill, after the thickly wooded state forest that runs almost the full length of that high but relatively level ridge. Whatever the name, this is an area that quickly can become a favorite for both day hikes and overnight backpacking.

Here you walk the well-marked Randall Hill section of the Finger Lakes Trail (FLT), which was constructed and is maintained by the Onandaga Chapter of the Adirondack Mountain Club. Running along the flattened crest of Randall Hill, making for easy-to-moderate walking, the trail meanders through tall, well-spaced hardwoods, stands of evergreens, swales of ferns, and cool glens with quietly flowing brooks. It is the central por-

tion of a 21-mile stretch of maintained and marked trails in this part of New York State; to the south the FLT leads a little over 10 miles to Mount Roderick near Solon and to the northwest, about 11 miles to NY 26 near Otselic Center.

The 7¾-mile loop recommended includes a short detour to a lean-to and a scenic overlook.

Access. To reach Cuyler Hill for the start of this hike, take NY 13 northeast from Cortland or south from Cazenova to Cuyler, a hamlet of two dozen homes slightly off NY 13. In the center of the hamlet, turn east onto Lincklaen Road, and drive for 2 miles to Cuyler Hill Road, on your right just beyond a small house. Turn here, and drive uphill for 1.1 miles to a cluster of farm buildings where the paved road intersects a dirt one. Turn left onto the dirt road (a continuation of Cuyler Hill Road), and drive 0.4 mile to Stoney Brook Road, the first dirt road on your left. Continue uphill on this road. At 0.3 mile you reach woods and the edge of Cuyler Hill State Forest. Looking back from here, you have a wide vista of long valleys, pastureland, and wooded hilltops. Two miles to the west rises Pease Hill and farther west the Morgan and Truxton Hills (see Hike 11).

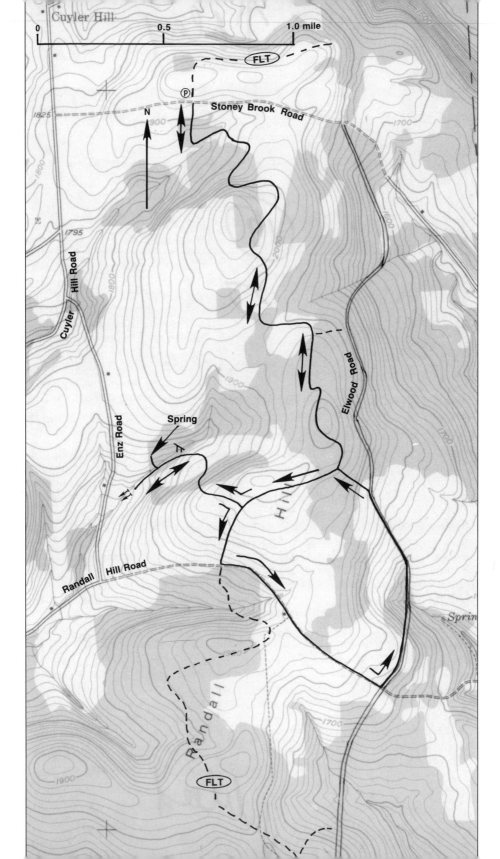

Cuyler Hill

0   0.5   1.0 mile

FLT

P

Stoney Brook Road

N

1825

1900

1700

1800

1795

1800

Cuyler Hill Road

2000

1600

Enz Road

Spring

1900

Elwood Road

1700

Hill

Randall Hill Road

Randall

Spring

1700

1900

FLT

Cuyler Hill State Forest

In another 0.2 mile, watch for the word "Hike" painted in white on a tree to your right. This is where the Randall Hill Section of the FLT crosses the road. Park your vehicle here.

Trail. Begin your walk by following the trail south, downhill into the forest. Within a few feet you come to several trail signs—white lettering painted on a large tree on your left—that read "Cuyler Summit 1 mi," "Rose Hollow 2½ mi," and "Randall Hill Rd 3 mi." The trail markers along the main FLT are white; those on spur trails are orange.

In about ½ mile the trail passes over what in spring and early summer is Bundy Creek, although by late summer it may be a dry streambed. Another ½ mile brings you to Cuyler Summit, the high point of Randall Hill (elevation 2080 feet). Beyond it, the trail is rela-

tively flat for a stretch before starting a gradual descent. In about ½ mile, after making a sharp left turn and then one to the right, you see an orange-marked spur trail forking to your left. This leads to Elwood Road, a dirt lane running parallel to the main trail. Continue on the main trail for another ¾ mile, through several fern swales, over another high point called Kiwi Summit (elevation 2020 feet) on the FLT map, and finally to a second spur to Elwood Road. Shortly the main trail passes over a third high point, called Accordion Summit (elevation 2020 feet) on the FLT map.

About ¼ mile beyond, the trail forks. Here, painted on a tree, a white-lettered sign reads "Rose Hollow" with an arrow pointing right. Bearing right and following the orange-blazed spur trail downhill for ¼ mile, you come to the Rose Hollow lean-to, which overlooks a small gully cut by Enz Brook. Near the lean-to look for two signs hand-lettered on trees; one directs you to an overlook to the southwest, the other to a spring. In summer the vista from the overlook is restricted by the full-foliaged trees. Try the spring trail for some refreshing cold water and a much better view. In ⅛ mile it leads you across the brook to the small productive spring and the trail's end. If you bear left here and walk another 100 feet through the woods, you step into a field, where you have an excellent view of the distant, wooded tops of Seacord and Allen Hills.

Retrace your steps to the main trail, turn right, and continue walking south. The trail now pitches gradually downhill through large stands of maples and smaller stands of evergreens to Randall Hill Road. The FLT heads across the road and into the forest, but to continue your hike, turn left and walk this road for a little under a mile, until it intersects Elwood Road. At the corner on your right you can see a clearing with makeshift fireplaces. This camping area is one of several spots, along with the lean-to, where you can stay on an overnight outing.

Turn left on Elwood Road and walk another mile to the orange markers and "Hike" sign that indicate the entrance to one of the spur trails you passed on your way out. Turn left here and walk the short distance (1000 feet) back to the main trail, where you turn right (north). You are now 2½ miles south of your starting point. In less than an hour you should be back on Stoney Brook Road where you left your vehicle.

This area is ideal for ski touring and snowshoeing. The main trail has enough variation in terrain to make skiing interesting, and it is long enough to allow you to ski all day. As the roads in the state forest are not plowed in winter, they too can be used for touring. The snowfall is heavy here and the forest holds it well to the end of March, and sometimes into early April.

21

Stoney Pond State Forest

Total distance: 2¼ miles

Hiking time: 1½ hours

Vertical rise: 14 feet

Maps: USGS 7½' Morrisville; USGS 7½' West Eaton

Stoney Pond State Forest is located a little over a mile south of US 20, one of the more scenic east-west routes crossing upstate New York. This parcel of land, elongated in shape, is one of the smaller state forests found in this region; it covers 1469 acres and is about 3 miles wide and 1½ miles deep. However, it is situated in a picturesque section of central New York—identified geographically as the Susquehanna Hill region—and is bounded on the east by the Susquehanna River and on the west by the Toughnioga River.

This area belongs to the highlands that dominate the landscape found south of US 20, with elevations averaging about 1800 feet. The hills, while not high, are many and irregularly arranged to give the terrain a rugged, craggy appearance; from the base to the top, most hills rise only about 200 feet, making for easy climbs. In Stoney Pond State Forest, you find seven such peaked hills, all forested.

The state forest's small size belies its many assets. One is proclaimed as you enter the forest, by a sign that reads: Stoney Pond Nordic Ski Trail. "Trails" would be the more appropriate term; since the late 1980s, 13 miles of Nordic ski trails have been built here. The 16 sections of the trails have been numbered. Administered by the state's Department of Environmental Conservation, Stoney Pond is one of the finest state-run Nordic ski areas in central New York. In winter two sections of the trail system, Trails 13 and 15, are reserved for snowmobilers; all the rest are used by cross-country skiers.

During the warm seasons, these maintained and marked trails become hiking and biking routes. Stoney Pond State Forest also allows camping, but permits must be obtained for the 12 designated camping sites; these may be acquired from the Lands and Forests Office of the Department of Environmental Conservation in Sherburne between 8:20 AM and 4:30 PM Monday through Friday, or by calling 607-674-4036.

Swimming is not allowed in man-

0   0.25   0.5 mile

N

Willowvale Road

Old State Road

1500

1600

S   O   N

1700

Trail 17

Trail 19

Alternate Route

1600

Jones Road

Trail 1

Trail 1

Trail 6

1600

dam

Trail 1

Trail 3

Stoney Pond

P

Trail 2

dam

Trail 4

Stoney Pond Road

camping area

Trail 3

Payne

made Stoney Pond, but fishing and boating are; fish include bass, bluegills, and bullheads. A boat-launching site is found in the day-use area across the road from the camping area; motors, however, may not be used on boats. With the exception of snowmobiles, all motor-powered vehicles are prohibited from trail use.

Construction of the Nordic ski-trail system was begun in 1989; the trails were laid out so that skiers in winter, and hikers and bikers in summer, can travel to all sections of the forest.

Access. Stoney Pond State Forest may be reached via Willowvale Road, which runs south from US 20. Willowvale Road, in turn, lies 4.5 miles west of Morrisville and 7 miles east of Cazenova. From US 20 drive south on Willowvale Road 0.8 mile to the intersection with Old State Road. Turn right (west) onto Old State Road and drive 0.6 mile to the intersection with Jones Road. Turn left (south) onto Jones Road and drive 0.6 mile to the second parking area on the left of the dirt road. Here you will find the trailhead to Trail Section 1.

Trail. You will see a yellow disk with the numeral "1" on a tree to your right at the start of the trail. A little into the woods you will encounter a yellow arrow directing you to your right. The trail now follows a downhill course for a short distance to a level stretch before heading downhill again.

On your right is an old stone fence, a reminder that this land was cleared for farming early in the 19th century. You are now traveling on what used to be an old wagon road, long since abandoned. Through the trees you can see a small unnamed pond, which feeds, via a short stretch of stream, into Stoney Pond.

The trail now bends to your left and leads along the northwest edge of the pond, taking you through a large stand of pines. At the ¼-mile mark, you come to an open space and, just beyond it, an earthen dam. To your right is the small unnamed pond you have been seeing along the way.

Cross the dam to where an arrow directs you to turn left. Here you reenter the forest to reach the spot where Trail 2 intersects Trail 1 and stops. Continue north on Trail 1 for a short distance to a footbridge over the outlet stream coming from the pond you just passed.

From here it is an additional ¼ mile to a second footbridge crossing a small streamlet flowing into Stoney Pond; in a few steps you cross still another footbridge over a small feeder brook. Now the trail starts to turn to the right, with Trail 17 intersecting on your left. Continue on the trail ahead of you around the northern end of Stoney Pond and through a stand of hemlocks.

The trail now turns southward, with Trail 19 intersecting on your left. If you wish to extend your hike by 1½ miles, take Trail 19; it leads you to the northeast corner of the state forest, then south, and then west to the southern end of Stoney Pond. On the other hand, if you continue on Trail 1 it will take you south for ¾ mile to where you intersect Trail 3 and Trail 1 ends. Continue on Trail 3 as it takes you into an open area and then across an earthen dam at Stoney Pond's south end.

Once across the dam, you will encounter a dirt road that is part of Stoney Pond Road, forming a loop around the camping area. Bear to your right and follow the road which separates the day-use area on your right from the camping area on your left. Continue westward on the road for ¼ mile to where Trail 2 intersects on your right. Turn here and follow Trail 2 westward.

Looking north across Stoney Pond

Trail 2 follows an abandoned farm road for ¼ mile until you encounter a fork. Take the left leg; a short distance brings you to the small unnamed pond and dam you encountered earlier in your hike. From here retrace your steps uphill to a fork in the trail. In winter when cross-country skiers are on the trails, those going uphill use the right leg while those coming down use the left. In a few more minutes you are back at the parking area and your vehicle.

22

Kennedy Memorial Forest

Total distance: 9 miles

Hiking time: 4 hours

Vertical rise: 1523 feet

Map: USGS 7½' Harford

To the hiker, the high spot in this area is called Virgil Mountain; to the downhill skier it is Greek Peak. The hiker gets to the top by foot, the skier by chairlift.

Once on top in whatever season, you have a grand view to the north, east, and southeast. To the east and southeast is a deep cleft through which Gridley Creek runs. To the north across the narrow Gridley Creek valley is Tuller Hill. Looking northwest several miles, you can see the hamlet of Virgil nestled in Virgil Creek valley.

The 4554-acre state forest, named in memory of Jack Kennedy, the regional forester who developed this area, occupies the high terrain up to the western edge of Virgil Mountain. The hill's eastern side, with a sharp downhill drop of almost 1000 feet, is private land owned

by the Greek Peak Ski Center, which operates three chairlifts on that side of the mountain.

The highland area of the state forest is knobby, with six spots rising to elevations of over 2000 feet. Virgil Mountain is the highest at 2132 feet. Other high spots range from 2010 to 2070 feet, but the most spectacular view is from the top of Virgil Mountain. The terrain making up Kennedy Forest is also dissected by a half dozen streams that have cut narrow valleys, or hollows. The best known are Babcock Hollow in the central sector and Quail Hollow, 2 miles to the east.

Running through almost the entire east-west width of Kennedy Forest is the Finger Lakes Trail (FLT), a groomed and well-marked foot trail.

Access. The trailhead can be reached most easily from Virgil, which is on NY 90 6 miles south of Cortland. Once in Virgil, take the Virgil-Harford Road (County Route 128) south for 2 miles to its intersection with Babcock Hollow Road. Turn left (east) onto Babcock Hollow Road, which takes you east for a while and then south. From the intersection, drive 2.4 miles, where you will see a sign indicating the beginning of the state

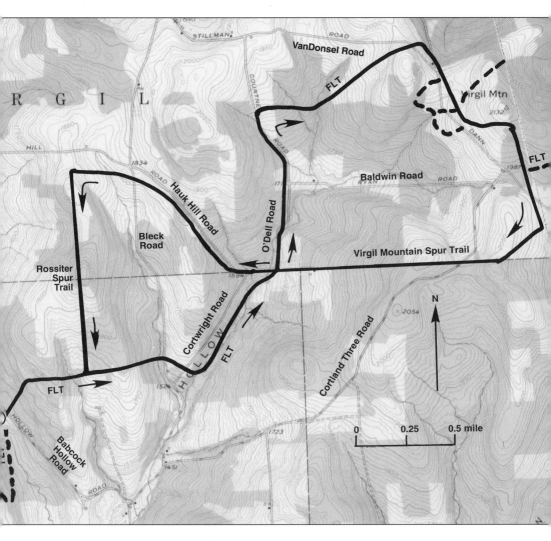

forest. White blazes on trees on both sides of the road also indicate where the FLT crosses the road. The FLT is just a short distance south of a mobile home on the right side of the road. This is the trailhead, so park here.

Trail. This hike uses the FLT as well as some of the dirt roads in the forest, allowing you to walk a loop. Starting at Babcock Hollow Road, you begin your hike on the FLT with an uphill climb of over ¼ mile; the vertical rise is 300 feet. The trail then makes a sharp descent, crosses a brook, and climbs another hill following the south edge of the woods. Here a footpath, the Rossiter Spur Trail, intersects on your left (north); this is the route you will use on your return trek.

Another ¼ mile brings you to the hill's top, and the trail now starts another sharp descent, dropping 230 feet

Looking west from Virgil Mountain

climb uphill brings you to Bleck Road; cross the road, and continue on the FLT as it reenters the woods. A short distance beyond, the trail crosses another dirt road, Cortwright Road, and descends a steep bank to a creek flowing south in a ravine called Babcock Hollow. Here the FLT turns north. Follow the creek on its east side for ⅝ mile to where it climbs a small hill, leaving the hollow as it intersects a dirt road, O'Dell Road.

The FLT continues north on O'Dell Road for ⅝ mile to where a dirt road, Baldwin Road, intersects on your right. After an additional ⅜ mile on O'Dell Road, the FLT diverges by turning right into a field. In a short distance you enter a wooded area and cross two gullies containing streamlets flowing south. For the next ⅝ mile it is uphill before intersecting another dirt road, VanDonsel Road; the vertical rise in this climb is 300 feet.

Starting here, the FLT cuts back and forth across VanDonsel Road for ½ mile before making its final turn east into the forest. For the first ¼ mile, stay on the FLT as it takes you uphill to the highest spot in the region, Virgil Mountain (elevation 2132 feet). At the top you will find the ends of several ski lifts; for the downhill skier, this is known as the Greek Peak ski area. From this lofty overlook you have an excellent view to the east that includes Tuller Hill State Forest.

The FLT, however, remains in the woods as it makes its way along the hilltop. Soon it turns slightly to the left to head downhill along the edge of the ski trail; in a few hundred feet it turns right and heads in an eastward direction until it reaches the right-of-way beneath some power lines. Here you have a fine view of the surrounding hills and valleys.

Follow the FLT as it turns right; an additional ½ mile brings you to where the FLT turns left and heads downhill. Continue straight ahead on what is now the Virgil Mountain Spur Trail. In ¼ mile, the spur trail reaches and crosses VanDonsel Road and starts an uphill climb. In the first ¼ mile, the trail runs in a southwesterly direction; then it turns slightly to the right to head in a straight westerly direction.

An additional ¼ mile brings you to Cortland Three Road, which the spur trail crosses to climb in ¼ mile to the top of the hill (elevation 2050 feet). From here the route is downhill through the forest for ¾ mile to where you intersect O'Dell Road. From the hilltop to this point the vertical drop is 500 feet.

A short walk on the dirt road brings you to an intersection with Cortwright Road and Hauk Hill Road. Turn right onto Hauk Hill Road and hike uphill for ¾ mile to where Bleck Road crosses Hauk Hill Road. Stay on the latter for an additional ⅜ mile to where the Rossiter Spur Trail begins its journey south.

A short climb on the spur trail takes you to a flattened knob (elevation 1900 feet). For the next ¼ mile the terrain remains level; then the trail takes you up a steep slope for ⅛ mile to the top of another knob (elevation 1970 feet). From here the spur trail heads downhill for ⅛ mile to where you intersect the FLT you walked earlier. The vertical drop from the hilltop to this point is 270 feet. When you reach the FLT, turn right (west) and follow the trail downhill for ½ mile to Babcock Hollow Road and your parked vehicle.

23

Pharsalia Wildlife Management Area

Total distance: 7¼ miles

Hiking time: 5 hours

Vertical rise: 220 feet

Maps: USGS 7½' Otselic; USGS 7½' East Pharsalia

Although much of the surrounding countryside boasts scores of small peaked and knobby hills, Pharsalia Wildlife Management Area seems to want to be different—it is flat. The state-owned portion of this general region sits on tabletop land and is the highest in the area, topping out at an elevation of 2000 feet.

From this tabletop, the land pitches downward on all sides into shallow valleys through which run the Otselic River on the west side, Canasawacta Creek on the south, the East Branch of Canasawacta Creek on the northeast, and Middletown Brook on the north.

The Pharsalia Wildlife Management Area is covered by thick forest, providing the hiker with a fairly good wilderness

experience. Of course, there are a few signs that humans have been at work here. The road system is one of these. Although all roads found here are one-lane dirt routes, they are extensive enough to enable the hiker to reach all sections of the management area. Another sign is the cluster of ponds found on top of this small plateau. These were constructed to provide watering holes for the region's wildlife, but they fit so well into the environment that the human influence goes unnoticed.

The only other sign of human presence is a section of the Finger Lakes Trail (FLT), a narrow footpath running fairly inconspicuously through the entire wildlife management area in a north-south direction. But for the most part the region is a haven for various game animals and woodland birds, including the white-tailed deer, wild turkey, red and gray squirrel, and ruffed grouse.

Even outside this managed haven the touch of civilization is barely noticeable, since the vast region surrounding it contains large tracts of state land. To be sure, people live here, but not too many. South of the wildlife management area you can find several hamlets (actually small clusters of houses), North Pharsalia, and East Pharsalia. To the east

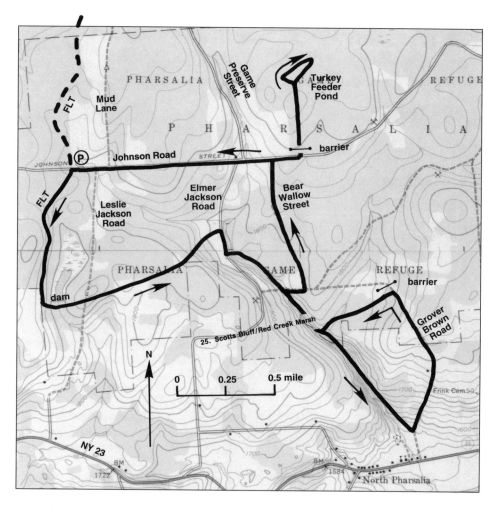

there is the even smaller community of Pharsalia and to the west, Pitcher. The nearest cities are Norwich, 15 miles to the east, and Cortland, 20 miles to the west. In between are hills and forests.

Pharsalia Wildlife Management Area is a fine place in summer for biking as well as for hiking. In winter these same routes, including the FLT, can also be used for Nordic skiing and snowshoeing; a winter access point is where the state's Johnson Road intersects NY 23 (plowed) on the wildlife management area's west side. The roads in the area are not plowed.

Access. The most direct route to the trailhead is via NY 12 running south from Utica to Norwich. NY 12 may also be reached by US 20 from Cazenova (southeast of Syracuse) where the two highways intersect at Sangerfield; from here it is 31 miles to Norwich. As you enter Norwich, NY 23 crosses NY 12. Turn right (west) onto NY 23. Drive northwest on NY 23 for 15 miles through the hamlet of South Plymouth to North Pharsalia. From here continue on NY 23 for 3.5 miles where a dirt road, Johnson Road, intersects on your right.

Jackson Pond

Turn here and drive east on Johnson Road for 0.8 mile. At this point the north-south-running FLT crosses the road; the footpath is marked by white blazes. Park here.

Trail. Enter the forest at the trailhead and walk south on the FLT. The terrain is flat for the next ¼ mile, and soon you see through the trees to your left a small body of water. This is Jackson Pond, ⅜ mile long. When you reach its south end, the FLT turns east. Once past the pond's earthen dam you emerge at a dirt road, known as Leslie Jackson Road (there are no street signs here).

The FLT crosses the road and takes a northeasterly course through the forest and over level land for ⅝ mile. The trail then starts a moderate descent to where it intercepts another dirt road, called Elmer Jackson Road (no street signs

here, either). You leave the forest at the north end of a small, unnamed pond and follow the FLT south along its western edge for ⅛ mile until the pond ends and the trail turns back into the woods on a southeasterly course.

The FLT now follows a gully that later deepens and takes on a gorgelike appearance; this is also the route of the pond's outlet stream. In ¼ mile you encounter a blue-blazed spur trail, which you'll use later, intersecting on your left. However, continue on the FLT for an additional ¼ mile until you encounter a second blue-blazed spur trail intersecting on your left (you'll also use this trail later).

An additional ¼ mile brings you to the end of the state land; after leaving it, the FLT passes through a deep ravine called Grouse Gorge and eventually intersects a dirt road, Grover Brown Road. The distance from the last spur trail to this point is ¾ mile.

Turn left onto Grover Brown Road and head north for ⅝ mile to where you encounter a barrier across the road; before reaching it you will see the beginning of the blue-blazed spur trail on your left. Take the spur trail southwest for ⅜ mile until you intersect the FLT you walked earlier. Turn right and retrace your steps to the other spur trail on your right; take it for ⅛ mile to where it intersects a dirt road, called Bear Wallow Street.

Turn to your left and head north and gradually uphill on this dirt road; ⅝ mile brings you back to Johnson Road. Turn right and walk about ⅛ mile to where a truck trail intersects on your left (north). The truck trail is barricaded but you can walk ½ mile to an artificial pond called Turkey Feeder Pond.

Retrace your footsteps back to Johnson Road. Turn right (west) on Johnson Road and follow it past Game Preserve Street on your right and a few steps more past Elmer Jackson Road on your left. An additional ⅝ mile brings you first past Mud Lane on your right and then Leslie Jackson Road on your left; ⅛ mile more takes you back to your parked vehicle.

ONTARIO DRUMLINS AND HILLS

24

Chimney Bluffs/East Bay Marsh Unit

Total distance: 2½ miles

Hiking time: 1½

Vertical rise: 150 feet

Map: USGS 7½' Sodus Point

Here's a place that delights the eye with the natural wonder of bluff sculpturing—the breathtaking sights of the "chimneys." Here, too, you can hike a Lake Ontario beach and the edge of a 150-foot-high bluff. You also can engage in a host of enjoyable activities: a picnic on the beach, a swim in the lake, a canoe trip in the large bay and its four feeder streams, or a hike around the point.

There are two differently administered state land areas here. Occupying the small forested hill, which is actually a glacier-produced drumlin, is the undeveloped Chimney Bluffs State Park; it is administered by the state's Office of Parks, Recreation, and Historic Preservation. Around the park's three sides is state land managed by the state's Department of Environmental Conservation; this is called the East Bay

Marsh Unit and includes a large tract of wetlands, open fields, abandoned orchards, and wooded areas. The marsh unit is one of six such units, collectively called the Lake Shore Marshes Wildlife Management Area, located in this section of land bordering Lake Ontario. The park is the smaller of the two areas of state land. Yet it has much to offer the hiker in trails and scenic attractiveness. When the state acquired it many decades ago, it planned to develop it similarly to other state parks, with a pay booth, parking lot, picnic area, and comfort stations. But the plans changed and state officials decided to leave the land undeveloped.

There are several bluffs here, but they all belong to a single large drumlin. Like the hundreds of drumlins scattered between Syracuse and Rochester, this one was formed by the forward movement of a continental ice sheet that spread over New York thousands of years ago. After the glacier retreated, this drumlin, like the others that make up the bluff system along Lake Ontario, was slowly eroded into its present form by wet weather and storms blowing off the lake's waters.

Access. Chimney Bluffs and East Bay Marsh areas lie 8.5 miles north of the

Bluff sculpture on Lake Ontario

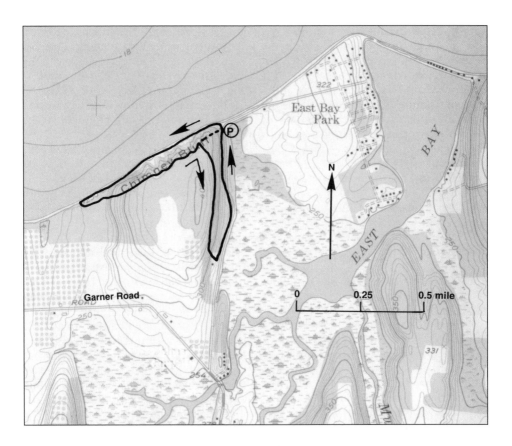

village of Clyde and a short distance east of Sodus Bay. You can reach these two areas from either Rochester in the west or Oswego in the east by taking NY 104 to where it is intersected by NY 414 which runs north from Clyde; NY 414 ends at the intersection, but the route continues north via Lake Bluff Road. Stay on this latter road for 2.8 miles where it is intersected by Lummisville Road. Turn right (east) on Lummisville Road and drive 0.9 mile to the intersection with East Bay Road. Turn left (north) on the latter road and continue north; an additional 2 miles brings you to a fork.

Take the right leg and continue on this paved road for 1 mile to the beach. En route to the beach at the 0.5-mile

mark a narrow dirt lane intersects on your left. This is one of the routes used to make either an ascent to or a descent from the top of the drumlin; it also is the easiest. However, continue on to the beach and park your vehicle in the parking area that overlooks it.

Trail. There are two ways to get a close look at the bluffs and their "chimneys." One is to start at the lane you passed while driving to the beach, climb to the top of the drumlin, descend to the shore, and return by way of the beach. The second reverses this route; you start by walking west ⅝ mile on the beach, intercept a footpath that leads to the top of the drumlin, and then descend to the highway via an abandoned lane. This is the recommended route; it is the more scenic of the two, and the easier to follow.

Once you have parked, you are at the base of Chimney Bluffs, which tower upward abruptly on your left. The face of the bluffs drops sharply to within 20 or 30 feet of the water's edge. Start your walk on the pebble-packed beach, heading left (west) as you face Lake Ontario.

Within a few hundred feet, you get your first glimpse of the "chimneys"—pinnacles, spires, peaks, saddles, and knifelike ledges that rise 150 feet above the water's edge. These landforms have been etched, eroded, molded, and shaped by constant exposure to wind, water, and the icy spray and wet snow that sweep across Lake Ontario with gale force each winter.

The bluff, a mixture of relatively hard and soft soils, is a drumlin, with its northern half eaten away by wind, rain, and waves of lake storms; it was formed centuries ago by the last continental glacier. The surface facing the lake is exposed earth. Here you see the effects of weathering and the work of erosion agents, which remove the soft, soluble soil and rock, leaving behind the more resistant strata in the forms of pinnacles, spires, and hogbacks.

With every step you take along the beach, the scene changes dramatically as new chimneys come into view or your angle of perspective shifts. The bluffs tower over you for about a half mile before tapering off into flat land, which edges the lake for another half mile. At the ⅝-mile point you can look back and view the entire coastline.

Now, leave the beach and climb the bank to a footpath. Turn left onto the path and head in the direction of your vehicle. You soon reach the top of the bluffs. Here, with every twist and turn of the bluffs' edge and along the narrow projections of the hogbacks, the view seems even more breathtaking. The contrast of the red-brown pinnacles with the blue-green water of the lake is most striking, especially on bright, sunny days.

Be sure to stop from time to time and drink deeply of all this. However, in the midst of the grandeur, don't neglect the simpler beauties that crowd around your feet. Take time, especially in late spring, to observe the vast array of wildflowers that fills the woods crowning the bluffs. Sprinkled throughout are the typical forest flowers: yellow wood sorrel, buttercup, coltsfoot, mandrake, miterwort, foamflower, and violets. But most striking is the profusion of painted trillium, Solomon's seal, and columbine. Columbine is found on both sides of the footpath for nearly its entire distance. So, too, is a variety of ferns, including large patches of sensitive fern, woodfern, and cinnamon fern.

You finally reach the eastern edge of the bluffs where a path descends to the parking area. It is a short but steep descent, and care is advised.

A second and easier route is to follow a path that slants to your right. This takes you a short distance downhill to an abandoned lane leading gradually down to the highway on which you drove earlier to get to the beach. Turn left on the highway and walk ½ mile to where you parked your vehicle.

At this point you can call it a day or, better still, continue to explore some of the area's other offerings. Either spring or fall, when the air is crisp, is a fine time to follow Garner Road westward on foot. Begin at the fork of East Bay and Garner Roads; this is just beyond the bridge over the stream flowing into East Bay.

A mile brings you to where Garner Road turns south. On the right side of the turn is a path leading northward, through a wooded area, to the beach.

Taking a right here allows you to walk east for a mile along the beach to your parking spot. A ¼-mile-long footpath also starts at the bridge and runs north, along the west side of the outlet stream.

The area's other assets include marsh areas and canoeable waterways. The marshes provide ideal habitat for a variety of bird species, especially waterfowl, that come here to nest and feed during the spring and summer.

If you are a canoeist by all means bring your canoe. Four marsh-draining streams feed into mile-long East Bay, which is separated from Lake Ontario by a narrow causeway. This makes East Bay a naturally impounded body of water—one of more than a dozen of such unusual phenomena found along the southern shore of Lake Ontario. The longest stream is Mudge Creek, which has its origin miles to the south.

You can spend an entire day canoeing these waters. You may cover more than 10 miles canoeing up and back each of the feeder streams, as well as around the bay. These trips will allow you to see birdlife and waterfowl aplenty, so bring your bird field guide and binoculars.

25

Scotts Bluff/Red Creek Marsh Unit

Total distance: 3 miles

Hiking time: 2 hours

Vertical rise: 240 feet

Map: USGS 7½' North Wolcott

The Red Creek Marsh Unit, a state-owned parcel of wetlands and woods fronting on Lake Ontario north of Clyde and Seneca Falls, encompasses a variety of natural wonders within its 2 square miles. Among them are Scotts Bluff and the naturally impounded Red Creek. The creek is ideal for flatwater canoeing and, if you like, even canoe camping along its upper reaches. The different habitats the tract encloses allow you to observe an array of both woodland and shore birds; so, beginner or expert, bring your field guide—you will find many opportunities to use it during 2 hours or so of easy walking around this loop. The Red Creek Marsh Unit is one of six such units acquired by the state to protect the wetlands in this section of Lake Ontario's shores. All of these marsh units are part of what is called the Lake Shore Marshes Wildlife Management Area. They are managed by the state's Department of Environmental Conservation.

Scotts Bluff, like the other bluffs along this part of Lake Ontario, is a drumlin, a glacier-produced landform, which over thousands of years has been weathered into its present shape by the winds, rains, and storms sweeping inland from Lake Ontario.

Access. Your walk begins by Scotts Bluff, 7.6 road miles from Wolcott, which is 25 miles north of I-90 Exit 41 off NY 89. Drive east out of Wolcott, toward NY 104, en route to the town of Red Creek. At 2.6 miles you cross Wadsworth Road. Another 0.8 mile brings you to Hapeman Road, where you turn left and travel 2 miles to an intersection. Turn right, drive 0.2 mile into the hamlet of North Wolcott, and turn left onto Broadway. In 0.6 mile you cross Younglove Road, 1000 feet beyond which is a sign marking the boundary of the Red Creek Marsh Unit. Another 0.5 mile brings you to a bridge across Red Creek, which on weekends is often lined with fishermen. All

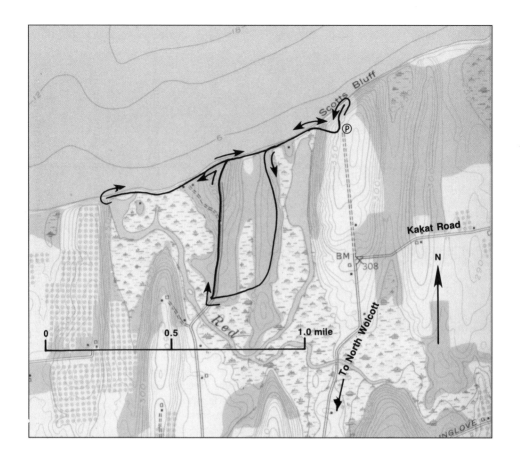

around you are wetlands where waterfowl nest, feed, and rest from early spring until late fall. About 0.9 mile beyond the bridge, the road, which turns to dirt after 0.4 mile, comes to a dead end. You are now on top of Scotts Bluff. Park your vehicle in the small parking area on the west side of the road.

Trail. At the road's end, a footpath bending slightly to the right leads to the edge of Scotts Bluff. Here, 100 feet above the water, by a process similar to the one that produced the edges, pinnacles, peaks, and "chimneys" of Chimney Bluff (see Hike 24), winds, rains, and spray driven across Lake Ontario and against the relatively soft earth of the cliff face have etched their marks in the form of peaks and saddles to produce this unusual landform.

Return to your vehicle. Facing west you overlook a hayfield that slopes down toward the marsh in the southwest and toward Lake Ontario in the northwest. Walk downhill to the steep trail that descends to the beach. Here an endless assortment of brightly colored pebbles and flat rocks cobbles the lakeshore. Most of the stones are of a bright reddish hue, with appealing designs on their

Scotts Bluff

smooth, worn surfaces. You may be tempted to fill your pockets with the most attractive ones—until you remember that you still have a mile to walk.

Back from the water's edge, tall, stately willows line the beach for ½ mile west to the next bluff. Amidst the willows, sand and dirt combine to form a natural path parallel to the lakeshore. Here, just south of the willow trees, you see what looks like a pond about ½ mile in length and 500 feet across. This is the east leg of naturally impounded Red Creek. When heavy waves sweep across Lake Ontario during storms, they roll up tons of rocks, stones, and pebbles to form a breakwater several feet high. This breakwater then acts as a dam, preventing the water in Red Creek from emptying into the lake.

Walk west along the natural path for ¼ mile until a jeep trail angles off to your left. Follow this trail through a wooded area along the edge of the marsh. You are now heading south on a fingerlike spit of land. In ½ mile, the trail turns to your right, heading over some high ground and then through a small stretch of marsh. In just over 100 yards you come to a dirt road. Turn right and walk north, back toward Lake Ontario. This is a most pleasant place to pass through, particularly on a sunny morning when the birds are most active. The road is completely canopied by trees, mostly white oaks and maples, and there is always a cool breeze coming off the lake. Cedar waxwings, vireos, scarlet tanagers, and towhees are among the many species you might see or hear. Spring through autumn, this wood is a noisy place, filled with the calls and songs of the feathered inhabitants.

Another ½ mile brings you to the road's end, at the edge of a 90-foot bluff, where you have an excellent view of the shoreline. To your left a footpath leads for several hundred feet into a wooded area, skirting a small clearing often used by campers. Then it bends right toward the bluff edge and slopes down to the beach, passing two summer cottages that occupy a small tract of private land.

Once on the beach, continue westward another ¼ mile. Again you find willows lining the upper shore. To your left, a narrow neck of water, part of the west leg of Red Creek, comes almost to the beach. Here you can see the interaction of water, land, wind, and waves changing the landscape almost before your eyes: One day the water may be held back by the piled-up pebbles; the next the waves may have washed some away, allowing the impounded waters of Red Creek to spill through the small breach into the lake.

Retrace your steps along the beach, up the path, and back to the road at the dead-end turnaround on the 90-foot-high bluff. Cross the road and walk down the field between the bluff edge and the wooded area on your right. Near the bottom a path leads through a stand of trees and back to the beach. Continue walking east for about 1000 feet, until you see, on your right, the jeep trail you walked earlier. Take the path under the willows to the base of the bluff, and go up the footpath to your vehicle.

26

Howland Island Wildlife Management Area

Total distance: 4 miles

Hiking time: 2½ hours

Vertical rise: 440 feet

Map: 7½' Montezuma

The state-owned Howland Island Wildlife Management Area serves as a wildlife refuge, providing a suitable habitat in which waterfowl may rest, feed, and nest. It is also home to a large number of resident Canada geese, who raise their young on the numerous ponds found on Howland Island.

When winter arrives and the ponds freeze, these resident geese head for Cayuga Lake, about 10 miles south of Howland Island, making this probably the shortest migratory route on the Atlantic fly-way. The geese spend the winter on the lake's open waters.

Of course, during migratory periods nonresident Canada geese and, especially, ducks use the ponds of Howland Island as resting and feeding sites on their way north in spring and south in fall.

Several features set Howland Island apart from other nearby wildlife refuges. For one, this 3600-acre preserve is truly an island, though an artificial one. The Seneca River flows in a huge semicircle around its northern portion, while its southern edge is bounded by the New York Barge Canal—more commonly called the new Erie Canal—which replaced the old Erie Canal after the turn of the century. At that time, the engineers cut a waterway at the bottom of the Seneca River loop to shorten the distance and thereby created an island.

Another characteristic of Howland is that most of the island is best described as "upland"—fields separated by large stands of hardwood—although it is marked by a strip of marsh wetland along the sides facing the river and canal. The open field areas are planted with corn to provide food for wildlife, including white-tailed deer, geese, and ducks. The ponds, which were constructed for waterfowl, are found in the island's upland section, not the lowland rim. Small hills are also found on the island. Actually, they are clusters of glacier-produced drumlins, giving variety to the landscape and good vantage sites to the hiker.

Still another difference is Howland's many ponds—11 in all. These artificial impoundments, most of them interconnected, serve as the setting in which management techniques are employed by the state's Department of Environmental Conservation to provide food, cover, and shelter for over 460 species of wildlife.

This is a place to bring your bird guide and field glasses, as well as your camera.

Try hiking the island during early or late spring when both land birds and waterfowl are migrating. You may see several species of hawks, including red-tailed, sharp-shinned, Cooper's, and harriers. The island is laced with a network of maintenance roads that is closed to unauthorized vehicles, so you can reach any part of the island on foot to do your bird watching.

There are some periods when hikers are not allowed here: During the waterfowl nesting season in April and May, when the entire refuge except for the first mile of the main road is closed to the public; and during the October and November hunting season, when controlled hunting hours prevail. These hours are usually imposed on Tuesday, Thursday, and Saturday from early morning until noon. For more information call the regional office of the state's Department of Environmental Conservation in Cortland (607-753-3095).

Access. Howland Island is about 8 miles northwest of Cayuga Lake and about 5 miles north of the New York Thruway (I-90). If you come via the Thruway, use Exit 40 at Weedsport to pick up NY 31. Drive west on NY 31 to Port Byron and then north on NY 38 for 2 miles to Yellow Schoolhouse Road (0.5 mile beyond a set of railroad tracks). Follow this road to your left. At 1.8 miles, you cross a one-lane steel bridge over the canal. On the far side, to your right, is a public boat launching site, used extensively by fishermen and canoeists.

You are now on Howland Island. Continue on the two-lane dirt road for 0.9 mile past a dirt road intersecting on your right to a large parking area marked off by a line of large, round boulders. Park here. At the north end of the parking area where the road con-

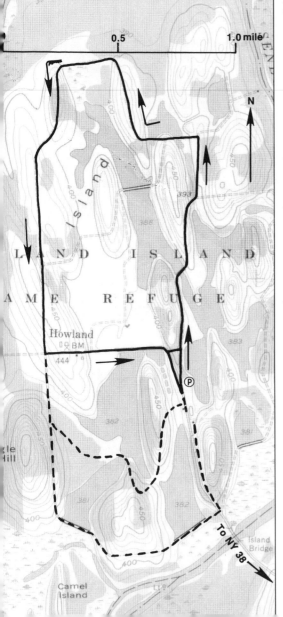

Pond at Howland Island Wildlife Management Area

northward on the two-lane dirt road for 0.9 mile, past a wooded hill on your right, to a dirt service road intersecting on your right.

Follow the service road to a barrier erected to keep out unauthorized vehicles. Walk around the barrier and continue hiking eastward on the service road. This road now turns northward; a short distance ahead another dirt road intersects on your right. Bypass it and continue north for a quarter of a mile to the top of a wooded hill.

The road is tree-lined. On your left is a small, elongated, tree-covered hill—one of more than a dozen drumlins found on the island. As you walk northward you are actually traveling along a peninsula formed by the drumlin and the ponds on either side. Before you reach the end of the peninsula in about a mile from your starting point, the road bends slightly to the right to cross a causeway to another peninsula. Here the road makes a

gradual but short ascent before pitching downward to cross a brook.

Beyond this brook, another road bears off on your right. Ignore it by keeping left past another wood-covered drumlin. About ¼ mile farther on you come to a T-junction.

Here you are on high ground. Ahead, looking northeast, you can see still another pond, where, as elsewhere in the preserve, you may spot a family of geese during the summer. Turn left at the junction and head downhill (west); this brings you to more water, with the road passing over a causeway at the southern end of the pond.

You now turn north and walk over a small hill to a lowland stretch. In a short distance you may notice some swampland through the trees on your left. Soon the road starts up a gradual rise, passing a right-branching lane as it begins its loop south. You are now walking through a relatively thickly wooded area where trees canopy the road.

Shortly the trees give way to fields on both sides. This is high ground where only small patches of trees obstruct the view. The road bends slightly to the right and then to the left, setting you on a straight southerly course; 1¼ miles more bring you a cluster of buildings, the Howland Island staff headquarters, and another east-west road.

Turn left here. This road now runs gradually downhill for ¼ mile and then crosses another impoundment. Beyond the causeway, the road turns right (south) and in a little over ¼ mile returns you to your starting point.

One of the other pleasant trails you can follow on the island takes you south past the staff headquarters to a fork. If you bear left, you pass through a heavily wooded area, cross a narrow neck of another impoundment, and eventually return to your starting point.

To lengthen your walk a bit, you can bear right at the fork and continue south past Eagle Hill on your right, across a dam, along the southern edge of still another impoundment, uphill to the main road, and then left along the road back to your starting point. For a good view of the island, climb the short distance to the top of Eagle Hill, the highest point on the island at 570 feet.

Howland is a fine place for snow-shoeing and ideal for ski touring. The terrain, with its small rolling hills, provides a whole series of short downhill runs to add a bit of excitement. Howland Island Road is plowed in winter. The snow conditions on the island are generally good, and in January and February the snow is plentiful.

27

Verona Beach State Park

Total distance: 4 miles

Hiking time: 2 hours

Vertical rise: 12 feet

Maps: USGS 7½' Sylvan Beach; Park Brochure

Verona Beach State Park has two personalities, each quite different, separated by a two-lane highway, NY 13. On the west side of the highway is a long sandy beach facing Oneida Lake, with a picnic area and camping sites. This is the side associated with summer crowds, excitement, laughter, and fun.

On the east side of the highway you will find a far more subdued environment—lush, cool forest and the most diversified flora found in central New York. Around and over a quiet pond and lily-filled waterway that looks like an elongated lake run more than 16 miles of hiking trails. In summer the east side offers the quietude and peace of a forest glen, in which you may hear, if you listen, the soft voices of nature. In winter, the

snows bring a hush broken only by the sound of winds whispering in the pines.

The state park is located at the east end of Oneida Lake, as is the hamlet of Verona Beach, situated between Oneida Creek in the south and the Erie Canal/Fish Creek waterway in the north. Flowing through the park is Black Creek, a slow-moving stream that begins in a swamp at the park's northeast rim and empties into Oneida Creek, almost at the lake's edge.

The park is relatively new, having been constructed in the late 1950s. However, the park land and the land around it is old, formed more than 12,000 years ago when a continental ice sheet called the Wisconsin Glacier covered virtually all of what is now New York State. As the glacier started to melt back it dammed the St. Lawrence River and, in the process, flooded much of central New York, turning it into a huge lake, called by geologists and glaciologists Lake Iroquois. When Lake Iroquois finally drained into the St. Lawrence and Mohawk Rivers, it left behind the Oneida flood plain, which today surrounds Oneida Lake. This land is flat, marked by scattered cattail marshes, hardwood swamps, and large areas of sandy soil brought here when glacial meltwaters flooded into Lake Iroquois.

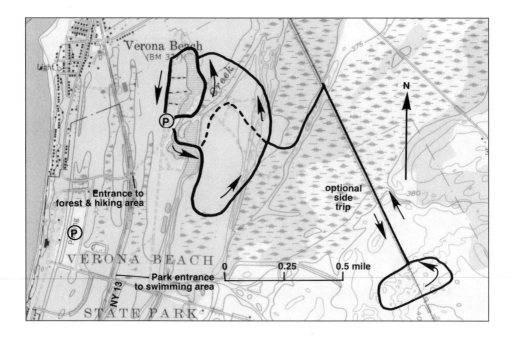

All these remnants of the glacial and postglacial periods can be found in the state park, from sand-filled beach to swampy habitat. At one time the sands from the beds along the shore were shipped by railroad to various glass-making industries.

At an earlier time, the Iroquois called this their land since it sat astride a principal water transportation route that ran from the Mohawk River—via a 4-mile carry at what today is Rome—to Wood Creek, which emptied into Oneida Lake. From here Lake Ontario could be reached via the Oneida and Oswego Rivers. Today this route is still being used, but the Erie Canal at the north end of the state park has replaced Wood Creek, and locks along the Oswego River permit the movement of large power boats from Lake Ontario to the 31-mile-long Oneida Lake.

The park boasts abundant wildlife, including white-tailed deer, wild turkey, and other small game. It is also home to a wide variety of shore birds, as well as wetland and woodland birds; these include hawks, woodpeckers, warblers, herons, and an occasional osprey. Resident fish include smallmouth and largemouth bass, yellow perch, walleye, and bullheads.

There is much here to see and enjoy, especially with children; the park is ideal for a family trek. The park's east side is heavily wooded by a wide assortment of evergreen and broad-leafed trees; there are many species of ferns here. Identification can prove to be a challenge; tree and fern field guides will prove helpful.

The pond at the start of the hike is stocked with game fish. Numerous access points along the pond's shore allow anglers to spin-cast for their catch; there are even several spots that allow fly-casting.

During migratory seasons, the wooded area of the park becomes a resting and feeding site. Many birds stay the summer to nest and raise their young; be sure to bring your binoculars and bird field guide. You will find many species of mushrooms along the sides of the hiking paths, as the moist soil and shaded ground encourage them to flourish at any time during the summer. Be sure to bring a mushroom field guide if you are interested in mushroom identification.

Fall is an especially fine time to hike the state park. Autumn foliage in the forest brings a blaze of color to the eye and the brightness of sunlight lifts the spirits.

Access. From Syracuse in the west and Rome or Utica in the east, you can get to the state park by traveling the New York Thruway (I-90). If you use the Thruway, ramp off at Canastota (Exit 34) and drive 5.7 miles north on NY 13 to the park entrance on your left. You also can take NY 31 from Syracuse or Rome. In either case, drive until you intersect NY 13 at South Bay. Turn left (north) onto NY 13 and drive 1.7 miles to the park entrance. If you enter the park here, you must pay a parking fee.

However, by continuing north on NY 13 past the park entrance for ⅜ mile, you can drive into the park's undeveloped part by turning right (east) onto a dirt road. There is no parking fee charged here. A short distance on the dirt road brings you to a fork. Bear to your left and drive a few hundred feet to an open area with a sign that reads: Fisherman Parking. Park here. (In wintertime it is best to drive into the main park and leave your vehicle in the plowed parking area; there is no parking fee charged in winter.)

Trails. The park's trail systems are such that they may be used year-round. Designated routes have been established for Nordic skiers and snowmobilers in winter, and in the park's eastern woods are a 4-mile cross-country ski trail and an 8-mile snowmobile trail. During the other seasons, these serve as hiking and biking trails.

After you park, follow the dirt road as it forks to your right. Continue on this road as it circles a fair-sized artificial pond (unnamed). A mile brings you to the pond's northern end, where the road loops around to intersect another dirt road running north and south.

Turn south on this road and head back to your vehicle. En route you will encounter four paths leading from the road to the pond; these are used by fishermen to get to the water's edge.

When you reach your vehicle, turn right and walk up the road you drove earlier until you come to a fork. The right leg takes you back to NY 13. Instead, turn left and continue south for several hundred yards to a small parking area with a hiking and skiing sign pointing ahead. On the road that runs off to your left is a sign informing you that this is a "service road," restricted to use by park vehicles only.

Follow this service road as it crosses a causeway over Black Creek, which is filled from shore to shore by aquatic plants. Once over the causeway, the road splits, with one route going north and the other south. In winter the southern route is designated as the Nordic ski trail and the northern one as the snowmobile trail.

Continue on the south-bound route, which takes you in little over ½ mile through a mixed forest of hardwoods and evergreens along the southern edge of Black Creek and past several beaver lodges. At the ¾-mile mark, the trail begins turning eastward, and in an additional ¼ mile it completes the turn and begins to run straight in a northeasterly direction for another ¾ mile; here it intersects another road used in winter by snowmobilers.

Mallard ducks at Verona Beach State Park

If you want to do some more hiking, turn right onto the snowmobile trail; a 1½-mile walk will bring you to a road running on what was once a railroad right-of-way, but is now a tree-canopied footpath with all signs of the old railroad gone. A right turn and a mile farther brings you to an intersection; the road on your left, as well as the one on your right, form a loop, coming together farther down on the abandoned railroad right-of-way. Retrace your steps to the ski trail and turn right.

If, on the other hand, you wish to stay on the Nordic ski trail, cross the snowmobile trail and continue in a northeasterly direction. From here it is ¾ mile to where the trail gradually turns to your left; when you reach the mile mark, you pass a firing range reserved exclusively for law-enforcement officers.

From here it is a little over ½ mile to a causeway over Black Creek; an additional ¼ mile brings you to an intersection with the road circling the pond—the route you followed at the beginning of your hike. Turn left and follow the road back to your vehicle.

28

Klondike State Forest

Total distance: 5 miles

Hiking time: 2½ hours

Vertical rise: 630 feet

Map: USGS 7½' Panther Lake

Klondike State Forest, although relatively small, is a delight to hike; it provides you with a wooded landscape, varied terrain, an attractive pond, and several easily accessible roads that allow you to walk through the entire forest, as well as to several remote spots in the forest.

Its name makes you think of the cold and forbidding Klondike region in the Yukon district of northwestern Canada, site of the greatest gold rush the world has ever known. There is little the state forest has in common with its northern namesake, though. It takes its name instead from a low swampy area tagged as "The Klondike" for reasons that are now forgotten. This piece of wetland lies in the northern part of the state land.

The small, 875-acre state forest is located about 7 miles north of Oneida Lake between the hamlets of West Amboy in the north and North Constantia in the south. It is situated in what is known as the Oneida Lake Plain, which in turn is in the Ontario Lowland Region.

This low-relief land was once part of an old glacial lake bottom thousands of years ago. The area's low rolling hills consist primarily of ground moraine deposits left behind by the retreating glacier of the Pleistocene period. Because the land is poorly drained, it is dotted with numerous swamps and shallow ponds.

On the southern edge of the state forest are two such ponds—Chase Pond and South Pond, both located on posted private land. To the west, with the state property line passing through its eastern part, is North Pond. Immediately north of the state land is the swampy area known as "The Klondike," whose water drains into North Pond.

The highest spot in the state forest is Chase Hill with an elevation of 673 feet. While the hills are not high, the region has an abundance of rolling terrain that adds variety and attractiveness to your hike.

Access. The state forest lies south of NY 69, which runs east and west between

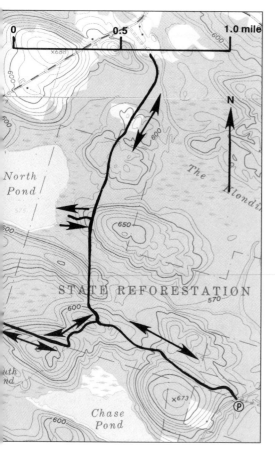

road as a westward continuation of Starks Road. It is here that you begin your hike. Head westward up a gentle slope. After the first 100 yards, the road levels out. On both sides of the road are stands of hardwood, primarily maple, interspersed with evergreens.

About ¼ mile down the road, you will see a stone fence paralleling the road on your left, about 20 yards away. As soon as you see another stone fence intersecting at a right angle, turn left off the road, and follow a foot trail south through a break in the stone fence and up a slight rise. The ascent is a modest one, and after 100 yards the trail levels out as it passes through a stand of pines.

Suddenly the trees give way to a large field on your left. You are now on top of Chase Hill, which gives you an attractive overlook across the field to the southeast. The field pitches gradually downward toward a house at the far end. Hidden from view, but located in the shallow valley to the west, is Chase Pond. Far ahead to the east is tree-covered high ground, with a couple of houses visible in the distance.

Retrace your steps to the road, and continue your hike to the west. In the next ½ mile, the road dips and rises several times; it then turns to your right (north) and heads gradually downhill. At the turn, a jeep trail runs uphill (south). Take the jeep trail for a short excursion to the southwestern corner of the state forest. Once it reaches the top of the hill, it makes a short but sharp descent, only to climb a second hill, at the top of which you meet posted signs indicating you have reached the southern boundary of the state forest.

Intersecting from your right, however, is another jeep trail, paralleling the state boundary line. Turn here, and follow this trail for a little less than ½ mile, until the trail ends as it reaches the state forest's

Parish and Camden. NY 69 can be reached easily via I-81, exiting onto NY 69 at Parish (about 22 miles north of Syracuse). Once on NY 69, drive east 7 miles to West Amboy. Continue 1 mile beyond West Amboy to where Tanner Road—a two-lane dirt road—intersects on your right. Turn here, and follow Tanner Road for 1.8 miles to the intersection with Starks Road, a single-lane dirt road. Park here.

Trail. What was once just a walk trail has been widened into a single-lane dirt

Quiet fall day on the Klondike Trail

western boundary. The jeep trail is canopied by tall trees to make this a most pleasant hike. When you reach the trail's end, retrace your steps to the main road.

The road is now heading in a northerly direction, dipping into a small depression, rising to the top of a small hill, and then pitching more steeply downward, about ¼ mile from the jeep trail you hiked earlier. Look along the bank on your left as you head downhill; soon you spot a discernible hiking trail heading uphill and west from the road.

While this is not a heavily used tail, its outline is clear enough to allow you to follow it; ¼ mile brings you to the southern edge of North Pond and a nice overlook of this small but attractive body of water. You are also at the western boundary of the state forest, so reverse direction and return to the main road, where you turn left to continue.

As you reach the bottom of the hill on the main road, you cross a small stream draining water from the Klondike Swamp to North Pond. Once across the stream, you ascend a small hill. At the top, the woods have been cut back on your right to permit vehicle parking.

Across the road from the parking area is a foot trail, which you can follow as it leaves the road and heads downhill, taking you a short distance to the eastern edge of North Pond.

Back on the main road again, continue northward for almost ½ mile; here the state forest ends and private property begins, although the line of transition is not discernible because all is heavily forested. You can continue following the road to the end of the woods, about ⅝ mile from the state forest boundary.

Here the forest gives way to a field, on the far side of which are several houses at the south edge of a paved road, County Route 26, just short of a mile south of West Amboy. From here you can retrace your steps through the state forest along the main road to your parked vehicle.

Klondike State Forest also is a good spot for such wintertime activities as snowshoeing and Nordic skiing. Snowshoeing allows you to explore several of the jeep trails, as well as several abandoned logging roads radiating off the main road. The rolling terrain is ideal for ski touring, including a number of sporty downhill runs.

29

Selkirk Shores State Park

Total distance: 3½ miles

Hiking time: 2 hours

Vertical rise: 120 feet

Maps: USGS 7½' Pulaski; Park Map

Selkirk Shores State Park is 1000 acres of forested land fronting Lake Ontario on the west, bounded on the north by the Salmon River and on the south by Grindstone Creek. The state park has many natural assets that make it an attractive setting for hiking.

You can do a lot of other things here as well—swimming, sailing, canoeing, picnicking, camping, and fishing, more than can be crammed into one day. It is best to plan a weekend outing, or even a longer one.

Like all state parks, Selkirk charges an entrance fee, and if you plan to camp there is a daily camping fee. But you get a lot for your money. Both Grindstone Creek and Salmon River are popular fishing streams. Trout running up to 20 pounds can be found

here, as well as Coho and Chinook salmon. More recently the state has begun stocking lake trout and Atlantic salmon in the lake.

The lower reaches of both streams also can be canoed, and of course Lake Ontario is ideal for sailing. The parking area that adjoins Grindstone Creek serves as a boat-launching access. The entire park is woodland right to the water's edge, and most of it is evergreens, with rows of Scotch pines, large stands of tall hemlocks, and a number of spruce and pine plantations that keep the park green the year-round.

In winter, the park is a popular spot for cross-country skiing. Park personnel maintain groomed and marked ski trails that serve well during the summer as hiking trails. If you combine the ski trails with the park's regular hiking trails and road systems, you have over 15 miles of hiking trails.

The park's other asset is its abundance of wildlife. Hunting and trapping are not permitted here, so the park acts as a game refuge sheltering a surprisingly large number of ruffed grouse, varying hare, red and gray fox, and white-tailed deer. If you are on the trail early in the morning, be prepared to meet some of these local inhabitants.

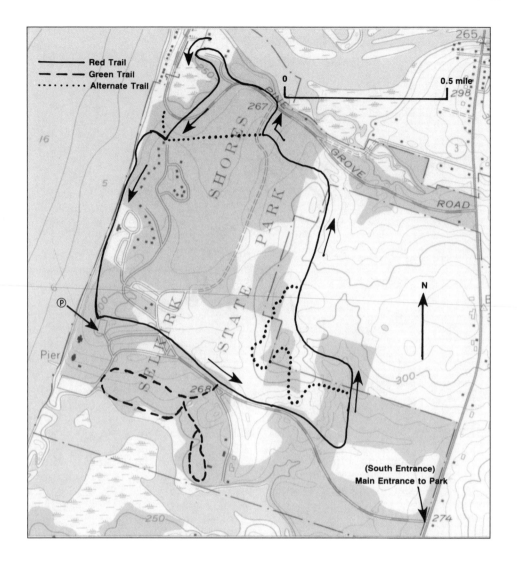

Red Trail
Green Trail
Alternate Trail

0   0.5 mile

N

(South Entrance)
Main Entrance to Park

The park has two entrances. The north entrance leads to an area called Pine Grove, next to the Salmon River, where there are a number of three- and four-room cottages rented to the public by the state. Rental applications are taken in January, and cottages are assigned by lottery. Here, too, you find a boat-launching site. There is no entrance fee to this section of the park. The south entrance brings you to the areas where you can swim, picnic, and camp, and here a fee is charged.

Access. The state park is on the east shore of Lake Ontario, 4 miles due west of Pulaski. Entrances are on NY 3, which parallels the shoreline and runs from Fulton to Watertown. The park can

Looking over Salmon River

also be reached via I-81; exit at Pulaski, and follow NY 13 westward past the southern part of the town to Port Ontario, where it intersects with NY 3. Turn south on NY 3, and drive 1.6 miles to the park's southern (main) entrance. A mile west on this access road brings you to the ticket booth.

From the ticket booth, bear to your right. This road takes you in less than ¼ mile to a parking area on your right. Park here.

Trail. Your hiking will be primarily on cross-country ski trails that are marked as such. You will see these markers near the northeast corner of the parking area, where you follow a trail east; it parallels the entrance road you used to reach the parking area. This is the Red Trail, the longest of the two loop trails, which run

through the central and northern portion of the park. The short loop, the Green Trail, is in the southern part.

In less than ¼ mile, the trail crosses a park road, and then for the next ¾ mile it runs through a wide cut in a stand of Scotch pines, paralleling but well away from the park's entrance road. Soon the Scotch pines give way to a large and impressive stand of red pine. The trail now turns to the left and enters a more open area. To your right are hardwoods and to your left are pines; ahead the field is dotted with small Scotch pines.

A short distance downtrail, you see a marker pointing to a trail intersecting on your left. This is part of the Red Trail's inner loop, which runs about a mile before rejoining the main trail. The main trail soon also turns to the left, heading west for ¼ mile, where it then turns right and runs north; ¼ mile more, and you encounter the second intersection with the inner loop.

In another ¼ mile, the trail turns to the left and heads west. A short distance ahead, you enter an attractive open area and then a stand of tall hemlocks, where you encounter an intersection with a north-south trail. Turn right onto this new trail, and follow it north for ⅛ mile, where it intersects a blacktop road off the park's northern entrance route. Turn left onto the blacktop entrance road, and walk west ⅛ mile, where a dirt road intersects on your right; en route you see several parking spots among the trees on the Salmon River side of the road, providing some nice views.

Turn right onto the dirt road, and a short distance brings you to Pine Grove with its summer cottages and boat-launching site. Retrace your steps to the north entrance road, and continue walking west as the road swings to the left and then to the right; at this spot you should see a hiking trail on your left. You can take this trail or the one farther down the road at a spot where the road turns more sharply to the right.

Either of these trails runs to the south and quickly brings you first to the park's cabin colony area and then to the camping area. Continue southward paralleling the beach to the parking area and your vehicle.

If you have time, you may wish to hike the shorter Green Trail. You pick up the trail markers on the south side of the entrance road about ⅛ mile east of the Park Office, where a service road intersects the entrance road on your right. This trail consists of a western loop and a short eastern loop.

30

Lakeview Wildlife Management Area/ Southwick Beach State Park

Total distance: 11¼ miles (2 days)

Hiking time: 6 hours

Vertical rise: Minimal

Maps: USGS 7½' Henderson; USGS 7½' Ellisburg

At first sight of Lakeview Wildlife Management Area from NY 3, you see what looks like any other wetland—a large marsh and acres of cattails. There's more here, though, than first meets the eye. While it is true that about 90 percent of the wildlife area is marsh, the total variety of terrain and vegetation will surprise you. You will encounter a natural barrier beach, high sand dunes covered on the back side with dune vegetation, upland woods, juniper fields, meadowlands, abandoned fields, cultivated fields, conifer forest, and hardwood forest.

The wetland area, 5 miles long and just over 1½ wide, lies between Lake

Ontario on the west and the upland (made up of woods and fields) on the east. In the middle is a marsh with a variety of different-sized ponds—Lakeview, Floodwood, Goose, and North and South Colwell Ponds. Here exists a freshwater ecosystem protected from the erosive effects of lake storms by a natural barrier beach with impressively high sand dunes. Feeding this system are several streams—Filmore Brook and Sandy Creek in the north, Mud Brook in the central sector, and South Sandy Creek in the south. All finally empty into Floodwood Pond and thence into Lake Ontario.

The canoeable routes include several creeks and ponds: These are Sandy Creek and South Sandy Creek, with put-in spots where NY 3 crosses the streams; Lakeview Pond at the end of Pierrepont Road and its outlet stream feeding into Sandy Creek, Floodwood Pond, and then into Lake Ontario; and South Colwell Pond, North Colwell Pond, and the outlet stream leading into Lake Ontario.

This area, with its waterways, wetlands, and upland woods provides shelter for a variety of animals including the white-tailed deer; spawning habitat for a variety of fish; and, above all, a breeding, resting, and feeding area for migratory

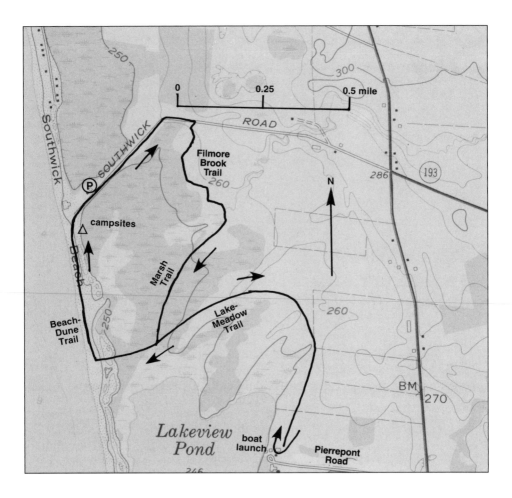

waterfowl, including ducks of more than a dozen species.

Another factor that makes this area especially attractive to the hiker is that Lakeview abuts Southwick Beach State Park in the north. While relatively small compared to Lakeview, Southwick has a large picnic area, an attractive sandy beach, and a dozen camping sites where you can pitch a tent for a weekend stay. The park charges an entrance fee.

As the Lakeview area is an excellent place for long or short day hikes, plan to spend several days camping at Southwick. Together, the two areas pro-

vide you with much to see whether you are hiker, naturalist, birdwatcher, fisherman, or canoeist.

Access. The wildlife area and park are in the southwest corner of Jefferson County, about 10 miles north of Pulaski and 20 miles southwest of Watertown off NY 3. NY 3 can be reached from I-81 at the Pulaski exit, where you drive west on NY 13 to NY 3 at Port Ontario. From Port Ontario, drive north on NY 3 for 10.2 miles, where Pierrepont Road intersects on your left; this road takes you to Lakeview Pond, a half mile west of NY 3,

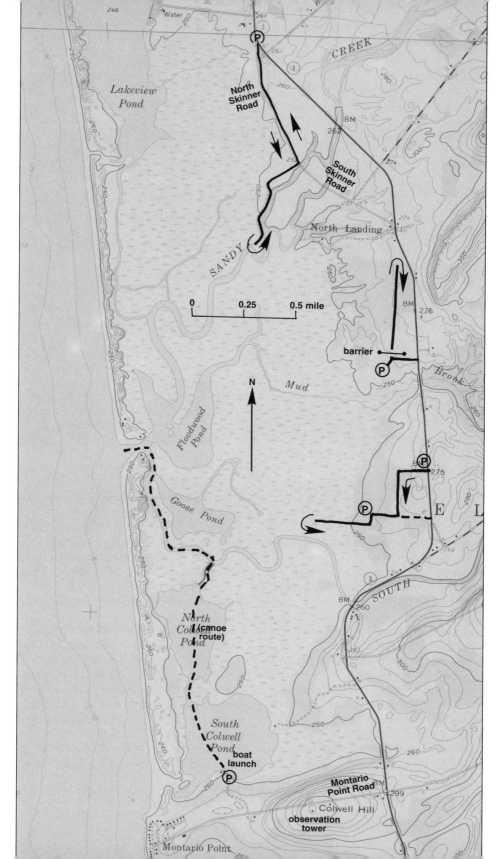

Water 250

246

261

CREEK

Lakeview Pond

North Skinner Road

South Skinner Road

SANDY

North Landing

BM 262

274

274

300

350

BM 276

barrier

Brook

0   0.25   0.5 mile

N

Mud

Floodwood Pond

275

266

Goose Pond

E   L

250

SOUTH

BM 260

3

283

300

North Colwell Pond

(canoe route)

South Colwell Pond

boat launch

Montario Point Road

BM 299

Colwell Hill

observation tower

Montario Point

and to the southern trailhead of the groomed trail system. Continue north on NY 3 for another mile to the intersection with Southwick Road. Turn left onto Southwick Road; 0.8 mile brings you to the entrance of Southwick Beach State Park. If you are planning a weekend outing, make arrangements at the entrance booth for a camping site.

Trail. The northern part of Lakeview Wildlife Management Area that adjoins Southwick offers 3 miles of marked and groomed trails. You can walk from the state park to the wildlife area or vice versa on trails marked by small white squares with a silhouette of a hiker.

The trailhead to the Filmore Brook Trail is located near the state park's entrance booth, allowing you to enter the wildlife area from the north. The trailhead to the Lake-Meadow Trail is found near the boat launching site at Lakeview Pond in the south. Here you find a small frame building with a sign reading "Lake Meadow Trail" on the east side of the building.

The Beach-Dune Trail starts at the park's western campsite and runs south. It takes you to the wildlife area's 3¾-mile-long natural beach, a broad, sandy beach that is restricted to walking to preserve its attractiveness. Many activities are prohibited on this natural beach, including camping, swimming, driving motorized vehicles, picnicking, playing radios or other recording devices, and making fires. If you wish to engage in these activities you can do so in Southwick Beach State Park.

The first day's hiking is on the trail system and natural beach in the northern part of the Lakeview Wildlife Management Area. The second day's walking in the southern half is on a series of unconnected short trails, whose starting points must be reached by vehicle. In three short expeditions, you will be able to inspect the wildlife area from several different vantage points, and in one instance to penetrate into the middle of the marsh area on a trail running on high ground.

First Day
Southwick Beach State Park to Lakeview Pond and back via the natural beach
Distance: 5⅝ miles
Hiking time: 3 hours

From your camping site, follow the blacktop road to the state park's entrance gate, where the Filmore Brook Trail enters the woods on the south side of the road. As you turn onto the trail, you see immediately on your left an abandoned orchard, which quickly gives way to a large hardwood forest. The trail runs south for a short distance, then swings southeast, eventually crossing Filmore Brook at a small waterfall.

The trail now turns sharply to the right, leaves the woods, crosses the southern edge of a cultivated field, runs through a conifer forest, and then enters a hardwood forest to become the Marsh Trail.

In little less than ½ mile, you reach the intersection with the Lake-Meadow Trail, which cuts back sharply to your left. The trail running to the right takes you to the Beach-Dune Trail, which you'll walk later. Turn onto the Lake-Meadow Trail and head northeast.

The next ¼ mile is a trek through a thick stand of hardwood, suddenly giving way to an attractive ¼-mile-long meadow and juniper field. The trail, once across this open area, passes through a stand of hardwood, crosses an open area with cultivated fields on your

Entering the "natural beach" area

left, and then reenters another wooded area on an abandoned wagon trail.

In ½ mile farther, you come to an open area. Ahead you can see a small frame building. As you reach the building you see the boat launching site on the south side and Lakeview Pond on the west. Here, too, you find a large parking area graced by tall trees to provide cool shade as you take a rest break to enjoy the scenery surrounding the pond.

When you are ready, retrace your steps on the Lake-Meadow Trail for a mile to the intersection with the Marsh Trail. On your left is a sign indicating that the trail you are walking will take you to the sand dunes and beach a short distance ahead where the Beach-Dune Trail begins. Continue past the Marsh Trail. Ahead you see the back side of the sand dunes of the barrier beach, as you cross a small brook that at this point is a combination of water from Filmore Brook and the outlet stream of an unnamed pond into which drain the waters of Southwick Marsh.

As you cross the brook, the hardwoods quickly give way to dune vegetation growing on the east side of what is called the "back dune." A dune area usually is made up of two high spots—the fore dune and a higher back dune with a depression called a panne in between. The dune vegetation stabilizes the dune, preventing the sand from shifting and drifting. Such a stabilized dune area is called a barrier dune, for it acts as a barrier against the wind and storms coming off a large expanse of water, in this case Lake Ontario.

At this point you come to the beginning of a wooden bridge spanning the dune area, from the back dune over the fore dune to the beach on Lake Ontario. The bridge is there to protect the dunes from foot-travel erosion. In your walk so far you have come through seven different ecological areas—uncultivated fields, cultivated fields, woods, meadowland, juniper field, dunes, and a natural beach.

From the water's edge inland, the beach is wide and flat with the sand well packed. The flatness gives way as the dune area is reached; the amount of sand that is piled to form the dunes is impressive, with a fore dune about a story high and a back dune about two stories high. The top of the back dune is covered with trees, predominantly aspen as well as some impressive white pines standing like sentinels guarding the marshlands behind the dunes.

The natural beach is quite scenic and invites walking. You might try it by turning left at the end of the bridge and walking south for, say, a mile.

After your mile walk, retrace your steps north along the beach. Pick up the Beach-Dune trail, and continue north on the beach. In little less than ½ mile, you pass a sign marking the boundary between the wildlife area and the state park. A little farther ahead are the beachfront campsites, concession building, and picnic area of Southwick Beach State Park.

Second Day
Southwick Beach State Park to
Colwell Pond via NY 3
Distance: 5⅝ miles
Hiking time: 3 hours

Leave the state park by vehicle for NY 3, and drive south on NY 3 for a little over a mile past Pierrepont Road to North Skinner Road, a dirt road intersecting on your right. Park here. A mile walk along this dirt road will take you to and then along Sandy Creek, one of two main streams that flow into and through the wildlife area. The other is South Sandy Creek.

As you walk along the road you notice that you are on high ground, in an ecosystem typifying an upland environment, while less than ¼ mile to your right is the marsh with vegetation associated with wetlands. After reaching the end of the road, retrace your steps.

Back in your vehicle, drive south on NY 3 for 2 miles, where a single-lane dirt road intersects on your right. Park here and start your walk going west on the road; ¼ mile brings you to a turnaround area, once the site of an observation tower. To your right (north) is a metal barrier gate across an abandoned road that runs north for ⅝ mile through a forested area. Good times to walk this route are in early summer before the grass gets too high and in late summer after the state has mowed it.

Head back to your vehicle, and drive south 0.8 mile on NY 3, where another dirt road intersects on your right. Walk west on this road for ¼ mile to the end, where you can turn south and walk across the field to another east-west dirt road.

Turn west on this dirt road, and follow it to a parking area. A footpath begins at the south end of the parking area. Follow this into the middle of the marsh itself along high ground that has the appearance of a dike. There is water on both sides of the high ground, and, if your timing is good, you may see a lot of waterfowl in the area. Be sure to bring your binoculars.

The predominant vegetation of the marsh is cattails, but the marsh also contains rice cutgrass (*Leersia oryzoides*),

pondweeds, arrowhead (or duck potato), bulrushes, bur reeds, sedges, waterweed, musk grass, and swamp loosestrife. A short distance to the south is South Sandy Creek and just ahead is Goose Pond, but all around you is thick vegetation in which red-winged blackbirds and marsh wrens as well as ducks find protection and an ideal habitat to rest, feed, and nest.

In little less than ½ mile the path ends; retrace your steps to your vehicle. Continue south on NY 3 for 1¼ miles to the intersection with Montario Point Road on your right (west). Turn here and drive uphill for ⅜ mile to the top of Colwell Hill. On your right is a state-built observation tower with a fine view of the entire wildlife area. From the observation tower it is ⅜ mile westward to a dirt road intersecting on your right. Turn here and follow the road into a wooded area and to a state boat-launch site and put-in point for canoeists on South Colwell Pond.

If you brought a canoe, you can add some paddling to your day's outing. Head north on South Colwell and then on North Colwell Pond to the connecting outlet stream that brings you to Lake Ontario and to the broad, sandy beaches on either side of the outlet. It is 1¾ miles one way from the put-in point to Lake Ontario.

After returning to the state launch site, you are ready to head back to your campsite at Southwick Beach State Park and, perhaps, to enjoy a swim before supper.

TUG HILL

31

Happy Valley Wildlife Management Area

Total distance: 7½ miles

Hiking time: 4 hours

Vertical rise: 1220 feet

Maps: USGS 7½' Dugway; USGS 7½' Williamstown

Happy Valley is heavily forested, sprinkled with small and large ponds, and crisscrossed with dirt roads, jeep trails, and abandoned logging roads—an ideal setting for short strolls, long day hikes, and even weekend backpacking. Happy Valley Wildlife Management Area is a multiuse area where the State Department of Environmental Conservation emphasizes maintenance of ideal habitat for game such as white-tailed deer and ruffed grouse. Here also one can fish, hunt, snowmobile, cross-country ski, and snowshoe, as well as do some serious hiking.

The state forest covers 8624 acres of land in Oswego County 6 miles northeast of Parish on the southern side of Tug Hill. It is the second largest of the four Tug Hill wildlife management areas.

Geologically, it is located in a landform region called the Ontario lowlands, marked by low ridges and swamplands. The North Branch of the Little Salmon River rises here as a small stream flowing south to eventually empty into Little Salmon River.

The two highest places in the forest are the mile-long ridge officially called Stone Hill (elevation 750 feet) and a more peaked hill unofficially called White Hill (elevation 700 feet). The latter has the highest vertical rise, 160 feet—a climb that obviously is not very demanding. There are dozens of small man-made impoundments and several large ponds, including almost-mile-long Whitney Pond, mile-long Long Pond, half-mile-long Mosher Pond, and the smaller St. Marys Pond.

Spring and fall are the best times of year to hike Happy Valley. May is an ideal month, when the hundreds of apple trees throughout the region are in full bloom. Or pick a time in October for hiking when the fall foliage is at its peak; the splash of color is worth the trip.

Camping is allowed here, and there are some ideal spots along Whitney and Long Ponds. You must obtain a camping permit from the regional office of the DEC in Cortland (607-753-3095). All the

Whitney Pond

large ponds have a good supply of large-mouth bass and pan fish, so bring along your fishing gear.

Access. The trailhead can be reached from I-81. Exit at Parish and take County Route 26 northeast for 0.9 mile where it turns right and east. Continue on the county road for 3.6 miles until it is intersected by Churchill Road, a two-lane dirt road on your left. Drive 0.5 mile down Churchill to its intersection with Pucker Road, and park here.

Trail. There are no marked walking trails on the state land, but you can put together a route combining dirt roads, jeep trails, and fire lanes. Three dirt roads run the full length of Happy Valley from north to south.

Starting at their intersection, you can follow either Pucker or Churchill Road. The Pucker Road route is a 5-mile round-trip hike; it takes you past St. Marys Pond for 2 miles to where Pucker Road turns sharply left. On your right is a narrow lane, which in ½ mile leads to a ½-mile-long elongated impoundment, a haven for waterfowl especially during migratory periods. Another route to the impoundment follows Churchill Road north past White Hill Road for a little over a mile. A narrow, intersecting lane on your left takes you in ½ mile to the east side of the impoundment.

On the other hand, the recommended route covers a 7½-mile loop. It follows Churchill, White Hill, Happy Valley, and Whitney Roads to Long Pond; it returns by several unnamed lanes to complete the loop.

From your parking place, proceed northeast on Churchill Road. The field on your right quickly gives way to woods, and a mile down the road you reach White Hill Road, intersecting on your right. Turn here and head uphill;

¼ mile and a 70-foot ascent bring you to the top of the hill. The summit of White Hill lies to your left. You can follow the first jeep trail intersecting on your left to the tree-covered top. From the road, however, you have an overlook to the east.

Continue on White Hill Road as it goes downhill and crosses a small brook and then uphill to intersect Happy Valley Road. Turn left (north) here, and follow the road a short distance to a fork, where the main dirt road (now Whitney Road) makes an elbow turn to your right. The left, unnamed fork that runs due north probably was once the continuation of Happy Valley Road.

Hike eastward now on Whitney Road for almost ½ mile where you meet another fork. If you turn left, a short distance brings you to the west side of the Whitney Pond spillway as well as to a fair-sized open area frequently used for camping. At the spillway, you have a nice view north along Whitney Pond. The scenery looks a little like that in the Adirondacks.

Return to Whitney Road, and continue north across the pond's outlet stream (actually the North Branch of the Little Salmon River) to a small parking area on your left. From here a path takes you to the east side of the spillway. Back on Whitney Road, a mile walk brings you to a lane intersecting on your left. It leads you in ¼ mile to the east edge of Whitney Pond, where there's a nice spot to pitch a tent.

Return to Whitney Road again. About ½ mile northward, the road begins to turn to your right (east), and a short distance beyond brings you to a road intersecting on your left (Happy Valley Road). Continue east past the intersection, where you will see a small cemetery with headstones dating back to the 1830s and 1840s, a reminder of the early settlers who transformed forest into farmland. Their community now is completely gone.

Another mile of hiking brings you to a causeway across Long Pond; again the scenery is very Adirondack-like. On the pond's east side, there are good camping spots. You can turn around here and head back to the cemetery.

Just beyond the cemetery, turn right (north) onto Happy Valley Road, and walk for almost ½ mile to where an unnamed dirt road intersects on your left. Turn here and walk west for a mile. At a mile's end, you intersect a single-lane, little-used north-south road. Turn left (south), and in little less than 2 miles you are back on the main dirt road (the southern end of Happy Valley Road). From here you can retrace your steps 2 miles to your vehicle.

32

Buck Hill State Forest

Total distance: 11 miles

Hiking time: 4 hours

Vertical rise: 959 feet

Maps: USGS 7½' North Western; USGS 7½' Boonville

Buck Hill State Forest is ideal for a short day hike. To add a few more miles to your trek and to enjoy some additional vistas from this high region, you can include Buck Hill's next-door neighbor, Clark Hill State Forest. And if you're contemplating a weekend camping trip, you might as well include Penn Mountain State Forest, a few miles to the east (see Hike 33).

All three state forests occupy high country making up an escarpment overlooking the Mohawk Valley to the south. Because the land pitches fairly steeply to the south, the high spots provide fine views in virtually all directions of the compass.

Buck Hill is a good example. It is the highest spot in the southern end of the state forest, with an elevation of 1401

feet. While this height may not seem much compared with some of the other nearby hills, it certainly is enough to give you some fine views to the east and to the north.

Looking northward, you should be able to spot Jackson Hill and, a little to its east, the Boonville gorge, dug out by the large volume of water released by the last continental ice sheet to cover New York as it retreated over 12,000 years ago. Each of the four glaciers that overran New York contributed to the deepening of the Boonville gorge.

The Pleistocene Ice Age of North America began 2 million years ago. Four successive glacial advances and retreats were triggered by fluctuations in the climate. As the glaciers advanced, they rounded off hilltops and deepened existing valleys and gorges, and as they melted back they released torrents of water that continued the down-cutting work in such places as the Boonville gorge.

Buck Hill State Forest is relatively small—only 1494 acres. However, the forest's several truck trails permit you to hike not only to the summit of Buck Hill but also throughout the entire length of the state forest.

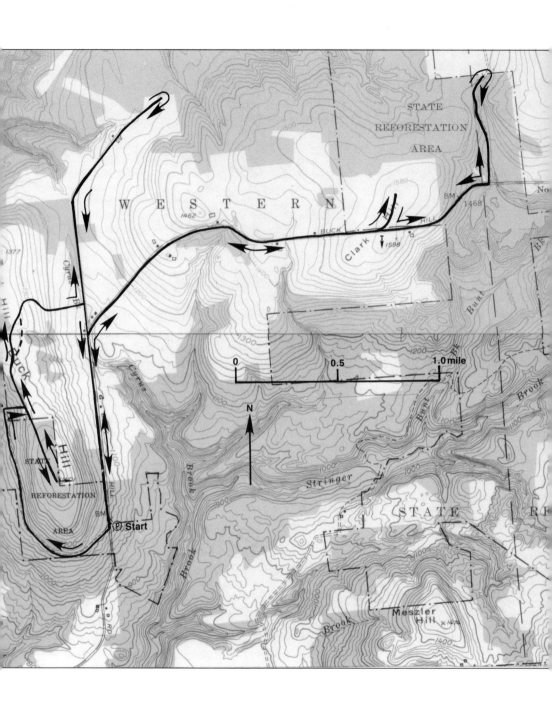

Access. Take NY 46 to the village of North Western, which is 12 miles north of Rome and 13 miles south of Boonville. Just ½ mile north of the village is a bridge crossing Stringer Brook; once over the bridge, Buck Hill Road branches east and heads uphill. Follow Buck Hill Road 1.5 miles to the top of the hill where a sign indicates the start of the truck trail. Park here.

Trail. Your hiking here is entirely on truck trails. One such truck road begins on the north side of Buck Hill Road. This dirt road climbs uphill a short distance and then levels out as it loops to the south. The road continues looping until eventually at the ½-mile mark it is heading in a straight northerly direction.

A ½-mile hike brings you to a road intersecting on your right. A short but steep uphill climb takes you to the intersection with another dirt road, running north and south. The land pitches down ahead of you, giving you a fine view to the east as you look over Cyrus Brook and Stringer Brook gorges. A mile to the east you see the forested hilltops of Clark Hill State Forest, specifically Meszler Hill, Maple Mountain, and Oakes Hill.

Turn right here, and follow the road as it takes you south and uphill. In a little less than ½ mile, you reach the summit of Buck Hill. As the road follows the forest edge, the land to the east is open, giving you some nice vistas. Retrace your steps to the intersection, but continue due north on the road you are hiking.

In ¼ mile you come to a fork. Actually, the road splits here only to come back together again a short distance ahead. This part of the land is level, but soon the road turns right and heads downhill for a little over 1¼ miles to intersect with another north-south dirt road.

Turn left here and follow it northward. This road is relatively level for the first ½ mile; then it turns slightly to your right and begins a gradual descent as it takes you to the boundary of the state land. A little-used lane or jeep trail continues beyond this point on private land. From here you should retrace your steps to your vehicle.

If you would like to add more mileage to your day's outing, you can hike from where you parked your vehicle first north and then east on Buck Hill Road to the summit of Clark Hill, a distance of 2¾ miles.

At the top of Clark Hill, you stand at an elevation of 1598 feet. The state land is on the north side of the road. On the south side is an open field that allows you an unobstructed view to the south. On a clear day you can see miles from this spot. Here too you find a dirt road leading north into Clark Hill State Forest, but it takes you into the forest only a short distance. If you continue east on Buck Hill Road for another ½ mile, you see a truck trail intersecting from your left. Turn here and walk north; ½ mile brings you to the edge of the state forest and a turnaround area from where you can now retrace your steps to your vehicle.

33

Penn Mountain State Forest

Total distance: 10 miles

Hiking time: 5 hours

Vertical rise: 1320 feet

Maps: USGS 7½' North Western; USGS 7½' Boonville

If you're looking for a large, peaking mountain similar to those found in the Adirondacks, Penn Mountain won't measure up. Yet compared to the other hills in this region, Penn Mountain is the big fella, with a commanding view of the local countryside.

Penn Mountain is actually a knob on top of the high terrain that makes up the escarpment overlooking the Mohawk Valley, 15 miles to the south. This knob, once the site of a fire tower, is 1813 feet high, a good-sized hill for these parts. It occupies the northern part of the 2646-acre state forest that is named after it.

The state forest includes several other hilltops—Bowen Hill (elevation 1773 feet), a little over a mile to the southwest of Penn Mountain, and Starr Hill (elevation 1793 feet), at the southern end of

the state forest. These last two give you fine overlooks to the west and to the south. Penn Mountain itself is tree-covered, so visibility from there is a bit restricted.

Geographically, Penn Mountain State Forest sits between the Tug Hill region in the northwest and the western Adirondack foothills in the northeast and between the Black River Valley in the north and the Mohawk River Valley in the south.

This land is the source of several streams that feed into the upper reaches of the Mohawk River in the west. It also serves as a watershed, directing the waters of Stringer Brook and Big Brook to the west into the Mohawk and the waters of Cincinnati Creek to the east into West Canada Creek.

Penn Mountain State Forest has several close neighbors that also appeal to hikers—Buck Hill State Forest (see Hike 32) and Clark Hill State Forest, about 2 miles to the northwest. Just south of Clark Hill State Forest, in the Boonville gorge, is Pixley Falls State Park, a delightful place to picnic and take short hikes. From Pixley Falls State Park to Boonville is the route of the old Black River Canal (see Hike 42), whose towpath is used for hiking and cross-country skiing.

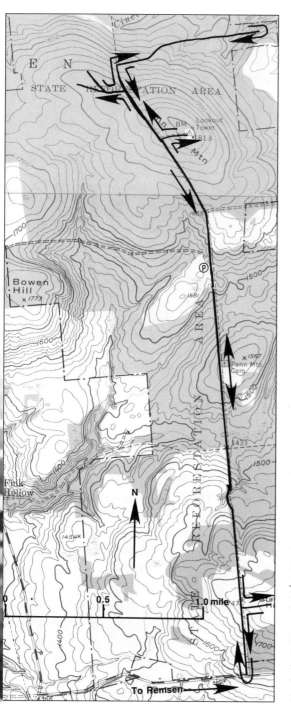

Access. Penn Mountain State Forest is reached most easily via NY 12/28 for 20 miles to an intersection with a road running west out of the village of Remsen, which is a short distance east of NY 12/28.

On the left side of the road you see a sign directing you to Steuben Memorial. Turn left here, and drive west 0.6 mile, where a road intersects on your left. Turn here, and drive south for another 0.6 mile, where a road intersects on your right; take this road, and drive west 3.1 miles, where NY 274 intersects from the south. Continue straight ahead on what has now become NY 274 for a mile, which brings you into the hamlet of Steuben. Turn right here, and drive north 4 miles to the top of the hill. On your right (east) is a dirt road that takes you into the state forest.

Take this dirt road, and drive east 1.4 miles, where you intersect with another dirt road. Park here.

Trail. The high terrain gives you a number of excellent overlooks beginning at the highway–dirt road intersection. On the way into the state forest, you drive on the northern edge of Bowen Hill, whose crest is about ¼ mile south of the road. A mile to the west is Clark Hill State Forest with its several hills—Oakes Hill, Maple Mountain, and Meszler Hill. As the land descends steeply to the south, you also have a fine view in that direction.

At the spot you parked your vehicle, you find a large open area immediately south of the road. Here too you can enjoy a fine vista to the south. After enjoying the sights, you can begin your hike, which is on dirt roads and truck trails.

At the intersection, turn left on the north-south dirt road, and head north uphill. A little less than ¼ mile brings you to another dirt road intersecting on your right; take this road, and walk east for a little less than ½ mile. This brings

View to southwest from Starr Hill toward Meszler Hill

you to the edge of the state forest and to open country where you have a good view to the east.

Retrace your steps to the main dirt road, and continue your hike north for ½ mile to where a lane intersects on your right; turn here to go to the site of the old fire tower on the crest of Penn Mountain. Back on the main road, continue walking north. The terrain here is level for the next ¼ mile, where you intersect with a truck trail on your left. This does not go into the forest very far before it forks, with each leg of the fork running a short distance to a turn-around area.

Returning to the main road, you now start a gradual descent as you continue north for a little less than ¼ mile; here the road turns east. If you proceed straight ahead and down a steep hill, you soon encounter an impoundment—an elongated pond containing the water of Cincinnati Creek, which starts about ½ mile to the west.

Continue on the dirt road toward the east, and a little under a mile farther brings you to the road's end. From here you retrace your steps to your parked vehicle to hike the southern portion of the state forest. Stay on the same north-south road. After heading downhill ¼ mile, you start a modest climb for another ¼ mile. When you reach the top, you notice headstones in an open area on your left: Penn Mountain cemetery, where earlier residents of this land are buried.

The road now begins to slope downward, and in little less than ½ mile you are in a small valley with a lane crossing the road. Continue due south on the main dirt road; soon you cross two spots where, in early spring, you find the headwaters of Big Brook.

The road now runs uphill. It is a steady climb for the next ½ mile for a vertical rise of 214 feet. When you reach the top, you can take the lane on your left to the top of Starr Hill, where you can enjoy a fine vista to the south. The hill is named after David Starr, who served as a captain in the American Continental Army and settled here in 1791. If you continue south on the main dirt road for a little over ¼ mile, you will intersect with an east-west highway marking the end of the state forest. The view here to the south is also good. From here you can retrace your steps to your parked vehicle.

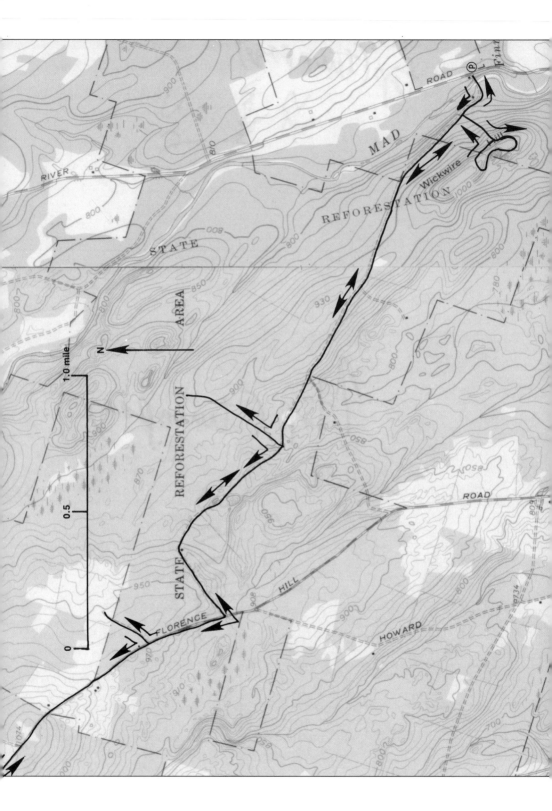

34

Mad River State Forest

Total distance: 8½ miles

Hiking time: 5 hours

Vertical rise: 1400 feet

Maps: USGS 7½' Florence; USGS 7½' Westdale

In Mad River State Forest you can do some hill climbing. Florence Hill and Wickwire Hill dominate the landscape. You reach the top of Florence Hill (elevation 1074 feet), the highest spot hereabouts, by making an ascent so gradual that you are hardly aware you're doing any climbing at all.

Wickwire Hill is another matter. At 1060 feet, it is not quite as high as Florence Hill, but it is peaked with steep sloping sides that will make you well aware of climbing. The distance from the trailhead at Mad River to the top of Wickwire is a little less than a half mile—far enough to make the climb challenging but not tiring.

The state forest is located on the southern edge of the Tug Hill region on land that rises fairly abruptly from the Oneida Lake plain in the south. Most high places here are merely bumps on the landscape, but Wickwire Hill, which from a distance stands out distinctly, has a personality all its own.

The 2700-acre state forest, something of a crazy quilt in layout, takes its name from Mad River, which tumbles down from the higher terrain in the north and rushes through the eastern portion of the state forest. Those who named rivers in this part of New York were either overly fond of the name "Mad River" or confused, for there are two Mad Rivers in the Tug Hill area. One, which has its beginnings in the central region of Tug Hill, flows south for 10 miles to empty into the west-flowing Salmon River. Little over a mile south of the Salmon River Reservoir, you find the headwaters of the second Mad River, the one we refer to here. It too flows south beyond the Mad River State Forest to empty into the East Branch of Fish Creek in Camden.

The state forest is about 3 miles north of Camden and easy to reach from NY 13. Farmland here is confined to space along the main highways in the area surrounding the state forest. Otherwise, about 85 percent of the land is thickly forested, so the region has more of a wilderness feel than a cultivated appearance.

There are no designated hiking trails in the state forest, but instead a single-lane truck trail that runs through the central section, with several roads radiating off it. All are well shaded during the summer to make walking a pleasure.

Access. Either NY 13 or NY 69 brings you into Camden. At the traffic light in the center of Camden, drive north on NY 13 four blocks to where the road forks. NY 13 bears to the left. Take the right leg, which is Empey Avenue, where you will see a sign to the village of Florence. Follow Empey Avenue north out of Camden; as soon as the road crosses Mad River on the edge of town, its name changes to River Road.

Drive north on River Road for 3.6 miles, where the road crosses Mad River for the third time since leaving Camden.

From the bridge continue north for 0.3 mile, where a single-lane dirt road intersects on your left (on the corner is a house). Pull off River Road and park.

Trail. You begin your hike by turning onto the dirt road. A couple hundred feet brings you to a bridge crossing Mad River. Once across the bridge, you enter the forest. Immediately on your right is a small house, the last one you'll see before the state forest, which starts a short distance uphill.

As the road passes the house, it swings a little to the right and heads uphill. Looming high on your left is Wickwire Hill. About ¼ mile uphill, you see a broad, well-used trail intersecting on your left, which has been made by users of all-terrain vehicles (ATVs). On weekends you may see ATVs on this trail, but

Old stone fence paralleling trail

during the week usually you can have it to yourself.

The climb to the top of Wickwire Hill is relatively short—only ¼ mile from the truck trail—but it is fairly steep, especially as you approach the top, with a vertical rise from the trail to the summit of 260 feet. Near the top, the trail forks. Bear to your left, and follow this trail to the hill's top. The trail turns right, runs a short distance along the narrow ridge, and then loops right and heads downhill to intersect the second trail coming uphill. Turn left onto this trail and follow it to the top, where the trail makes a tight loop.

The top of Wickwire Hill is completely forested. During the summer, you don't have much of a view, but in early spring or late fall you'll be able to see to the west.

Retrace your steps downhill to the truck trail, and turn left. Continue your uphill hiking for a little over ¼ mile, at which point the road flattens out, making walking easy for the next ½ mile. At the 1⅝-mile mark, a small open area appears on your left. In summer, the area is grassed in, but you might discern the outline of a trail that would take you back into the forest and onto the private land.

For now, continue on the truck trail in a northwesterly direction. The terrain now becomes more uneven, with the road dipping down for a short distance and then rising to climb the next ridge; ¼ mile more brings you to an intersection with another single-lane dirt road coming in from your right.

If you wish to add a little more distance to your hike, follow this road as it runs almost due north. It forks in ½ mile, and you can stop and reverse direction. Once back on the main truck trail, turn right and continue on your northwesterly route.

At the intersection, the road dips once again, and a short distance beyond it crosses a wooden bridge over a small brook. At ½ mile from the bridge, the road makes a sharp turn to your left to head southwest. In ¼ mile, you emerge onto a blacktop highway, Florence Hill Road.

To reach the top of Florence Hill, turn right and head uphill; ¼ mile brings you to a dirt road intersecting on your right. Turn down this road, which ends at ¼ mile where two gates indicate that the state land has ended. This is a nice spot to take your lunch break.

Back on the blacktop highway, continue north for another ½ mile. You are now on top of Florence Hill. There is a house on your left; between it and the trees lining the road there is an open spot, giving you a fine long-distance view to the south and west.

Continue on the highway for another ¼ mile, where another blacktop road intersects on your left. At this intersection with Westdale Road, you have a nice overlook to the west before you retrace your steps to your parked vehicle.

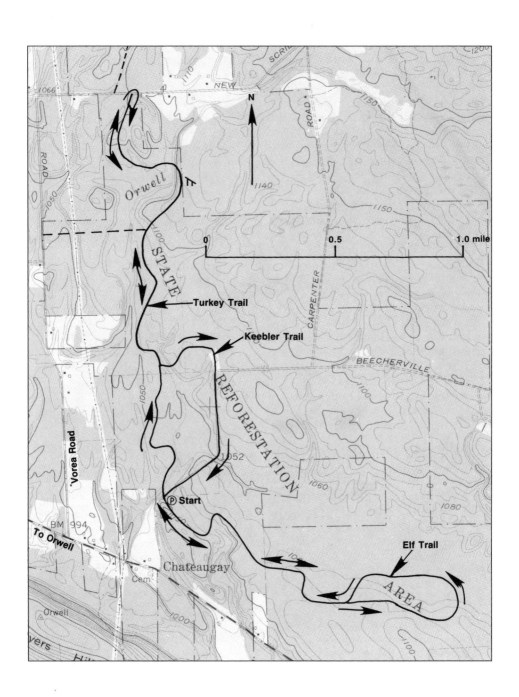

35

Chateaugay State Forest

Total distance: 5 miles

Hiking time: 2½ hours

Vertical rise: 240 feet

Map: USGS 7½' Orwell

Chateaugay is a land of tall pines, white-tailed deer, rocky soil, and stone fences. In summer it is full of ferns, acres and acres of all kinds of ferns—wood ferns, bracken ferns, sensitive ferns, ostrich ferns—soft green in the sunlight that slants through the forest canopy.

It is the stone fences that give Chateaugay its special character; they are a reminder that what is today a dense forest was once farmland. It was hard farming, however, in what is still rocky soil. Some of the rocks are rounded and polished, shaped long ago by glaciers; others are flat and angular, unearthed by the plow only a half century ago.

Whoever built the stone fences did so with care and patience, piling and fitting each stone snugly to make the fences almost a work of art. These fences were the

boundaries of small square fields. Given the stony land, you can't help appreciating how much toil and sweat went into keeping these fields cultivated.

That's all past now. Hardwoods and tall conifers have replaced the grain fields and hayfields, and the stone fences now have only trees for neighbors. In this wild forest, the stone fence seems to exert a taming effect on the environment. The swales of ferns, which cover the ground everywhere, give the forest an even more groomed appearance.

Chateaugay has two more attractions for the hiker—water and a walking trail. Two small but attractive streams, Pekin Brook and Orwell Brook, give the woods the soft sounds of water splashing over rocky ledges and into quiet pools. You can savor all this when you walk the several loops that make up Chateaugay's trail system.

The trail system, built in 1978–1979 under the sponsorship of the Oswego County Cooperative Extension Service, was constructed for cross-country skiing. In winter, when the snow lies deep in the state forest, this becomes a skier's mecca. In the off-seasons of spring, summer, and autumn, the trails are ideal for hiking. They can be used either for a day's trek or for an overnight backpacking outing.

In the northern part of the state forest about 2 miles from the trailhead you'll find an Adirondack-style lean-to, should you come to Chateaugay for a weekend.

Access. Chateaugay State Forest can be reached via I-81 by exiting at Pulaski or from US 11, which runs through Pulaski village. Find County Route 2 on the east side of the village, and drive east 5.7 miles past Richland to the hamlet of Orwell. From Orwell, continue east for 1.8 miles where Beecherville Road intersects from your left, across from a small cemetery. Drive north on Beecherville Road (a dirt road) for 0.2 mile to a small parking area on your right. Park here.

Trail. Two trails, one running north, the other east, start at the spot where you park. The Chateaugay ski-trail system is groomed and marked by yellow disks with a silhouette of a skier. Also, red, yellow, and blue plastic strips are tied around trees to help the skier (or hiker) follow the various trails.

Cross the road and enter the path on the west side of the road, where you will see a signboard with a map of the trail system. The trail on which you are hiking now runs due north 2 miles; it is designated "B" and called the Turkey Trail. Off this trail loops the mile-long "C" or Keebler Trail. On the east side of Chateaugay (where your car is parked) is a trail designated as "A," the Elf Trail, a little over 1¾ miles long.

Four unmarked trails that radiate off the Turkey Trail can be used for skiing or hiking also. They are not shown on the map here, so if you try them be sure you have map and compass with you. Chateaugay also has several truck trails (Beecherville Road and Carpenter Road) that tie into the ski trails and can be used for hiking. The land is relatively flat with a few small hills that don't rise more than 50 feet.

A short distance downtrail you cross a narrow wooden bridge over Pekin Brook, and in less than 50 yards from the bridge you see your first stone fence on your left. The trail follows along the stone fence for 100 yards, where you turn left and pass through a fence opening. You are now in a stand of pines, and the trail continues north, this time with the stone fence on your right. A short distance ahead, you pass through another opening in the stone fence, and soon thereafter through two more openings, all about the same distance apart.

The trail now intersects the stone fence. Turn left here, keeping the fence on your right and walking through a fern swale. In a short distance, you find an opening in the fence on your right and two signs nailed to a tree on your left. The sign pointing north indicates the continuation of the Turkey Trail, and the other points to the east at the beginning of the Keebler Trail.

Continue on the Turkey Trail, where just ahead is another wooden footbridge at the foot of a small slope. Soon you pass through another stone fence opening on your right, and in a short distance through the last one. You are now almost a mile uptrail, and the path turns left and then right, bringing you to Orwell Brook.

In spring the brook is full and running swiftly, but by midsummer the water flow is reduced considerably. Continue along the east side of the brook for ½ mile, and then the trail turns eastward away from the brook. In less than ¼ mile, the path forks. To your right and uphill a short distance, you see the lean-to.

To your left, the trail continues westward over another wooden footbridge into a clearing. Turn to your right here, and follow the markers as the trail swings west again for less than ¼ mile and then heads north; a little over ¼ mile brings you to New Scriba Road, a blacktop highway and the end of the ski trail.

Retrace your steps 1½ miles to the junction with the Keebler Trail. Turn left onto it, and follow the trail east for a little over ¼ mile to where it intersects a dirt road (Beecherville Road). Continue south for just over ½ mile to the trailhead and your parked vehicle.

If you want to do more hiking, try the 1¾-mile-long Elf Trail, which runs from the parking area eastward. It is best to hike the Elf Trail in late spring before summer growth of the ostrich fern and other vegetation fills the trail to make walking somewhat difficult.

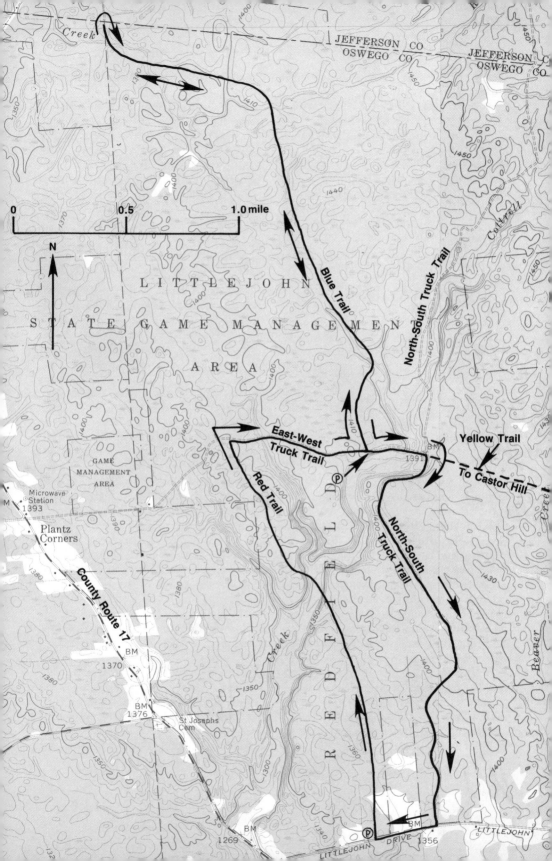

36

Littlejohn Wildlife Management Area

Total distance: 10⅜ miles (2 days)

Hiking time: 5¾ hours

Vertical rise: 700 feet

Maps: USGS 7½' Boylston; USGS 7½' Worth Center

Save Littlejohn for autumn when the fall foliage is at its peak. With the sun streaming through the treetops, you'll be walking through a cathedral of color, drenched in bright yellows, reds, and browns.

The 8022-acre Littlejohn Wildlife Management Area is completely forested; so is the land around it, especially to the east and the south where you find an almost trackless wilderness—no communities, no homesteads, not even any roads. It is solid forest.

This is the "Big Woods" or, as it was once called, the "Lesser Wilderness," about 25 miles wide and 30 miles long, making up 750 square miles of dense, wild forest. Only the local population of bobcats calls it home.

The expression "Lesser Wilderness" served to distinguish the Tug Hill forest from what lies east of the Black River Valley, namely, the Adirondack forest, then called the "Greater Wilderness." Actually, there are more foot trails in the Greater Wilderness area than in the Lesser Wilderness, which should give you some idea of the latter's remoteness and primitiveness.

Littlejohn holds down the western flank of the Tug Hill wilderness area. Although part of the wilderness, it is not all that intimidating and actually appears friendly. Littlejohn's forest is predominantly maple, with well-spaced trees that allow considerable visibility and a feeling of openness. An additional asset is the flatness of the terrain, which makes your hike an easy one. While it will give you a taste of what this wilderness area is like, Littlejohn is easy to reach and to traverse. Roads penetrate from three directions, and a north-south road runs the full length of Littlejohn.

Topographically, the state-owned area is much like the rest of the Tug Hill region; it is high, with an elevation of 1400 feet, but as flat as a tabletop. It is the latter characteristic that leads some to speak of the Tug Hill plateau. It is in fact a hill, rising from Lake Ontario (elevation 260 feet) to over 2100 feet in the region's eastern edge so gradually that you are unaware of the climb.

Access. Littlejohn Wildlife Management Area can be reached via I-81 and Smartville. Leave I-81 at exit 39, and drive through Sandy Creek and Lacona, picking up Smartville Road (County Route 15) at the eastern end of Lacona. From here, drive 8.1 miles east through the hamlet of Smartville to an intersection with the paved Lorraine-Redfield Road (County Route 17). Turn right here, and drive 0.8 mile to where Littlejohn Drive (a dirt road) intersects on your left. Turn and drive 0.6 mile on Littlejohn Drive to a parking area on your left, adjacent to a stand of pines. Park here.

Trail. Littlejohn has several hiking trails and roads that can be combined to make an excellent trail system for the weekend hiker. In the southern part is a 2-mile hiking trail marked with red disks. This Red Trail begins where you are parked and runs north to end at what the state foresters call simply the East-West Truck Trail, a one-lane dirt road. The Blue Trail begins ½ mile east on this truck trail. The 2¾-mile-long Blue Trail runs north until it ends at Town Line Road.

Of the two, the Blue Trail is more pleasant to walk in the summer as it is virtually weed-free. The Red Trail, which passes through more open areas and receives more sunlight, soon fills up with weeds as the summer begins. The trail does remain discernible and easy to follow, though.

In the eastern part of Littlejohn is the Yellow Trail. It too starts at Littlejohn Drive on a little rise that, interestingly enough, has a name, Castor Hill (once the site of a fire tower). The Yellow Trail ends at the intersection of the East-West and North-South Truck Trails.

To explore several of these trails may require a weekend campout, although any of them will make a good 1-day hike.

First Day
Littlejohn Drive to East-West Truck Trail and back
Distance: 4¾ miles
Hiking time: 2½ hours

Begin your hike on the Red Trail. On one of the pine trees at the parking area is a sign reading "Hiking Trail." Enter the pine stand at this point. The trail turns northward and soon crosses a small brook (which usually goes dry in summer), a tributary of Cottrell Creek.

In about 100 yards, the trail leaves the pines and enters an open area that was once a hayfield or pasture and is now slowly reverting to woodland. At the end of ¼ mile, you leave the open area and reenter the woods. The Red Trail actually follows an abandoned road that may have been either a wagon lane or a logging road.

The terrain is quite flat. If it is midsummer, your travel may be slowed a bit by tall weeds in the lane. You'll encounter some wet spots en route if you are hiking in spring, but by summer most have dried out. At 1¼ miles, you come to a gully where a narrow log footbridge crosses Cottrell Creek. By midsummer the creek is down to a trickle, and you'll have little trouble stepping over what little water remains.

Climb the other side of the gully, and continue on the trail northward as it follows the high ground on the west side of a gully through which flows a tributary of Cottrell Creek. In little over ½ mile, you intersect the East-West Truck Trail. Turn right onto this dirt road and hike east. In ½ mile you come to a sign reading "Hiking Trail" on the north side of the road. This is the beginning of the Blue Trail, which you'll hike later.

For now, continue east on the truck trail, which starts a gradual descent to again cross Cottrell Creek in ¼ mile. Chances are that the water has been dammed by beavers (unless they have been trapped) to create a small pond on both sides of the bridge. On the north side of the bridge about 50 yards away, you will see a huge mound of sawdust, left many years ago by a sawmill that operated around the turn of the century when the area was intensively logged.

A short distance beyond the bridge, you intersect the North-South Truck Trail. Turn right here, and follow the one-lane dirt road southward. The road is well shaded by maple trees on both sides to make this an attractive route to walk. While it makes a number of slow turns, the road is 2 miles long, the same as the Red Trail. You come out on Littlejohn Drive. Turn right (west), and head back to your starting point ½ mile away.

Second Day
East-West Truck Trail to Town Line Road and back
Distance: 5⅝ miles
Hiking time: 3¼ hours

From the intersection of Littlejohn Drive and County Route 17, drive north 2 miles to the second intersection. The road on your left is Center Road. The one on your right is the East-West Truck Trail, the main access road to Littlejohn. Drive 1.6 miles east on the East-West Truck Trail to where the Blue Trail begins. There is an area on your right where you can park.

When you enter the woods, you are walking on what looks like a jeep trail, rutted by four-wheel-drive vehicles. Don't let this introduction to the Blue Trail disappoint you. A short distance into the woods, the rutted lane gives way to a single-path walking trail. It is wide, well used, easy to follow, and virtually weedless.

In little less than ½ mile, you cross your first stream, a small brook that feeds into Cottrell Creek in the south. A mile of hiking brings you to the second brook, which feeds into Raystone Creek in the north. Your hiking here is on level terrain through a woods of widely spaced trees, and the trek is a most pleasant one.

In ¼ mile, you come to Raystone Creek itself. In summer, the water is so low that it is easy to cross the creek. The trail now turns gradually to the left and heads in a northwesterly direction. A mile more brings you to the end of the state land and to a turn-around area that marks the southern end of Town Line Road. Retrace your steps on the Blue Trail to the parking area.

37

Tug Hill State Forest

Total distance: 11 miles (2 days)

Hiking time: 6 hours

Vertical rise: 220 feet

Map: USGS 7½' Barnes Corners

Tug Hill State Forest is an 11,688-acre tract of state land sprawling in crazy-quilt fashion over the northern slope of Tug Hill and sitting astride the boundary of Jefferson and Lewis Counties. Contiguous to the state forest are 971 acres of Jefferson County Forest. This puts a lot of public land at your disposal and gives you plenty of forested terrain to explore. The big attraction for the hiker is a trail system of loops both in the northern and the southern sections of the state forest.

Actually, the trail system was constructed for cross-country skiers, so you'll find the trail markers to be yellow disks with the silhouette of a skier. These are nailed to trees about 8 feet above the ground in anticipation of the winter snows, which in this part of New York come early and in large amounts. Total annual snowfall here averages about 200 inches (over 15 feet), the highest snowfall east of the Rockies.

While the trails are used heavily during the winter by hordes of Nordic skiers, hikers don't use them much during the off-seasons, even though they are excellent for hiking; so you have a lot of trail to follow without someone stepping on your heels. Plan a weekend trip, covering one section each day. A good time to hike in the area is in late spring or early summer before the weeds grow too high on the ski trails.

The state forest displays many of the features of the Tug Hill region that are something of an anomaly. While it is located literally on top of Tug Hill, the state forest appears to be relatively flat; you'll find no peaked hills or deep valleys here, just a few bumps and depressions. Many of the depressions are soggy, while others are water-filled, producing ponds and wetlands where there ought not to be any. This happens because Tug Hill's sandstone cap is so close to the surface that it prevents water from draining off.

The land may be flat, but there are some surprisingly unexpected gorges that in this region are called gulfs. The gulfs seem to appear out of nowhere, as if some giant had driven a huge ax into arbitrary places throughout the land. The results are deep, straight-walled gorges, some over 200 feet deep.

Inman Gulf, which acts as the northern boundary of Tug Hill State Forest, is a good example. On the southwestern edge of the state forest is Lorraine Gulf, which also will impress you with its depth. When the streams in these gulfs are low in late summer, try walking into one of the gorges as a contrast to walking the flatlands above.

Access. Tug Hill State Forest can be reached from I-81 on the west by exiting at Adams, or from Lowville in the east via NY 177. From Adams, take NY 178 at the south end of the village, and drive east 12 miles to its intersection with NY 177. Turn right onto NY 177, and drive .75 mile to where you see a large parking area and a small shed on your left. Coming from Lowville on NY 177, you will find this area 2.2 miles west of Barnes Corners. Park here.

Trail. Three marked trails begin at the storage shed amid a stand of European larch and red pine. Each ski trail has a name, and some of them are a little unusual. The Home-run Trail follows a truck trail north; the Snowbird Trail runs west; and the Link-up Trail goes south. Two additional loops run off the Home-run Trail: the Whiteway Loop Trail and the Electric Loop Trail. All are well marked with yellow disks, as well as with directional trail name signs and road name signs when a trail crosses a road.

First Day
From Parking Area loops on four trails and back
Distance: 5½ miles
Hiking time: 3 hours

At the storage shed, start by taking the Snowbird Trail. Signs for it are found both at the storage shed and on a tree as you enter the trail. A few steps down-trail, you see a sign that this trail was built by the Black River Chapter of the Adirondack Mountain Club.

The Snowbird Trail, which runs for 1¾ miles, parallels NY 177 for ½ mile, taking you through plantations of red pine, white pine, and larch, and then up a small hill. Here the trail turns north, making a gradual descent through evergreens before rising to a knoll of hardwood. It next makes a steep descent and crosses a footbridge over Fish Creek.

In the next ½ mile, the uphill climb is steady, for a vertical rise of 110 feet. After reaching the top, you then make a short but gentle descent through stands of black cherry, white ash, and beech, until you intersect the Home-run Trail just north of the truck trail.

Turn left and continue north. You go gradually downhill for ¼ mile, cross a tributary of Fish Creek, and pass through a mixed stand of hemlock and hardwood trees. A short distance farther brings you to what on the ski-trail map is called Times Square, the junction of Electric Loop Trail, Whiteway Loop Trail, and Home-run Trail.

Turn left, and follow the Electric Loop Trail, which is 2¼ miles long. It takes you west for almost ¼ mile, where it picks up a Fish Creek tributary. It follows the stream for a while, and at the ¾-mile mark the trail loops northward, running parallel with the overhead power line (the Lighthouse Hill Transmission Line) from which the trail takes its name. You follow the power line for ½ mile, and then swing away from it, heading first northeast and then looping southeast until the trail reaches Times Square.

Here you turn left onto the Whiteway Loop Trail, which covers a distance of 1¾ miles. As the trail leaves Times Square, it passes through a stand of ever-

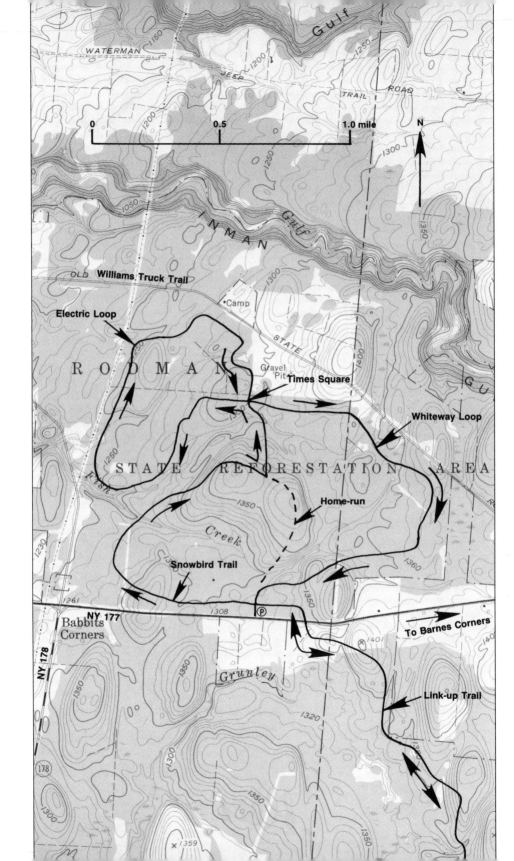

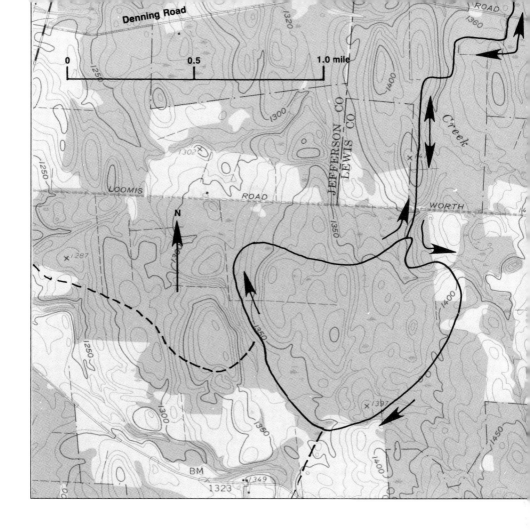

greens. At the ¼-mile mark, it turns right to run parallel with the Williams Truck Trail a short distance to your left.

You are now hiking over relatively level terrain. At the mile mark, the trail turns right and goes south for about ¼ mile, then turns right again to run in a southwesterly direction. Soon you climb a small hill, and in about ¼ mile intersect the truck trail that is the Home-run Trail. Turn left here, and head south back to your starting point, which is 700 feet away.

Second Day
From Parking Area on Link-up Trail and back
Distance: 5½ miles
Hiking time: 3 hours

At the storage shed, a sign directs you to the Link-up Trail, which runs 2½ miles to the south. The trail goes past the storage shed for a short distance, turns right, and crosses NY 177. Once across the road, the trail turns left and heads up a steep hill for a vertical rise of 100 feet.

At the top, the trail turns slowly to your right, running over fairly level terrain in a southerly direction. It passes into an open area with young white spruce trees, climbs a small hill, and moves through a stand of white spruce and white pine.

At the mile mark, you make a fairly steep descent, cross a tributary of Grunley Creek, and climb a small hill, where you turn right onto what was once a wagon road. In a little more than ¼ mile, you reach a single-lane, east-west truck trail marked as Denning Road.

Cross this road, and continue on the trail as it turns right, climbs a hill, and after a couple more turns makes a gradual descent to a bridge over Grunley Creek. A short uphill climb brings you to a ridge that you follow due south for ½ mile to Loomis Road.

This road marks the edge of the state forest; across the road is the Jefferson County Forest, where the trail continues with yellow disk markers. In less than ¼ mile along the trail, you intersect a loop trail built by the Youth Conservation Corps in 1978. Bear to your left, and follow this loop as it heads south to where it is intersected by a trail coming from the south, which in ¼ mile brings you to Waite Road. The main loop, however, swings in a northwesterly direction, crosses a Grunley Creek tributary, and after ½ mile turns right uphill. It is ¼ mile to the top of this small hill, and ¼ mile more to the lead-in trail that brought you into the loop earlier. Retrace your steps along the Link-up Trail to the storage shed and your parked car.

If you have time and feel a bit adventuresome, try a walk in Inman Gulf. An easy access point is at Barnes Corners 2¼ miles east of the storage shed. From NY 177, turn north on Whitesville Road, and in a short distance you come to a bridge over the Gulf Stream. This is the beginning of Inman Gulf. Enter the gully on the east side of the bridge.

The gully quickly deepens to become a gorge. At the mile mark, the gorge walls run straight up for more than 120 feet. In this short distance, you have witnessed the birth of one of the many gorges that cut deeply into the sides of Tug Hill. Other gorges nearby are Shingle Gulf, a mile north of Inman Gulf, and Bear Gulf, a little farther northeast. Through all these gulfs flow streams that eventually feed into Sandy Creek in the western part of Tug Hill.

Still another way to approach Inman Gulf is along the southern rim. Drive west from Barnes Corners on NY 177 for 1 mile, where Williams Truck Trail intersects on your right. Turn here, and drive 2.2 miles to an open area, where the power line crosses the road. Walk north on the right-of-way for a little less than ½ mile to the south rim of Inman Gulf. Peek over the rim, and 200 feet straight down you see the stream snaking through the gulf below.

38

Sears Pond State Forest

Total distance: 16⅜ miles (2 days)

Hiking time: 8¼ hours

Vertical rise: 920 feet

Maps: USGS 7½' Sears Pond; USGS 7½' New Boston; USGS 7½' Worth Center; USGS 7½' Barnes Corners

Sears Pond State Forest is an environment in transition: farmland reverting to forestland. Here you are walking through a history of a changing relationship between the land and the people. The state forest also serves as a divide between civilization in the north and east and wilderness in the central and western parts of Tug Hill.

Sears Pond is located in the north central part of the Tug Hill region. This is a region that is surprisingly flat, so flat that you are never aware you are ascending a hill as you drive to the trailhead at the mile-long Sears Pond. Nonetheless, when you drive east from the shores of Lake Ontario to Sears Pond, you go from an elevation of 260 feet to 1765 feet, for a vertical rise of 1505 feet.

A little farther east of Sears Pond is the Tug Hill escarpment overlooking the Black River Valley; this is the hill's highest point at 2110 feet, making Tug Hill the highest ground west of the Adirondack Mountain region.

Throughout the 1800s, people pushed up the slopes of Tug Hill in search of more land to farm, cutting back the forest as they went, until finally they reached the top of the hill. Here, however, farming became difficult. The growing season is short, and the soil is thin and poorly drained—conditions that made farming uneconomical.

In the last 50 years, the farmers have been slowly retreating down the hill and abandoning the farmlands that they had so laboriously attained. The picture of land use today is interesting. On the hill's north slope downhill from NY 177, about 90 percent of the land is farmed. A few miles south of NY 177 and uphill, only 50 percent of the land is farmed. In another mile or two, the percentage drops to 10, and as you enter the Sears Pond area less than 1 percent is farmed. In this short distance you see an abrupt change in the land's appearance and in the ecological relationships among the land, vegetation, wildlife, and the few human beings who still inhabit the area. The farmers are long gone, and what was once farmland lies fallow, with shrubs and young trees taking over.

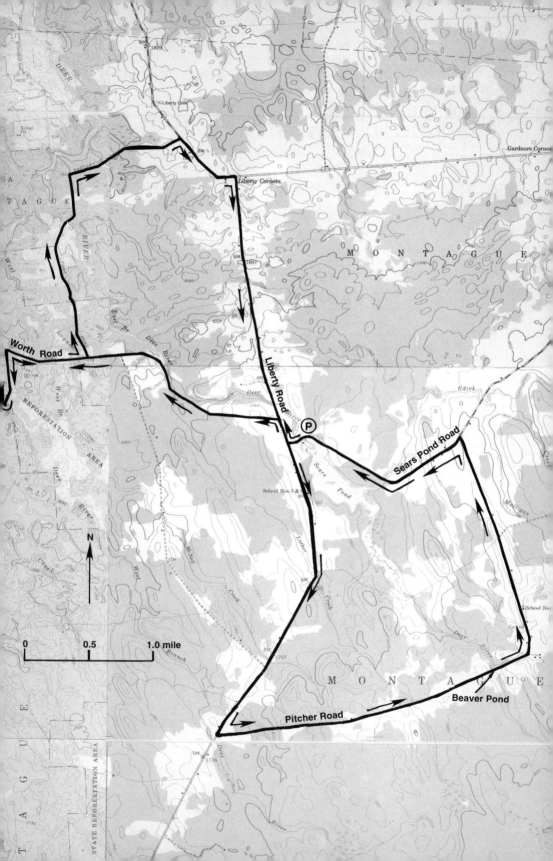

Gardners Corners

DEER

MONTAGUE

Liberty Cem

Liberty Corners

BM

RIVER

Worth Road

Edick

Liberty Road

REFORESTATION AREA

Sears Pond Road

Sears Pond

School Nos 3 &

N

School No

0   0.5   1.0 mile

Beaver Pond

M O N T A G U E

Pitcher Road

STATE REFORESTATION AREA

MONTAGUE

To get a good taste of this interesting area, it is best to do it in two bites by hiking two loops. The northwestern loop takes you into wilderness, where all signs of civilization quickly disappear and only a trackless forest remains. The southeastern loop, on the other hand, takes you through the transitional area where people still live (many only in summer) and where evidence of past farming can still be seen as the forest slowly creeps back.

Access. The trailhead at Sears Pond lies 6.4 miles south of NY 177. Either from Adams Center in the west or Lowville in the east, take NY 177 to the little hamlet of Bellwood. Turn here onto Sears Pond Road, and drive south until you reach a small parking area near a wooden dam at the north end of Sears Pond. Park here.

Trail. The hiking trails are made up of the several roads and access truck trails that run through the state forest. You can camp in and around the Sears Pond area, with no camping permits required.

First Day
*Loop from Liberty Pond Road via
Factory Road
Distance: 8¼ miles
Hiking time: 4¼ hours*

Begin your hike by walking west from your parked vehicle across the pond's outlet stream to where the one-lane, blacktop Sears Pond Road intersects Liberty Road, another single-lane blacktop road. The outlet stream is really a continuation of the East Branch of the Deer River, which originates several miles south in the Tug Hill Wildlife Management Area (see Hike 39).

Once at the intersection, turn right and head north on Liberty Road for about ¼ mile to where a single-lane dirt road, Worth Road, intersects on your left. Turn onto Worth Road and hike west. You are going through an area that was once farmed, but you will see little evidence of that today, as the forest has replaced the fields. The road parallels the course of the East Branch of Deer River; at the ¾-mile mark, the road bends a little to the right, and in ½ mile more it turns a little more to the right, coming to the stream's edge.

The terrain here is relatively flat, hence the hiking is easy. In slightly under ¼ mile from the stream edge, the road turns sharply to your left taking a due west course. In the next ½ mile, you pass two dirt roads, one intersecting on your left and another on your right, then cross a bridge over the West Branch of Deer River. The second road, Fork Road, is the one you will hike later.

Continue ½ mile east of the West Branch on Worth Road to where another dirt road intersects on your left. Turn here, and follow this road south to an impoundment. You are now on the northern edge of Tug Hill, a wilderness area about 30 miles wide and 20 miles long. Nothing is found here except trees.

Retrace your steps to Fork Road; turn left here and follow it north. At the mile mark, the road crosses the East Branch of Deer Creek, and ⅜ mile more brings you to Factory Road, intersecting on your right. Turn onto Factory Road, and hike east for a mile where you intersect Liberty Road. Turn right, and walk south on this single-lane blacktop road back to Sears Pond and your parked vehicle.

Second Day
Loop from Sears Pond via Pitcher
Road
Distance: 8 miles
Hiking time: 4 hours

For the second loop, return to Liberty Road, and follow it south for 2⅜ miles. The blacktop road gives way to a two-lane dirt road. En route, you see that the area is quite open, with fields on both sides of the road. You also see more evidence of civilization here, in contrast with the first day; there are quite a few homes along this road.

At the 2⅜-mile mark, a single-lane dirt road, Pitcher Road, intersects on your left. Turn here, and hike Pitcher Road eastward. Initially it takes you through a thickly wooded area, but after a mile's walk you leave the state forest and again see abandoned fields on your

right. Another ½ mile brings you to a large beaver pond.

The pond extends south from the road for almost ½ mile. The beavers constructed their dam along the edge of the road; it is 2 feet high, with water spilling over the road. A little over ½ mile down the road, you cross the headwaters of the East Branch of Deer River.

A short distance farther, you encounter a cluster of eight houses, most of which appear to be summer cottages. The road bends to your left here and heads north as you reenter the state forest. Fields on both sides of the road that were once cultivated today lie fallow, waiting for the forest to take over.

From the cluster of houses it is 1¾ miles to the intersection with Sears Pond Road. Turn left here, and follow the single-lane blacktop road over Edick Creek, which flows into Sears Pond on your left, then finally to your parked vehicle.

Overlooking Sears Pond

39

Tug Hill Wildlife Management Area

Total distance: 8½ miles	
Hiking time: 4 hours	
Vertical rise: 400 feet	
Map: USGS 7½' Sears Pond	

Before the farmers and lumbermen came, early in the 1800s, the entire Tug Hill region was heavily forested. It was frequently referred to as the "Lesser Wilderness" to distinguish it from the Adirondack forest region, which was called the "Greater Wilderness."

Today, while the slopes on all sides of Tug Hill are farmed, the region's central portion—600 square miles—is still as it once was, a wilderness. There are no homes, no roads, not even a hiking trail. This is an area of dense woods, virtually impenetrable. No one ventures into the heart of the region, which is more remote and more primitive than anyplace in the Adirondacks.

Yet you can get a taste of this unusual wilderness by hiking in the Tug Hill Wildlife Management Area (not to be confused with its close kinsman, the Tug Hill State Forest, located about 10 miles to the northwest—see Hike 37). The wildlife management area, in turn, is part of the much larger Tug Hill wilderness, which occupies 4985 acres in the north central part of this wilderness area.

A 4-mile-long, single-lane dirt road runs through the central part of the wildlife management area, with a foot trail continuing a mile beyond the road. This allows you to walk from one end to the other of this large parcel of state land.

En route you pass a large, mile-long impoundment and cross two streams that make up the headwaters of the north-flowing Deer River. The land of the game management area is also a drainage area. From the top of Tug Hill at an elevation of 1900 feet, the land drains water into the Deer River flowing north, Mad River flowing west, and Fish Creek flowing south.

It is the home of the white-tailed deer, red and gray fox, Eastern coyote, fisher, bobcat, and an occasional stray black bear that wanders into the area from the western Adirondack foothills. Here and there on beech trees you can see old claw marks of such a visitor. The deer here are not present in plentiful

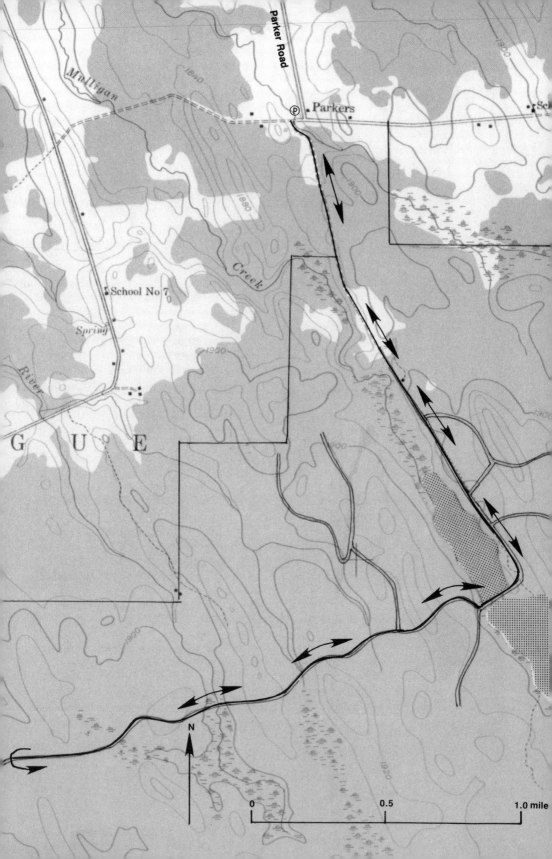

numbers, and in winter they move southeast to lower elevations to yard in what is called the Highmarket area, where the snow is not so deep.

The predominant trees are beech and red maple. Mixed in with the hardwoods are fairly large stands of conifers, primarily pine, spruce, and hemlock. Also found here is the relatively rare black spruce, variously called "bog spruce" or "swamp spruce." This is the environment for it, with a number of large bog and swamp areas throughout the area.

If you are a bird-watcher as well as a hiker, you will enjoy hiking here, for the area has received high marks by birders, especially in spring and autumn. Here you see yellow-bellied and least flycatchers, kinglets, cedar waxwings, hermit thrushes, mourning warblers, and white-throated and Lincoln's sparrows, not to mention migrating waterfowl. Goshawks nest here, and so do several different species of owls. Late spring and early summer, when the woods are full of wildflowers, is the time for spotting northward-migrating hawks.

Access. The wildlife management area can be reached most easily from NY 177, which runs along the north slope of Tug Hill between Watertown and Lowville. About 10 miles west of Lowville is a cluster of several homes that make up the hamlet of Bellwood. Turn south here onto Sears Pond Road; continue on this road for 3.6 miles to Rector, where Sears Pond Road turns right. Straight ahead, however, a dirt road (Parker Road) continues due south. Follow Parker Road for 1.8 miles to its intersection with another dirt road (Flatrock Road). Here you will see a sign that you are entering the Tug Hill Wildlife Management Area. Park here.

Trail. The single-lane main dirt road takes you to the southwestern corner of the management area. Running off this main route are several access roads, each about a mile in length. You can hike in the area for a 1-day trek or for a weekend outing. There is a fairly large open area at the end of the main road that can serve as your camping area.

From the parking spot, the road runs straight in a southeasterly direction for 2¼ miles to the impoundment. The trees have been cut back from the road to make the road look wider than it is. Beyond the impoundment, however, the trees grow to the edge of the road, providing cool shade for the hiker on a hot summer day.

After you have hiked ½ mile down the road, you can detect wetlands lying about 200 to 300 feet off the right side of the road; running through the elongated swamp is a small stream, Mulligan Creek. A mile farther brings you to the first of a series of access roads running off the main road. This one intersects on your left. Another lane intersects on your left ½ mile farther, and in less than ¼ mile you encounter the third, also on your left.

Continue on the main road for little over ¼ mile, where the road turns right and crosses high ground that dams a large impoundment on both sides of the road. Here you can find various species of nesting ducks; during spring and autumn migratory periods, the pond will be filled with geese as well, as they stop to rest and feed.

Along the road on the other side of the impoundment, a lane intersects on your left; it runs about ½ mile south. Continue on the main road, and in a little over ¼ mile you encounter still another access road, this time intersecting on your right; ⅜ mile farther brings you to a small stream flowing over the road,

Man-made impoundment in Tug

and another ⅜ mile leads you to a second and somewhat larger stream that also flows over the road. In summer the water is about 4 to 6 inches deep, and you need high waterproof boots to cross.

A mile more brings you to the road's end and a fairly large open spot used as a turnaround area. A mound of dirt across the road forms a barrier against further vehicular travel. Trail bikers, though, have circled around it to continue south on what is an extension of the main road. This gives you a walking path if you would like to continue your hike farther. The little-used road ends in a mile at the wildlife management area's western boundary.

You can now retrace your steps, exploring en route all or some of the access roads you passed earlier.

40

Whetstone Gulf State Park

Total distance: 4⅝ miles

Hiking time: 3 hours

Vertical rise: 567 feet

Maps: USGS 7½' Glenfield; USGS 7½' Page

On a scale running from the commonplace to the spectacular, Whetstone Gulf State Park lies at the top. While throughout the Tug Hill region you find gullies and gorges (called gulfs) cut into the slopes of the "Hill," you can see one of the most impressive examples in this state park.

As gulfs go, Whetstone's is relatively short, only 2 miles long; what it lacks in length it makes up for in depth. The upper (western) end is narrow and breathtakingly deep. The walls of the gorge go straight down, cut by glacial waters just as a hot knife goes through butter. From the rim's edge, you look down 400 feet to the bottom where the waters of Whetstone Creek bounce over rocks and boulders. Anything this deep really qualifies as a canyon.

What surprises you at first is how so deep an incision could have been made in a hillside that otherwise looks so gentle and benign. That is a characteristic typical of Tug Hill—juxtaposition of the unexpected with the expected, the gentle with the rugged, pastoral cultivated fields with thick forests rimming yawning gulfs. What brings the hiker to the Hill is the search for the unexpected, or still another surprise.

When you plan to hike Whetstone Gulf's rim trails, you might consider a hike into the park's neighbor, the Lesser Wilderness State Forest (see Hike 41), which adjoins Whetstone Gulf State Park. A dirt road, Corrigan Road, on the western edge of the park's gulf, takes you straight into the central part of the Lesser Wilderness State Forest.

Whetstone Gulf has facilities for camping and swimming, so you can make a weekend of your visit to the area. There is a charge for entering the park, but camping reservations are not required.

As you walk the rim trails, you will notice that the layered rock of the canyon is almost entirely black shale with thin interbeds of grayish siltstone and sandstone; fossils are prevalent in the silty beds. It is the softness of this formation that contributed to canyon-cutting.

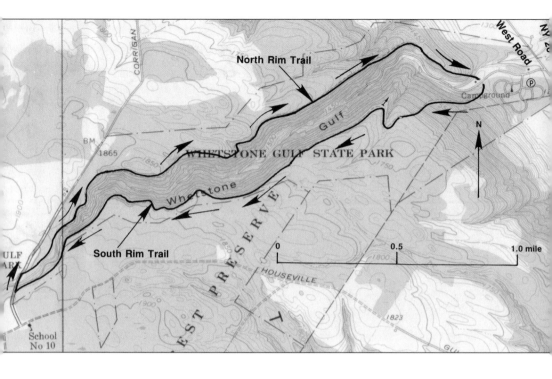

The eastern entrance to the park marks the contact between the underlying limestone and the overlying Utica shale; resting on top of the Utica shale is the Lorraine rock group and Pulaski rock formation. These formations are well exposed in the upper end of the gorge.

Access. Whetstone Gulf State Park is located 6.3 miles south of Lowville on NY 26. Lowville, in turn, can be reached via NY 12 from Watertown in the north or Utica in the south, or via NY 26 from Rome. The park's entrance is on NY 26.

Trail. A foot trail completely encircling the gorge is divided into the South Rim Trail and the North Rim Trail. Once you are inside the park, signs direct you to the trail beginnings. The South Rim Trail begins on the south side of a recreational building adjacent to Whetstone Creek; the North Rim Trail starts on the north side of the creek. It doesn't make any difference which trail you take, for they join one another at the road at the western edge of the gorge, allowing you to loop back to the park entrance. Let's begin with the South Rim Trail.

Once you are on this trail, it is a steady uphill climb through a forest area that provides cool shade during the hot summer months. At about the ½-mile mark, you will have climbed the steepest part, for a vertical rise of 400 feet.

The trail now levels out and then makes a sharp right turn; a short distance brings you to the rim edge, allowing you for the first time to get a good view of this lower end of the gorge. The walls are more slanted here than those you will see at the upper end. A short distance off the trail to your right is a

View of Whetstone Gulf with its almost vertical walls

wooden observation platform. From here you have a fine view of the Black River Valley and surrounding countryside to the east.

The trail now follows the gulf's southern rim, letting you look into the gorge as you walk. It continues uphill, with a gradual rise for the next ½ mile, flattening out when you reach the halfway mark. From here on the hike is on level ground.

At about the 1½-mile mark, the gorge begins to narrow and deepen; the walls become perpendicular. You now reach a spot where the trail bends a little to your right, bringing you to a huge boulder left here by the retreating glacier some 12,000 years ago. The boulder sits literally on the edge of the rim. From this spot you have a fine view of the gorge to the east.

A short distance farther brings you to a single-lane dirt road (Corrigan Road).

At this point the gorge has been reduced to a gully containing a series of small falls as Whetstone Creek makes its way into the gorge. Turn right onto the road, and cross Whetstone Creek. On the other side the North Rim Trail begins.

The trail on the north is pretty much a repeat of what you saw on the south. The terrain is about the same too; the first mile is relatively flat, and then the trail starts a gradual downhill descent.

At the 1½-mile mark, the downward pitch becomes more pronounced, and the last ½ mile is very steep. Before you start the final descent, the trail turns to the right, or southeasterly. It eventually breaks out of the woods as you reach bottom on the north side of Whetstone Creek. A bridge over the creek brings you to the south side and the parking lot where you left your vehicle.

41

Lesser Wilderness State Forest

Total distance: 9⅝ miles

Hiking time: 5 hours

Vertical rise: 390 feet

Maps: USGS 7½' Glenfield; USGS 7½' Page

The Adirondack Region, which spreads over a vast area east of the Black River Valley, has been called the "Greater Wilderness." To the west of the Black River Valley is a much smaller area on Tug Hill called the "Lesser Wilderness." The state has preserved this old terminology in the name of one of the state forests on the eastern edge of Tug Hill, the highest land west of the Adirondack High Peaks. The Lesser Wilderness State Forest is the largest state holding on Tug Hill—13,740 acres.

The foot-traveler who calculates distance in what his or her feet can cover in a day will regard this state forest as an impressive amount of territory. Actually it is broken into five pieces with the center parcel the largest at 8 miles wide and

6 miles long. Connecting roads and jeep trails permit you to hike from one parcel to the next with ease, and, if you have the stamina, from one end to the other—16 miles one way.

Even though the state forest is located on the highest place on Tug Hill, its topography is relatively flat. It serves as a drainage area for streams flowing to all directions: Roaring Brook, Whetstone Creek, Alder Creek, House Creek, Mill Creek, and the East and North Branches of Fish Creek.

One of the larger parcels of Lesser Wilderness adjoins Whetstone Gulf State Park (see Hike 40). If you are planning a weekend outing, you can combine hikes in the state forest and the state park. The state park includes campsites, so you can make it your base.

The southern half of the Lesser Wilderness State Forest is solid woods. The northern part is a land in transition from farmland to woodland, but the area is still fairly open. In the north, you find Whetstone Creek flowing out of an impoundment that represents one of the largest bodies of water on Tug Hill (at an elevation of 1902 feet). A couple miles south is Gomer Hill, the highest spot on Tug Hill, with an elevation of 2110 feet. For a good appreciation of the area's

1964

WHETSTONE GULF
STATE PARK

Graves Corners

McGraw Corners

Creek

School
No 10

STATE FO

BM
1946

JEEP

TABOLT

BM 1904

BM
1902

Tabolt
Corners.

920

1900

1950

1909

2000

2000

T
U
R
I
N

2000

1950

N

0   0.5   1.0 mile

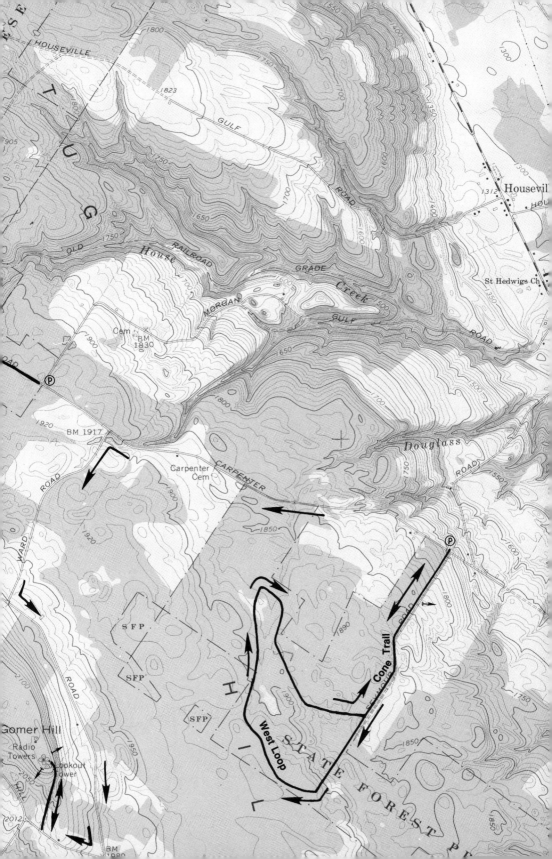

diversified landmarks, plan your hiking route carefully, and try to spend at least a full day.

Access. The state forest entrance on Carpenter Road can be reached via NY 26, which runs from Rome in the south through Turin to Lowville in the north. Carpenter Road is 8.8 miles south of Lowville and 3.4 miles north of Turin. Driving north from Turin, you'll pass the Snow Ridge Ski Center on your left.

Where Carpenter Road intersects NY 26 on the west, you see a sign to Gomer Hill and to a cross-country ski area. Turn here, and drive uphill on the dirt road for 1.2 miles, where the road makes a sharp turn to the right; 0.1 mile more brings you to a lane intersecting on your left, where there is a sign pointing to the cross-country ski area. Park here.

Trail. Your hiking is broken up into two stages, the first beginning in the parcel with the cross-country ski trails, the other several miles farther north. In between you can drive to the fire tower on Gomer Hill, where you can climb the tower to enjoy a fine view.

A short distance up the lane from the parking area, you see a booth where in winter Nordic skiers are asked to register. The ski trail parallels the lane on your right. However, weeds grow tall on it, making walking difficult, so stay on the lane (Seymour Road). For a little over ¼ mile it is a gradual uphill climb; another ½ mile brings you to where you can see the ski-trail markers on your right; here the West Loop and Cone Trails meet.

For the next ½ mile the terrain is flat; the lane continues straight in a southwesterly direction on the edge of the state forest. Through the trees on your left you can see an open field and beyond it a nice view of the Black River Valley. At ⅝ mile, the ski trail crosses the road, with the West Loop on your right. If the grass in the trail is not too high, try walking this trail. It is 2 miles long, bringing you back to Seymour Road at the spot you passed earlier. If you decide against the West Loop, you can retrace your steps on Seymour Road to your parked vehicle.

To drive to the manned fire tower on Gomer Hill, continue west on Carpenter Road for 1.6 miles, where Ward Road intersects on your left. Turn here, and follow Ward Road south for a mile to its intersection with Brenon Road. Turn left, and follow Brenon Road south for 1.2 miles to the intersection with Gomer Hill Road. Turn right on Gomer Hill Road, and 0.4 mile brings you to a road on your right leading to the fire tower.

Another 0.4 mile up this road brings you to the fire tower, which is surrounded by five radio towers, part of the Federal Aviation Agency Communication Facility. At the top of the tower, an observer can answer your questions and tell you about the surrounding territory. After you have enjoyed the view, return to your car and drive back to Carpenter Road.

Turn left here onto what is now called Tabolt Road; continue northwest on Tabolt Road 0.4 mile, where another parcel of the Lesser Wilderness begins. Park here.

Begin your second hike by walking west on Tabolt Road, a single-lane dirt road that passes through a heavily wooded section of the state forest. The trees keep the road shaded and cool in summer. After hiking ¾ mile, you reach an intersection with two other roads. One, which leads to Whetstone Reservoir, is fenced off; the other forks to your left and runs south. Follow Tabolt Road as it forks to your right; a mile brings you to an intersection with Houseville Gulf Road.

Field of "erratics" in Lesser Wilderness State Forest

Turn right here, and in a short distance you reach Corrigan Road intersecting on your left. Follow it north for ¼ mile to where it crosses Whetstone Creek. On the south side of the bridge you find the entrance to the South Rim Trail of Whetstone Gulf State Park. Take this trail to your right, and ¼ mile brings you to a spot where you can view the narrow, awesomely deep gorge that's called Whetstone Gulf.

Retrace your steps to Corrigan Road and then to Houseville Gulf Road. Turn right and follow Houseville Gulf Road for ⅜ mile, where a lane intersects on your left beyond Whetstone Creek. A short walk south on this lane brings you to the impoundment, Whetstone Reservoir, which is almost 2 miles long.

Retrace your steps to Houseville Gulf Road, and turn left. As you walk, notice that the forest has given way to more open land, which was once farmland. In ⅜ mile, you come to an intersection with an unnamed dirt road (Graves Corners on the topo map).

Turn left, and follow the dirt road west. On your right you have a full view of abandoned farmland that is slowly reverting to woodland; at the moment it produces a thick crop of shrubs and small trees. A mile from Graves Corners, you reach another intersection, known in the past as McGraw Corners. The elevation here is 2000 feet, so you have a fine view to the east and south. In the east the land is fairly open; to the south it is heavily wooded.

Retrace your steps 2¾ miles to your parked vehicle to complete your hike through three portions of the Lesser Wilderness State Forest.

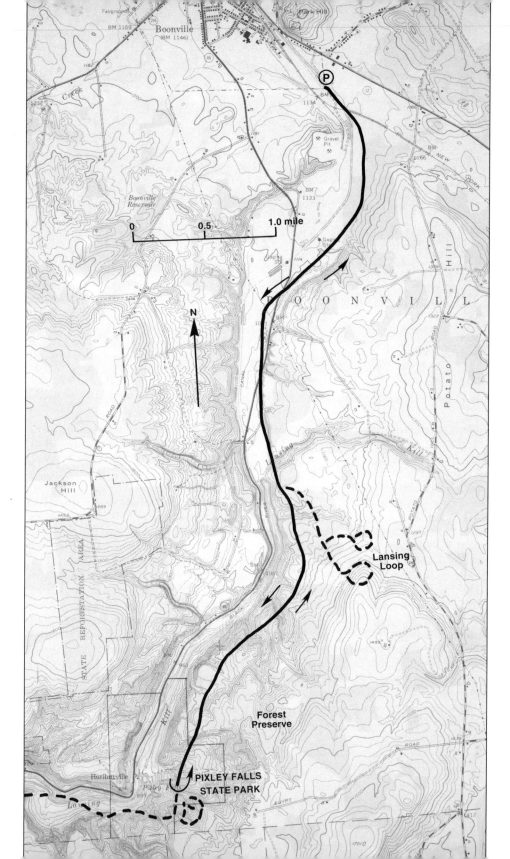

42

Old Black River Canal Towpath/Pixley Falls State Park

Total distance: 12 miles

Hiking time: 6½ hours

Vertical rise: 247 feet

Map: USGS 7½' Boonville

This piece of history almost got lost amid the tangle of saplings and thickening underbrush that blotted out what was once the pride of the North Country citizens—the Black River Canal. The North Country residents fought hard and long to get the New York legislature to finance the building of the canal; after a number of setbacks they finally succeeded in 1855.

The canal served the North Country well for 69 years before being officially closed. Abandoned to the vicissitudes of the times, the canal was in part filled in and in part simply left for nature—thickets, brush, and saplings—to reclaim.

In the 1980s, however, local residents felt that the old canal's upper portion could be rescued and made useful again.

They banded together to clear the canal's towpath for 7½ miles to make it one of the most popular Nordic ski paths in the region. In summer, the towpath is kept trimmed as a hiking trail.

The history of the Black River Canal goes back to the early 1800s, a time when getting products to markets south of Boonville was difficult and expensive. Many believed that if something were not done quickly, this part of New York would slip back into wilderness. Since this was the period of canal building in New York, the solution to the North Country's economic woes appeared to be a canal running from Rome to Carthage or even Ogdensburg.

Continuous agitation by North Country folks finally moved the legislature to action, although progress was slow and the legislature often indecisive. In the meanwhile, the Erie Canal was being enlarged. To obtain necessary water for this enlarged canal, it was proposed that a feeder canal be built from what is now Forestport (then called Punkeyville) to bring water from the Black River and send it down the Lansing Kill and the Mohawk River to the Erie at Rome.

This was the big chance the people in the Boonville area had been waiting for. Instead of running it down the Lansing

Abandoned lock on Old Black River Canal Towpath Trail

Kill and the Mohawk River, they proposed moving the water via a canal that would not only serve the Erie but also solve the North Country's economic problems. Finally, the legislature was prodded into building a canal from Rome to Carthage.

In 1838, work was started on a section running from Rome to the mouth of the Lansing Kill; 2 years later the canal was extended to Boonville and, still later, to Lyons Falls (then called High Falls).

However, work was brought to a halt in 1842 because the state was running into debt. Five years later it started up again. The Forestport-Boonville feeder canal was finished in 1848, and what was now known as the Black River Canal was extended first beyond Boonville and then to Lyons Falls in 1855.

The canal construction was an engineering marvel in its own right—it employed more locks than any other canal in the world. To get from Rome to Boonville, the canal had to rise 693 feet by using 70 locks. From Boonville to High Falls, the descent was 387 feet, using 39 locks. In short, over a stretch of 35 miles 109 locks were in use. Compare this to the Erie Canal, which ran 364 miles from Albany to Buffalo and only used 83 locks.

As the 19th century came to a close, competition from railroads drastically reduced the need for canals, forcing several of the lateral canals to close; even the Erie was abandoned and replaced by the current Barge Canal. The Black River Canal, however, managed to survive until 1924. Soon thereafter the lower section was drained and filled; only a small section south of Boonville carried moving water. The rest of the canal, in the Boonville Gorge, was abandoned to weeds and undergrowth.

But in the late 1980s, the old canal found supporters for its use. A group of Boonville citizens, organized under the name Black River Environmental

Improvement Association (BREIA), cleared the upper section of the towpath, converting it into a summer hiking path and winter cross-country ski route.

Today this towpath runs from the southern edge of Boonville southward through Pixley Falls State Park to where it intersects NY 46; parking areas are found at both ends. En route from Boonville to the trail's southern end you pass 13 abandoned locks, including the famous "5 combine locks," a series of joined-together locks that once gave the canal its highest lift.

Access. The trailhead at the canal's upper end is found just 0.5 mile southeast of the village of Boonville on NY 12. Boonville, in turn, can be reached from Utica via NY 12, or from Rome via NY 46. If you are coming from Rome you have to drive through Boonville, where you pick up NY 12 going south; follow this route to the village's southern edge. Here you encounter a large shopping mall on your right. Turn right onto a road on the mall's northern edge; 0.1 mile brings you to a building that serves as the BREIA headquarters and, in winter, a warming hut for cross-country skiers.

If you are traveling north from Utica on NY 12, look for Woodgate Drive (north) on your left. Across the highway is the shopping mall; turn left onto the road running along its northern edge to the BREIA building.

Trail. The starting point is found next to the old, water-filled Black River Canal; this water moves in the direction of the gorge portion of the canal. In its flow, the water runs under NY 46 twice and at the 2-mile mark leaves the canal bed, plunging down a steep hill to feed into the Lansing Kill; the remainder of the old canal bed is dry and brush covered.

From the BREIA building turn left (southeast) and follow the towpath running on the north side of the old canal. In summer the towpath is mowed to make walking easy; in winter tracks are set regularly for the Nordic skiers. Near the canal's southern end is Pixley Falls State Park, where you will find camping and picnic areas as well as short loop trails.

Since the distance to Pixley Falls State Park is 6 miles, you may wish to break up your hike to cover 2 days, camping overnight at the state park and then returning to Boonville the following day for the 12-mile round trip. Another option is to hike the towpath with one or more friends and leave a vehicle at Pixley Falls State Park; this cuts your hiking distance in half, since your journey is one-way.

You reach a control dam built at the first lock 1⅜ miles from your starting point. On your left side by a small inlet stream is a structure housing a gauging station. An additional ¼ mile brings you to NY 46. The canal water passes under the highway and past another gauging station on its downhill journey. About half a mile from the gauging station the canal turns south; this section passes through a large open area and then hugs the foot of a forested hillside until it reaches NY 46 again.

As before, the canal water passes under the highway and then runs through two abandoned locks; ¼ mile more brings you to a footbridge crossing the spot where the water leaves the canal to empty into the Lansing Kill at the foot of the hill. The highway, now running parallel with the canal, is several dozen feet above it. Here you enter the narrow part of the Boonville Gorge; the highway, like the canal before it, is cut into the gorge's side. Another mile brings you to the fourth abandoned lock.

From here the towpath runs relatively straight, with just a slight downhill pitch.

After hiking an additional 1 mile you cross the boundary into the 375-acre Pixley Falls State Park. From here ⅝ mile brings you to the fifth lock, and a short distance beyond to the entrance of the state park.

The Lansing Kill runs through the western edge of the park, a short distance from the towpath. Here you will find 22 streamside camping sites, each with its own table and fire ring. In addition, the park has several picnic areas, a softball field, and horseshoe pits. Just south of the entrance the waters of the Lansing Kill plunge over a 50-foot falls, putting on a spectacular performance in the spring, when the river is at its fullest.

The park also contains a ½-mile hiking trail that forms a loop. Starting at the far end of the park's south side, the trail takes you down to the foot of the falls, then along the stream's edge, and finally uphill and north, back to your starting point in the parking area. It is a fine forest trail to hike, especially in spring and early summer when four streamlets cascading down the hillside and over rocky ledges give you several attractive falls.

Here, too, you can find a variety of upland trees—American beech, yellow birch, sugar maple, eastern hemlock, and, around the falls, common alder, willow, and red maple. Pixley Falls also attracts those interested in its fossils, which were formed 500 million years ago during the Ordovician period. Fossils found in the park include brachiopods, trilobites, crinoids, and cephalopods.

The site on which the park is located was once owned by a dairy-farming family, the Pixleys, who sold the land in the 1920s. In 1935 the land was acquired by the state, and during the next several years the federally administered Civilian Conservation Corps cleared it and built the state park, naming it after the original property owners.

The park is a good place to reverse direction and head back to Boonville and your parked vehicle. However, there is still a section of the towpath running south from the park—from the entrance it is 1½ miles to the trail's end. En route you pass eight more locks, including the five combine locks. This set of locks and the towpath beside them are off-limits in summer. "No Trespassing" signs are erected during the summer months to discourage people from walking on top of the locks and to prevent a person from falling into their depths.

When you are ready you can start your 6-mile trek back through the state park and out, in a gradual uphill climb to where you started.

WESTERN ADIRONDACK HILLS

43

Aldrich Pond Wild Forest

Total distance: 17¼ miles (2 days)

Hiking time: 8 hours

Vertical rise: 640 feet

Maps: USGS 7½' Oswegatchie; USGS 7½' Oswegatchie SE

At the end of almost a 5-mile hike into Aldrich Pond Wild Forest are two beautiful lakes—like finding gold at the end of the rainbow. Streeter Lake and Crystal Lake lie a half mile west of Streeter Mountain (elevation 1767 feet), one of the many hills hereabouts that rise above 1700 feet.

The lakes, a tenth of a mile apart, are quite different. Streeter Lake is five times larger than Crystal Lake. Its water is dark-colored, as is so typical of Adirondack lakes. Crystal Lake, as its name implies, is transparently clear, with a white sandy bottom. The environment in and around the two lakes is also a bit different. Crystal Lake contains no fish; Streeter does. Play the role of naturalist and make a comparative study.

At one time, a large expanse of land surrounding these two lakes was owned by the Shuler family, and it is still frequently referred to as the Shuler Tract. The summer estate consisted of one large main lodge and several guest houses. A large field just north of the buildings was used to raise potatoes for the owner's potato chip business in southern New York.

This field, about ¼ mile square, is certainly an unusual sight in this wilderness region. It is the only open spot for miles around, although it is slowly reverting to forest, as young birch, aspen, and pine trees take root.

And if you don't know its history, the open area comes as even more of a surprise. There is no evidence now that it was once a potato field, much less that it was part of a large estate. All the buildings were razed and/or removed after New York State acquired the land in 1975. All you find here now is a lean-to overlooking Streeter Lake, a short distance from where the main lodge once stood.

When the state took possession of about 4000 acres of this estate in the St. Lawrence County town of Fine, it closed a gap in the northwest region of the Forest Preserve. The Department of Environmental Conservation has desig-

Lean-to facing Streeter Lake

nated the Shuler Tract and surrounding state land as the Aldrich Pond Wild Forest. Adjacent to the area on the east is the Five Ponds Wilderness Area, which surrounds Cranberry Lake.

Topographically, the terrain is rolling, with low hills, exposed outcrops of crystalline rocks, large glacial erratics, bogs and swamps, and a number of streams, including Little River, Tamarack Creek, and the Middle Branch of the Oswegatchie River.

The land now is covered with hardwood second growth that includes sugar maple, black cherry, and beech. In early spring, the forest floor is ablaze with flowers of every variety, making as attractive a scene as can be found anywhere in the Adirondacks.

Because of the low elevation and large number of wetland areas, a sizable deer population exists in the area, so it is a popular place in the fall for hunters, especially those who like to start hunting early in October with bow or muzzleloader; the rifle season starts later in the month.

In addition to the white-tailed deer, there are black bear, and in recent years moose have been sighted in this general area. A plentiful supply of the large Eastern coyote also is found here. Among the smaller mammals are fisher, beaver, porcupine, raccoon, and varying hare.

Access. The trailhead is found at the southern edge of the village of Star Lake. Star Lake can be reached via NY 3 between Watertown and Tupper Lake. In the center of the village, Griffin Road intersects on the south. Turn here, and drive south on Griffin Road for 0.8 mile, where Lake Road intersects on your right. Turn onto Lake Road, and drive

west 0.2 mile to the intersection with Amos Road. Turn left onto Amos Road, and drive 0.6 mile to the trailhead, which is on the left side of the road. Park here.

Trail. A sign at the trailhead indicates that the trail to Streeter Lake was built by the Youth Conservation Corps. It is groomed and marked with yellow disks. Once at Streeter Lake, you will continue hiking on abandoned roads that run south from the lake.

The first leg of your hike from the trailhead to Streeter Lake is 4¾ miles. The second from Streeter Lake to the other side of Bassetts Creek is 3¾ miles. To do both requires a weekend, so you should plan to backpack to Streeter Lake and stay overnight at the lean-to. On the other hand, the route to Streeter Lake and back makes a good day trek.

First Day
From Amos Road to Streeter Lake Lean-to
Distance: 4¾ miles
Hiking time: 3 hours

Your hike starts with a short downhill descent. Therefter the terrain stays fairly level for the next ¾ mile, where you cross a wooden footbridge over the slow-moving Little River. Once over the bridge, you intersect another trail running east and west. Turn to your left on what is actually a snowmobile trail, and count off 35 steps. On your right, the Streeter Lake trail continues uphill.

For the next ¾ mile you have a gradual uphill climb; the vertical rise in this stretch is 200 feet. In the next

¼ mile, you make a gradual descent to a low area and then start a relatively short and gradual uphill climb. The trail slopes downward again, and in less than ½ mile you enter a gullylike area, cross two log footbridges, and pass by several large impressive outcrops.

The first one may remind you of a fortress guarding a valley, the second more of pillboxes guarding the lowlands on your left. A short distance farther, you cross another footbridge. The trail now rises, swings to the left, and climbs a small hill, only to turn sharply to your right to make a descent to the north side of Streeter Lake Outlet.

At Streeter Lake is an abandoned single-lane dirt road from the hamlet of Aldrich several miles to the north. Where it crosses Streeter Lake Outlet, a gate now prevents access to the area by vehicle. Although it is no longer open to vehicles, the road still runs past Streeter and Crystal Lakes to end several miles to the south.

The trail runs along the edge of the outlet for a short distance and then crosses it on a wooden footbridge. Once across, the trail turns to the right, heading gradually uphill. In less than ¼ mile, it intersects an abandoned, weed-filled single-lane road, which is actually a loop that in either direction brings you to Streeter Lake.

For the shorter distance, turn to your left, and follow the road southward. In ¼ mile, the road, after looping to the east, intersects another abandoned, single-lane road, which in winter is a popular route for cross-country skiers. Another ¼ mile west on this road brings you to the edge of the forest and the start of the abandoned potato field; the road

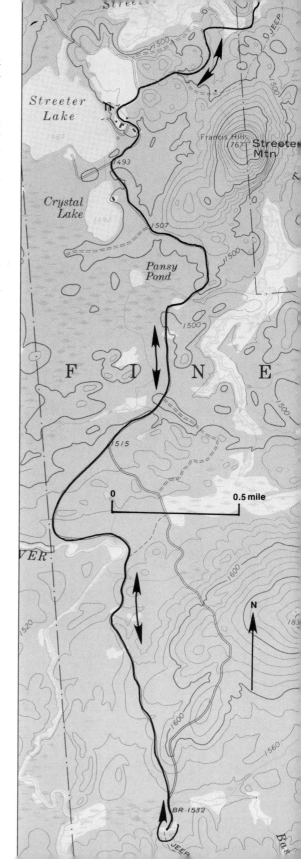

now runs along the southern edge of the field, and ¼ mile brings you to the lean-to and the bluff overlooking Streeter Lake. Here you can camp for the night.

Second Day
From Streeter Lake Lean-to to Bassetts Creek
Distance: 3¾ miles
Hiking time: 2 hours

For your second day's hike, follow the road immediately behind the lean-to south as it passes Streeter Lake and then swings around to the southern side of the lake. Here a road intersects on your right that leads to a small Shuler family cemetery.

The main road, however, continues south past Crystal Lake to where another road intersects on your right; this ⅜-mile-long road takes you along the southern edge of the lake. The main trail continues southward, crossing a small brook feeding into Tamarack Creek located a short distance to the east; ½ mile farther brings you to a road intersecting on your left. This road runs parallel to the one you are now walking for 1½ miles, and then swings west to rejoin it again, thereby forming a loop. To the east of this road is a peaked mountain, Francis Hill (elevation 1836 feet).

Bear to your right, and continue on the main route; ¼ mile brings you to the Middle Branch of the Oswegatchie River. The road turns left and follows the river for a little over ¼ mile, where it turns right and heads due south. A mile farther brings you to the intersection with the parallel road mentioned earlier. A short distance beyond the fork, the trail crosses a wooden bridge over Bassetts Creek, named after the land's earlier owner who had a deer hunting camp here.

A little beyond the bridge, the trail ends at an old circular log landing area. Originally the trail ran south all the way to the Herkimer County line; only bushwhacking with map and compass would allow you to reach this point now. From here you can retrace your steps, all the while enjoying this rare access to the headwaters of the Oswegatchie River and some of the densest wilderness in the North Country.

44

Greenwood Creek State Forest

Total distance: 7½ miles

Hiking time: 3 hours

Vertical rise: 280 feet

Maps: USGS 7½' Fine; DEC Pamphlet with Map

Greenwood Creek is not all that unusual a name, but it does have an appealing ring to it, and Greenwood seems to fit this small parcel of state real estate sitting adjacent to the Adirondack Forest Preserve. Appealing serves to describe everything about this state forest—the several stands of tall, well-spaced red pines, the attractive mix of birches and maples, the assortment of hiking trails, the picnic area, and above all the waterfall where Greenwood Creek tumbles down through huge boulders.

The state forest encompasses just 1009 acres spreading over an area 2 miles wide by 2 miles long. Yet by the time you have walked all the footpaths, lanes, and roads, and returned to your starting point, you'll have covered more than 7 miles—a good day's hike.

Flowing through the northern portion of the state forest is a small, cool stream, Greenwood Creek, which rises several miles to the east deep in the unpopulated Adirondack Park region. It meanders through the state forest, turns north, and eventually empties into Big Creek, a short distance from East Pitcairn.

The creek gives a good account of itself in the state forest, especially at the picnic site. Here you find a cluster of boulders piled on each other as if some giant had left a huge rock pile. Spilling over the boulders is Greenwood Creek, sparkling in the sunlight and splashing from rock to rock into a wide, clear pool. It's the perfect picnic spot.

Greenwood Creek State Forest is on the southwest boundary of St. Lawrence County, halfway between Harrisville and Fine on NY 3. Here you have entered the remoteness of the western Adirondacks, with its sparse population, few roads, and endless tracts of forest.

Access. Greenwood Creek State Forest is reached easily by NY 3 from Watertown, about 40 miles to the west. Traveling east from Watertown, NY 3 brings you to

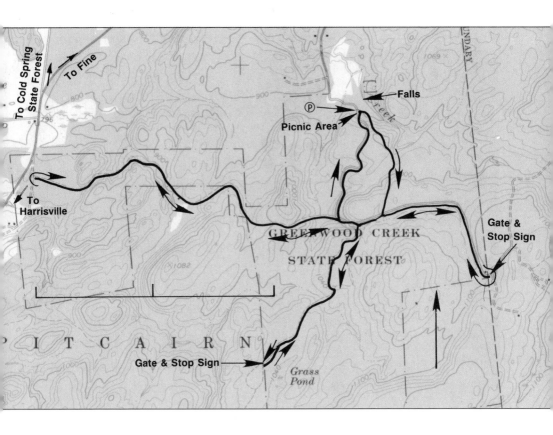

Harrisville and then to Pitcairn. From Pitcairn, continue east for 5.4 miles, where a dirt road marked by a sign to Greenwood Creek State Forest intersects from your right. Turn here, and drive 1.2 miles south; this will take you across Greenwood Creek and to the picnic area. Park here.

Trail. There is only one foot trail in the state forest. It is a 1¾-mile loop trail that begins and ends at the picnic area. The rest of your hiking is on hard-surfaced dirt roads and several lanes that serve as truck trails. All are shaded to make walking a pleasure even on a hot, sunny day.

Start your hike by following the trail

markers up along the edge of the falls at the picnic area. As you reach the top of this little hill, the trail turns right and heads uphill into the woods. After a short but steady climb, you make a short, gradual descent to the edge of Greenwood Creek.

The trail runs on the level for a short stretch and then begins to move up the slope of a hill; a 50-foot climb brings you to the top where the terrain levels out. You are surrounded here by tall red pines that create a most inviting forest setting—not too open, not too overgrown.

Soon you come to a dirt road. Turn left here, and follow the road as it heads east for a little over ¼ mile where it turns

Waterfall on Greenwood Creek

south. A half mile more brings you to a gate with a stop sign that marks the boundary of the state forest; beyond is private land. Retrace your steps to the intersection with the foot trail you hiked earlier.

Pass by the foot trail, and continue west of the dirt road as it heads downhill. A short walk brings you to a one-lane dirt road intersecting from your left. Turn here and head southwest. The terrain in this part of the state forest is flat. As you walk, you will be passing again through stands of red pine and then stands of hardwood, mostly maple and birch. A mile brings you to another gate with a stop sign marking the southern edge of the state forest. Retrace your steps to the main dirt road.

Turn left onto the dirt road, and continue walking westward. After ¼ mile, the trail turns north. At this bend, a lane intersects on your left, where disks nailed to trees mark this as a winter snowmobile trail. Turn onto this trail and head west.

The terrain in this section is a little more varied and rolling, which makes your hike even more enjoyable as you walk in the cool shade. The trail loops first to the right and then to the left, and at the mile mark it crosses a small brook. In the next ½ mile, the trail makes a gradual descent and levels out just before intersecting a north-south lane. Turn right onto this lane, and a few steps bring you to NY 3.

Retrace your steps to the main dirt road. Turn left onto it as it heads north. This section of the road wiggles a bit, making short turns to the right and then to the left as it heads gradually downhill. In a little less than ½ mile, you are back at the picnic area and your parked vehicle.

Camping is not permitted at the picnic area, but there are many other spots in the state forest where it is.

45

Wolf Lake State Forest

Total distance: 4⅝ miles

Hiking time: 3 hours

Vertical rise: 1120 feet

Maps: USGS 7½' Edwards; USGS 7½' Bigelow

This is outcrop country, where you find huge slabs of exposed rock that have been rounded and polished by the scrubbing action of glaciers as they crunched their way south into New York several times during the Pleistocene epoch. Technically, such bedrock outcrops are called *roche moutonnée* (from the French meaning "fleecy rock"), but more popularly they are referred to as "sheepbacks."

This is also talc country. Talc is usually formed when magnesium-rich rocks are altered, especially with heated water, and it is found in irregular deposits in metamorphic rocks along with serpentine, chlorite schists, and dolomite. Talc is used for talcum powder and paint fillers. It may be granular, fibrous, or soft, with a color between dull white to dark gray. At one time there were several talc mines near Talcville, and collecting sites of the mine dumps of the former United States Talc Company are found just a short distance west of town.

Geologically, the land belongs to the Adirondack Mountain Province, a small part of the much larger Grenville Province of the Canadian Shield, which extends south by a narrow neck under the St. Lawrence River by the Thousand Islands Bridge. Hence, you are encountering some very old rocks, indeed. Adirondack rocks originated over 1100 million years ago.

When the Adirondacks were created, they resembled the modern Himalayas. Over eons of time, they have been worn down to their present size, and in the Western Adirondacks today the land is in low relief, with low ridges, shallow depressions, and a terrain that is uneven and accented by boggy wetlands. The 4315-acre Wolf Lake State Forest, near the southwestern edge of St. Lawrence County, falls into what is called the Adirondack Lowlands. Here are found marble, syenite, and paragneiss rocks. Students of mineralogy know that St. Lawrence County is internationally famous for mineral collecting. The area in and around Wolf Lake State Forest is no exception.

Many of the depressions in this area are long and deep, resulting in rock-

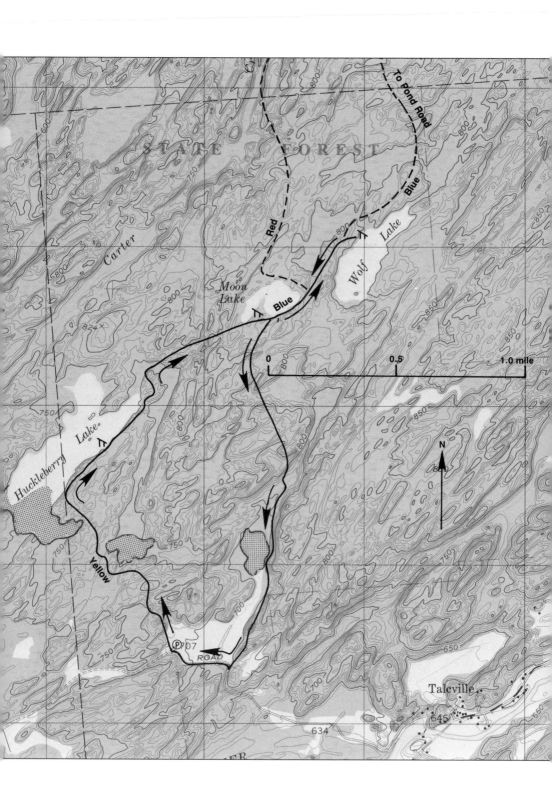

encircled lakes. Three beautiful examples occur in the state forest—Huckleberry Lake, Wolf Lake, and Moon Lake. The lakes are the real treat of this hike: rock-bound, graced by evergreens, and sparkling in the sunlight. Near each is a lean-to, so it is easy to stay a few days.

There are just over 10 miles of hiking trails in the state forest. All are groomed and marked, with trailheads at both the south and north ends of the state forest.

Access. Wolf Lake is reached via NY 58, which runs between Gouveneur in the north and Fine (near NY 3) in the south. If you are coming from Fine, you see at the 8-mile mark a sign directing you to the hamlet of Edwards. From this sign continue on NY 58 for 3.6 miles where you see a blacktop road intersecting on your right. Coming from Gouveneur, 8.5 miles bring you to a bridge crossing the West Branch of the Oswegatchie River. From the bridge, continue on NY 58 for 2.6 miles to the intersection of the blacktop road on your left.

Here a sign directs you to Talcville. A mile takes you to a bridge over the Oswegatchie River at the southern edge of the hamlet. Beyond the bridge, half a city block length brings you to a dirt road intersecting on your left. Turn here, and follow this dirt road for 1.2 miles, where it makes a 90-degree turn to your left. At this bend is the beginning of Moon Lake Trail. From here, continue for another 0.25 mile down the road to a fairly large parking area where the Huckleberry Lake Trail begins. Park here.

Those interested in mineral collecting should look for the collecting site a short distance after turning onto the dirt road in Talcville. Drive a little over 0.2 mile on the dirt road; after crossing the railroad tracks for the third time, you will see mining dumps on your left side, between the tracks and the river.

Here a whole talc deposit suite of minerals can be found: talc, hexagonite, wollastonite, serpentine, phlogopite, scapolite, diopside, pyrite, calcite, and various forms of tremolite, some of which fluoresce. Hexagonite is a rare manganese-bearing species of tremolite, with a distinctive lavender color. The unusual species for this area is groutite, a hydrous manganese oxide that takes the form of small lustrous black crystals.

Trail. Topographically, the land here is relatively flat, with the highest elevation being only 850 feet. When you are hiking, however, you find that you go forever up and down as the trail snakes its way through, over, and around the numerous large rock outcrops.

To get started is a bit of a challenge. The grass grows high in summer and almost obscures the entrance, but you soon pick up the signs of a discernible foot trail that you can follow north through the grass for about 100 yards. Here you see a post with a yellow trail marker. Another 50 yards bring you into the woods and onto a wide, well-used trail. As all the trail markers are yellow, we can refer to the Huckleberry Lake Trail as the Yellow Trail.

It is a mile via the Yellow Trail to Huckleberry Lake. Once on the trail, a short distance into the forest you pass between two large outcrops, a sample of the rocky landscape you'll encounter for the rest of your hike. The area is heavily wooded, predominantly maple with a generous sprinkling of white birch trees to make this a picturesque forest.

At the ½-mile mark, you see a body of water on your right through the woods, a pond filled with dead trees, the result of water backed up by a beaver dam. A quarter mile farther, the water that you see on your left is the low swampy southern end of Huckleberry Lake.

In less than ¼ mile, you climb onto a smooth rock bluff, and ahead of you is beautiful Huckleberry Lake, complete with several rounded glacier-scoured islands, where small shrubs and a few pine trees have been able to find a foothold.

The trail now runs on the bluff along the side of the lake. Brush-wide yellow stripes are painted on the rocks to keep you on course. A quarter mile brings you to a lean-to on a rock slab at the lake's edge.

In the next ¼ mile, the trail swings a little to the right and away from the lake until you are no longer able to see it. At another depression filled with water and dead trees on the right, the trail swings to the left, climbs a small hill, and descends to a log footbridge over the bog's narrow north end.

From here, it is ½ mile over even more smooth, rocky terrain to Moon Lake. You will see a lean-to as the trail circles the southern portion of the lake. A short distance uptrail from the lean-to, the Moon Lake Trail intersects on your right. This is the trail you'll take on your return.

The trail markers now change from yellow to blue. Continue in a northerly direction by following the blue markers. In a little less than ¼ mile, you come to another trail intersection. A sign here directs you to Wolf Lake toward the right and "Beaver Ponds Trail and Podunk" to the left. The Beaver Ponds Trail is 2¾ miles long and marked with red; at the 2-mile mark is a lean-to.

Continue northeast, though, on the backs of the smooth rocks and following the blue markers, for the next ¼ mile. On your right you see the water of Wolf Lake, and then the trail turns to the right and takes you a short distance to a lean-to on the lake's edge. This lake, like the other two, is rock-encircled and equally attractive.

From the lean-to, the Blue Trail runs 2⅜ miles north, ending at Pond Road. To complete your southern loop, however, retrace your steps to the Moon Lake Trail, and turn left. The markers you find here initially are blue, but a short distance downtrail yellow markers appear, which soon give way to red and then blue paint on trees, with the yellow markers reappearing near the end.

This trail is a bit more hilly and not quite as attractive as the Yellow Trail. At the ½-mile mark, you come to a narrow, V-shaped depression filled with water and dead trees. The trail weaves its way through rocks and boulders along the pond, and up ahead you see several beaver dams.

The log footbridge takes you over the outlet stream and then along the side of a long ridge, which, while not too high, nonetheless has steep sides. A little over ¼ mile brings you to still another fairly large beaver pond. The trail skirts the eastern edge and climbs higher up the hill. In little under ½ mile, you exit from the forest onto the dirt road over which you drove before. Turn right to follow the road west, past the open, fieldlike area, over the outlet stream, and back to your parked vehicle.

46

Frank E. Jadwin
Memorial Forest

Total distance: 11¼ miles (2 days)

Hiking time: 6 hours

Vertical rise: 520 feet

Maps: USGS 7½' Natural Bridge; USGS 7½' Remington Corners

Too much of a good thing, someone once remarked, is wonderful. While that may be true in the case of Frank E. Jadwin Memorial Forest, it is also something of a challenge. The challenge is to determine just what section of this large state forest to hike; it is hard to decide what options to take.

Jadwin is immense. At 19,964 acres, 10 miles wide and 14 miles long, it is one of the largest state forests in upstate New York. Yet it is easy to reach from either NY 3, which runs along its northern boundary, or NY 812, which runs south from NY 3 through the state forest's central portion.

While there is no designated hiking trail in Jadwin Forest, a network of dirt roads, truck trails, and jeep trails allows

the hiker to design a route of almost any length. These roads let you reach, explore, and—if you brought your angling gear—fish the upper portions of two rivers. Indian River runs along the western boundary. The West Branch of the Oswegatchie River runs through the entire length of the state forest, with several bridge crossings and fishing accesses.

In general, the state forest, like so much Western Adirondack land, is relatively flat and thickly forested. Creeks and rivers drain to the north and west. The terrain is characterized by low, irregular ridges and numerous depressions with swampy areas or water routes of the slow-moving creeks and rivers.

Geologically, Jadwin lies close to the boundary between the two sections of the Adirondacks, the highlands and the lowlands. This line runs through Natural Bridge, Harrisville, and Pierrepont, a short distance north of the state forest. The difference between the two regions is found in their rock formations. The highlands are underlain by metamorphosed igneous rock, while the lowlands are underlain by interlayered metamorphosed sedimentary and volcanic rock.

In this regard, Jadwin Forest is part of the highland region, while its close neighbor, Onjebonge State Forest (see

Indian River flowing along southern edge of Frank E. Jadwin Memorial Forest

Hike 47), less than a mile to the north, lies on the other side of the boundary in the lowland region. Topographically, of course, there is little difference between the two forests.

Jadwin's western portion between the Indian River and the West Branch of the Oswegatchie is flatter and lower (elevation 850 feet) than the eastern portion, where the terrain is irregular and higher, rising to 1200 feet.

To get a feel for the variety in this state forest, it is best to see it in two stages, hiking a section in the northwestern part and one in the southwestern part, so you should plan a weekend trip. Either section could serve as a 1-day hike, of course.

Access. The trailhead for the first day's hike can be reached from NY 3, which runs east from Watertown. From Natural Bridge, drive 1.2 miles until the road crosses a railroad track. On the other side, old NY 3 forks to the right. Take this fork, and drive 1.2 miles to the intersection with Henry Road. Turn right here, and follow Henry Road past Blanchard Pond to its intersection with Factory Road. Turn right onto Factory Road, and follow it for a mile, where a single-lane dirt truck trail, Aldrich Road, intersects on your left. Park here.

First Day
Factory Road to Indian River Flats
Distance: 7¼ miles
Hiking time: 4 hours

The road to Indian River Flats in the south runs on flat terrain with a vertical rise of less than 100 feet, a rise that is hardly noticeable during your hike. You are moving through a heavily forested area, and most of the time the road is shaded. The road heads in a southeasterly direction for the first 1⅜ miles, at which point another single-lane truck trail, Patchin Road, intersects on your left.

Continue south on Aldrich Road for another ¼ mile where you see a house on your left (marked by a sign reading "Whippoorwill Ridge") on a small triangular piece of private land whose point touches the road. Continuing for another ¼ mile, you see an abandoned building on your left, and ⅜ mile farther brings you to an intersection with another truck trail, Nelson Road.

Continue past Nelson Road. Aldrich Road swings more sharply southward and then turns southwesterly. In ⅜ mile, you reach a truck trail, Wahulula Road, that intersects on your left. At this point, Aldrich Road turns to the right, and a short distance beyond a narrow lane forks to the right.

Stay on Aldrich Road as it turns sharply to the south; ¾ mile brings you to the road's end at Indian River and an open, flat area called Indian Flats. Here you can take time to study the landscape while enjoying your lunch before retracing your steps to your vehicle.

Second Day
Jerden Falls Road via Truck Trail
back to Jerden Falls Road
Distance: 4 miles
Hiking time: 2 hours

To reach the trailhead for your second day, drive back to NY 3 via Henry Road. Where Henry Road intersects the old NY 3, turn right; in 0.4 mile you come to the present-day NY 3. Turn right onto NY 3, and drive 5.8 miles to NY 812, which intersects on your right. Turn here, and drive south on NY 812 for 7.8 miles,

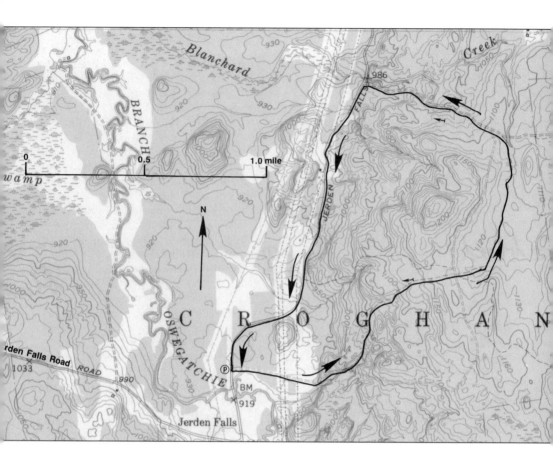

where Jerden Falls Road intersects on your left. Turn onto Jerden Falls Road, and follow it for 2 miles until it turns to the left and crosses the West Branch of the Oswegatchie River; 0.1 mile on the north side of the river, you see a single-lane truck trail that goes off to your right. Park here.

The truck trail makes a loop that will bring you back to your start. At the outset, the road is flat for the first ⅜ mile; en route you walk under power lines running in a north-south direction. Beyond the power lines, the terrain begins to slope upward. For the next mile you continue a steady, albeit gradual, uphill climb to an elevation of 1130 feet (200 feet vertical rise).

Before reaching a level area, you have a nice view to the west overlooking the West Branch of the Oswegatchie River. The land now levels out, and for the next ½ mile the road runs over flat terrain. At the 1¾-mile mark, the road touches the western edge of Blanchard Creek. Here the road turns westerly and starts a gradual descent. A downhill walk of ¾ mile brings you to Jerden Falls Road, where the west-flowing Blanchard Creek crosses under it. Turn left on Jerden Falls Road, and walk south on this dirt road back to your vehicle 1⅜ miles away.

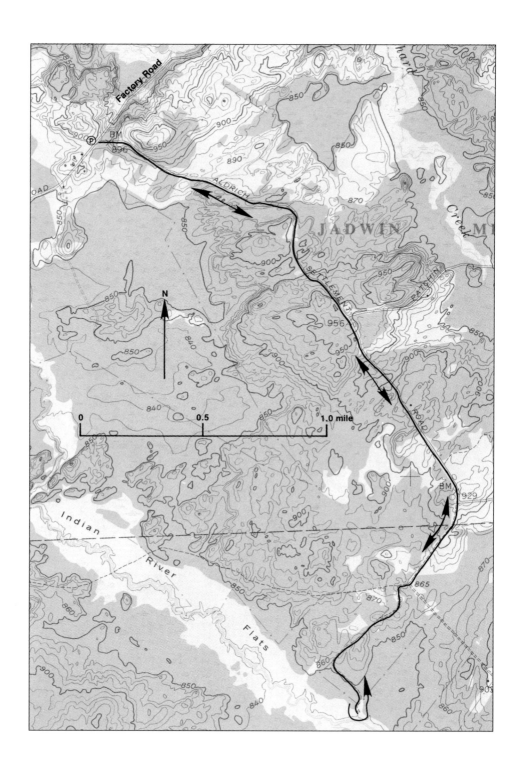

47

Onjebonge and Hogsback State Forests

Total distance: 8 miles

Hiking time: 4 hours

Vertical rise: 810 feet

Map: USGS 7½' Natural Bridge

Onjebonge State Forest and Hogsback State Forest, as close neighbors, are ideal for a day's trek in an area typical of the forested Western Adirondacks. Amateur geologists will find many rocks worth studying and minerals worth collecting nearby.

Both state forests are easy to reach via NY 3. Terrain in both is relatively flat for easy walking. Both have roads or trails running their entire length. The 624-acre Hogsback State Forest, 1 mile northeast of Onjebonge, is 4 miles east of Natural Bridge. Onjebonge lies a little over ½ mile north of Natural Bridge (so named because a branch of the Indian River disappears just north of the village, runs underground for about ⅛ mile, and then emerges to rejoin the river's main branch). Crossing the river at this point,

you are driving over a "natural bridge," one of the many geological phenomena you find in this region.

The western edge of the 1826-acre Onjebonge State Forest lies on the Lewis-Jefferson County line. This also is the abrupt geological boundary separating the Adirondack lowlands from the Adirondack highlands, which runs northeasterly through Natural Bridge, Harrisville, and Pierrepont. To the north and west of this line are found underlying rocks making up the lowland region; to the south and east are a different set of rocks that make up the highland region.

Specifically, the highlands are underlain by metamorphosed igneous intrusive rocks such as granite, charnockite, syenite, gabbre, and anorthosite. In contrast, the lowland Adirondacks are mainly underlain by interlayered metamorphosed sedimentary and volcanic rocks that are tightly and plastically folded.

All the features characterizing the Adirondack lowlands are found in Onjebonge. Over eons of time, erosion has produced a surface of low ridges of gneiss rock with intervening marshy low areas underlain by marble. All through the state forest, there are low outcrops,

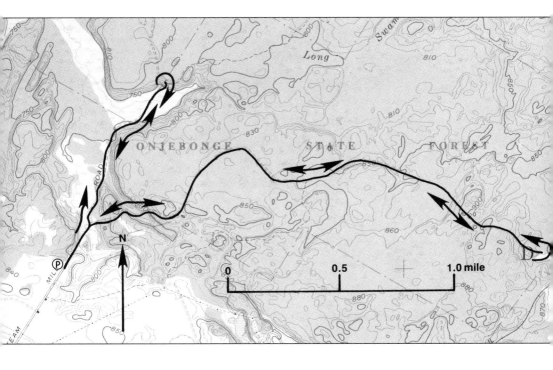

rounded and smoothed by the scouring action of advancing glaciers, four of which moved over New York during the Pleistocene epoch. Also found here are erratics, boulders from another region that were brought south with an advancing glacier and left behind when the glacier melted back.

Hogsback State Forest lies on the other side of the geological boundary in the highlands region. En route to it, you can stop to do some exploring for minerals at a famous old Dana collecting site, just off NY 3 when you drive east from Natural Bridge. (From the center of the village, drive 1.2 miles to where a dirt road intersects on your right. The collecting site consists of trenches about 75 yards into the field on the right side of the highway and the right side of the dirt road.) Mineralization has occurred here in marble-filled fissures in a syenitic gneiss. Crystals at this site are small but exceptionally well formed. You can find individual crystals or aggregates of all combinations of apatite, pyroxene, scapelite, titanite, wollastonite, and zircon.

The thickly forested terrain of the state forests is not well drained because of the underlying Precambrian rock. There are many swampy areas throughout Onjebonge; Long Swamp in the north is the largest. Hogsback differs a bit, containing instead two small ponds, Fitzgerald and Hogsback Ponds. Several small streams that eventually reach Indian River (which touches the western part of Onjebonge) rise in each state forest.

One road takes you through Hogsback State Forest. Onjebonge has a truck trail with a number of jeep trails radiating off it. All can be hiked and explored, but you'll need map and com-

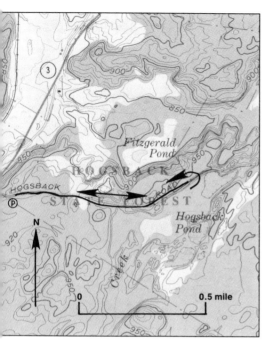

Trail. There are no marked hiking trails in Onjebonge State Forest. Truck trails and jeep trails make up a network of roads and lanes for hiking. The road system can take you well outside the forest and to such distant places as Indian Pond and Crooked Pond in the north.

Begin your hike on the main truck trail, Steam Mill Road. Head north for ¼ mile; here the road crosses a small stream, and just beyond you encounter a fork. Take the left leg of the fork first; this lane, a continuation of Steam Mill Road, is flat and shaded, making walking here easy and comfortably cool on a warm day. Continue north for ¾ mile, where you find a sizable wetland area flooded with water from the second tributary flowing into Indian River.

A short distance down the road, you encounter another fork. The right leg, which can easily be missed, leads northeast beyond the state forest to end at Crooked Pond 2¼ miles to the north. The main road, Steam Mill Road, forks to the left, and in over ¹⁄₁₀ mile leaves the state forest and heads north; 2¼ miles brings you to Indian Pond.

To stay within the state forest, make this fork your turnaround point and retrace your steps to the first fork. Here turn left (east); this unnamed dirt road runs an easterly course, taking you to the eastern boundary of the state forest.

As you head down the road, you pass a large outcrop of rock on your left. You'll see other such outcrops en route, with some just breaking the surface of the soil. At the ⅝-mile mark, a jeep trail intersects on your right. It runs south and just outside the state forest joins a road to a KOA camping area.

Continue on the road for another 1⅜ miles. Here another jeep trail intersects on your right; it runs southwest for a mile to the state forest boundary. Another ⅜ mile brings you to the road's end. Re-

pass to find and follow the unmarked Onjebonge trails, which together can add another 10 miles to your hike. One of these trails connects with a KOA campground a little over a mile south of the state forest.

Access. Onjebonge can be reached via NY 3, which runs east out of Watertown. From Watertown, it is about 24 miles to Natural Bridge, where in the center of the hamlet you encounter an intersection. Turn left (north) here. This road crosses the "natural bridge" and then a bridge over the east branch of Indian River. Once over the latter bridge, you immediately turn left onto River Road, and drive north for 0.4 mile where a dirt road, Steam Mill Road, intersects on your right. Turn here, and drive for 0.4 mile; this brings you into the state forest. Park here.

Hiker on large rock outcrop in Onjebonge State Forest

trace your steps 2⅝ miles to your vehicle.

To reach Hogsback State Forest, return to NY 3 at Natural Bridge. From Natural Bridge, drive east 4 miles, where a dirt road, Hogsback Road, intersects on your right. Turn here, and drive east for about 0.5 mile; this puts you just inside Hogsback State Forest. Park here, and start your hike by walking east on Hogsback Road.

In about ½ mile, you will see Hogsback Pond through the trees on your right; it lies below the level of the road. About ¼ mile to your left but hidden in the weeds is Fitzgerald Pond. While in Hogsback, you'll want to take some time to compare the rocks here to those in Onjebonge State Forest and to observe the difference in landscape, outcrops, and rock formations.

48

Independence River Forest Area

Total distance: 9¾ miles (2 days)

Hiking time: 6 hours

Vertical rise: 430 feet

Maps: USGS 7½' Crystal Dale; USGS 7½' Brantingham

Several elements make up the Independence River Forest Area. First, there is the Independence River State Forest, a small, 673-acre parcel of land just outside the state's forest preserve. Second, there is the huge land area within the forest preserve called the Independence River Wild Forest, which covers over 70,000 acres and includes more than 80 bodies of water. Flowing through the entire length of the wild forest and through the western part of the state forest is the Independence River, which the state has classified as a scenic river.

Happily for the hiker, lanes and dirt roads allow easy hiking from the small state forest to the much larger wild forest. (For the distinctions among "state forest," "wild forest," and "wilderness area," see the introduction.)

More importantly, hikers have at their disposal an extensive network of horse trails. These traverse not only the Independence River Forest Area, but also loop through Otter Creek State Forest (see Hike 50) and are all interconnected to form the 43-mile Otter Creek Horse Trail System. Color-coded as Red, Blue, and Yellow Trails, they make use of existing routes—old sandy roads, truck trails, jeep trails, and forest paths.

An Assembly Area with a trailhead parking site and roofed horse stalls is located just south of Chase Lake near an intersection of Chase Lake Road and a road called Blue Jog.

To obtain a map of the horse-trail system and general information about the state forests, contact the state's Department of Environmental Conservation office, RD 3, Box 22A, Lowville, NY 13367 (315-376-3521, weekdays 8:00 AM–4:45 PM).

In the Independence River forest region you have one foot in civilization and one foot in the wilderness, where only a thick forest, a few trails, and placid ponds are found. The infinite mosaic of lakes, streams, forests, and bogs makes a landscape of natural beauty with no equal anywhere in New York State.

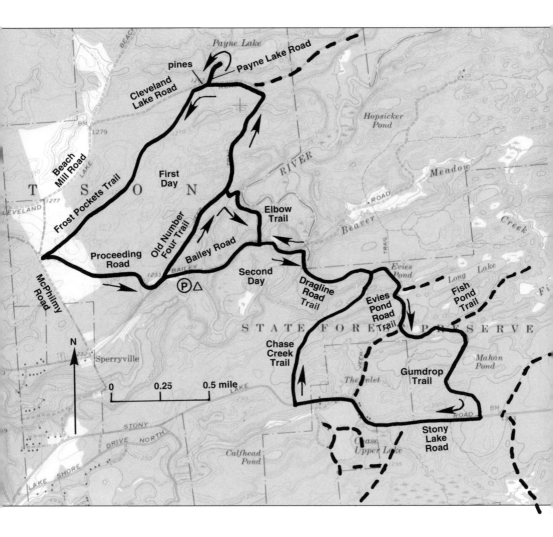

Exploring this attractive area, you walk through a lot of history, both natural and human-made. In the natural category, you'll find Precambrian bedrock that is the geological make-up of the Adirondack foothills, a landscape shaped and decorated by glaciation, and an environment of forests and wildlife that now is coming to resemble what it looked like before hunters, lumbermen, and farmers entered the area in the early 1800s. It is an area in transi-

tion as it slowly sheds its civilized past.

Geologically, this area includes eroded sedimentary rock and granitic igneous material that is generally associated with the Adirondack high peaks area. Topographically, the area is moderately high (elevation 1300 feet) and relatively flat and sandy—a gentle landscape in which evidence of glaciation is found everywhere in the form of worn-down hills, granite outcrops, a long narrow sand plain, a terrain covered with "erratics" (huge boulders left behind by the retreating glacier), and glacier-scoured low areas that make up today's swamps, bogs, and wetlands.

In the cultural category, the area has a colorful history of people who came to harvest trees, to build farms, or to be entertained as "sports" or tourists, who hunted, fished, and gave rise to summer communities such as those that still persist at Chase Lake and Brantingham Lake. These places once had larger hotels and fine cuisine for their visitors.

The area was lumbered and farmed throughout the 1800s, with the wood and grain shipped via the Black River Canal to such faraway places as New York City and Buffalo. The 85-mile-long Black River Canal with its amazing number of locks (109 locks for an average of almost two per mile) was completed in 1855 and operated continuously until closing in 1924. During its operation, it opened the North Country and thoroughly changed its forested landscape.

The most intensive logging operation in the Adirondacks to date was carried on here in the late 1800s. Once cleared of the trees, the land was heavily farmed, with evidence of farming still found here. Much of the abandoned farmland has failed to revert to woodland even after decades of nonuse.

As you hike through the western portion of the region, you find large open areas covered with spirea, a large genus of shrubs of the *Rosaceae* family, with showy white flowers. Such a setting stands in sharp contrast to the heavily wooded areas found in the region's more easterly sections.

To really appreciate this area, you should spend a weekend here. It is easy to find good camping sites along Independence River where you can camp without cost or a permit. You also can backpack to Payne Lake to camp, or try Chase Lake Resort and Trailer Park, a commercial camping area where you can swim, boat, and fish (for a small fee).

Access. To reach this area, take Number Four Road from the southeast end of Lowville, which is on NY 12 north of Utica and south of Watertown. Drive east on Number Four Road for 4.4 miles to a fork (Bushes Landing on the topo map). Bear to the right onto Pine Grove Road, and drive 0.8 mile to where Chase Lake Road intersects on your left.

Turn onto Chase Lake Road (a blacktop road), and drive 5 miles to a small summer community called Sperryville. From here you can either drive or walk 0.8 mile to a camping site off Bailey Road on the Independence River.

Trail. At times your hiking routes will follow a blue-marked horse trail that makes use of old roads, lanes, and jeep trails. Starting at Bailey Road, one section of this blue-marked route forms a loop in the north, allowing you to return to your starting point. The second section forms a loop in the southeast, making use of a series of connected blue-marked trails, a portion of Stony Lake Road, and a small, northern part of the red-marked Chase Creek Trail.

To allow enough time to explore both these loops, you had best plan for at least a 2-day outing; you might camp, perhaps, next to the Independence River just south of Bailey Road. There is only one motel in the area, located on Brantingham Road a short distance west of Brantingham Lake. Of course, there are numerous spots throughout the state land where you can pitch a tent without a permit and at no cost.

First Day
*Northern Loop, starting and ending
at Bailey Road
Distance: 3¾ miles
Hiking time: 2½ hours*

From your camping site next to the Independence River, walk north ⅛ mile to Bailey Road. Turn left and walk 100 feet or so to where a lane intersects on your right. This route is a blue-marked horse trail. On the topo map it is identified as a jeep trail and on the state's horse-trail map it is called Old Number Four Trail.

Take this trail and follow it north over a forested, rolling landscape. After a mile-long trek you will break out of the woods and enter a large open space with low-growing vegetation. This is a reminder that the area was once farmland, long since abandoned. A short distance farther brings you to a single-lane dirt road, Cleveland Lake Road.

The blue-marked horse trail turns right; you, however, turn left onto Cleveland Lake Road and head west for ¼ mile, until you see a lane intersecting on your left at a large stand of pine trees. Turn right here; a short walk north brings you to a typical Adirondack Pond, Payne Lake. Pause a while to enjoy the pond's beauty. When you are ready, retrace your steps to Cleveland Lake Road.

Turn right on the road. A short walk brings you to where the blue-marked horse trail crosses the road. On the state's horse map, this is called Frost Pockets Trail. The terrain ahead is fairly level and wooded. A mile brings you to where the forest gives way to open fields that once served as farmland.

An additional ⅛ mile takes you to an intersection of four dirt roads—Beach Mill Road, McPhilmy Road, Proceeding Road, and an unnamed spur road.

Turn left on Proceeding Road and head east. About half of this road passes through what was once farmland, while the last half runs through a forested area, eventually emerging on Bailey Road. Turn left on Bailey Road and walk back ⅛ mile to the road leading to your campsite.

Second Day
*Southern loop, starting and ending
on Bailey Road
Distance: 6 miles
Hiking time: 3½ hours*

As you did the day before, walk from your camping site to Bailey Road and then a short distance west to where you encounter a blue-marked horse trail. Turn right here and follow this trail (called Old Number Four Road on the state's horse-trail map) north for ½ mile to where another trail intersects on your right. This, too, is a blue-marked trail, called the Elbow Road Trail; after ⅛ mile it brings you to a scenic spot overlooking the Independence River, where the stream makes a sharp turn.

The blue-marked Elbow Road Trail continues south for ¼ mile where it ends after intersecting Bailey Road. The horse trail, however, continues by turning left (east) on Bailey Road; ¼ mile brings you to where the trail crosses Independence River and then turns south on what is now called the Dragline Road Trail (still with blue trail markers). In ¼ mile the trail curves eastward again; an additional ⅜ mile brings you to where it intersects a jeep trail and becomes Evies Pond Road Trail. Here, too, a red-marked horse trail intersects on your right; this will be the one you will use later, on your return trek.

In the next 1½ miles, the trail names

of the blue-marked route change several times, going from Evies Pond Road Trail to Fish Pond Trail to Gumdrop Trail, which intersects a dirt road called Stony Lake Road. Leave the horse trail and turn right (west) onto Stony Lake Road. Walk 1¼ miles, past a small pond called The Inlet on your right, and Chase Upper Lake on your left, to where a red-marked horse trail crosses the road. This is the Chase Creek Trail. Turn right onto this trail and follow it north for a mile to where it intersects the blue-marked horse trail you hiked earlier. Turn left and retrace your steps via the Dragline Road to Bailey Road. Turn left (west) on Bailey Road and hike ⅝ mile to the road leading to your campsite.

49

Gleasmans Falls

Total distance: 6 miles

Hiking time: 2 hours

Vertical rise: 510 feet

Maps: USGS 7½' Crystal Dale; USGS 15' Number Four

Gleasmans Falls is interesting to the hiker not so much for what it is but for where it is. The trail to Gleasmans Falls leads into the heart of the Independence River Wild Forest Area and through the quiet and solitude of a beautiful woods where the only evidence of civilization is the footpath that takes you there.

Gleasmans Falls is ideal for a day trip, for it is only 3 miles from the trailhead. The terrain is relatively flat, so walking is easy and you'll be able to reach the falls in an hour. Plan your hike to spend lunchtime at the falls, relaxing and enjoying the sights and sounds.

The falls is one of the more attractive sights along the Independence River, which has its source at several ponds 28 miles east, just south of the hamlet of Big Moose. At Gleasmans you find a series of waterfalls that drop a total of 60 feet, with the water then rushing through a flumelike gorge. Farther upstream, the river bottom is boulder-strewn as if the river were catch-gutter for some giant shooting marbles with a rival.

The contrast of the river's appearance with that of the surrounding forest is striking. The river here looks wild, rugged, primordial, even chaotic, and the noisy rush of water tumbling over the rocks adds to the river's wild independence. Indeed this character may have inspired the river's name. The forest, on the other hand, looks well ordered and gentle. There is a feeling of welcome about this woods with its well-spaced trees, fern-carpeted floor, and openness and brightness. There are no blowdowns or deadfalls to mar its appearance. Its appealing charm may be enhanced still more by a chance sight of a ruffed grouse hen and her chicks dusting themselves on the trail, or a deer eyeing you from a distance.

Put the woods and river together, and you have something that enlivens the senses and imprints the memory with scenes long to be remembered.

Access. The trailhead can be reached by Number Four highway, found on the

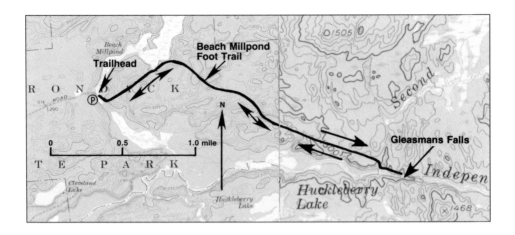

east edge of the village of Lowville. Lowville, in turn, can be reached via NY 12 from Utica in the south or Watertown in the north.

Once on Number Four highway, drive east for 4.4 miles to a fork (Bushes Landing on the topo map). Bear to the right onto what is now Pine Grove Road, and drive 0.8 mile, where Chase Lake Road intersects on your left.

Turn onto Chase Lake Road (a blacktop road), and drive 4 miles to the intersection with Erie Canal Road (0.25 mile back, Chase Lake Road switched its name to Brooklyn Square Road). Turn left, and drive north on Erie Canal Road (a blacktop road) for 0.6 mile where a single-lane dirt road (Cleveland Lake Road) intersects on your right. Turn here, and drive 1.2 miles to the second fork. Cleveland Lake Road follows the right leg. Take the left leg, Beach Mill Road, and follow it for 2.2 miles, where the road ends at a turnaround area where several cars can be parked. Park here.

Trail. The Beach Millpond Foot Trail runs in an easterly direction crossing three small streams en route to Gleasmans Falls. The trail is wide, well used, and easy to follow even without the trail markers, which are yellow disks nailed to trees. The trail is groomed and maintained by the state's Department of Environmental Conservation.

At the parking area, you can see Beach Millpond, once the site of a dam and sawmill, now only a beaver pond. The trail starts down a slight incline through an open area, swings a little to the right, crosses a wooden footbridge over Burnt Creek, and then enters a pine stand that is the beginning of the woods. A short distance uptrail, there is a place to register your name to indicate who is using the trail.

An 8-minute walk brings you to a spot where you can see on your left a vast open area through the trees. This is the Beach Millpond swamp and marsh area. A short distance farther, the trail bends to the right and moves more deeply into the forest.

The hiking here is most pleasant. This is a predominantly maple forest, with trees spaced so as to give you plenty of visibility deep into the woods in all directions. After hiking 1¼ miles, you come to another footbridge crossing Nickel Creek. Another 1½ miles over level ground bring you to a point where the trail begins a gradual downward pitch.

This descent is hardly noticeable, but you are heading southeast now toward Independence River. Soon you pass a large boulder on your left and then another sitting next to the trail. You turn a little to your right and start downhill, at which point you see and hear the river at the same time.

What you see, however, in the summer and autumn, is not the river but a boulder-strewn river bottom empty of water. Your first reaction is that the river has run dry. Actually, there is a small island here, where the water flows on the far side. Only during the spring runoff does the river rise high enough to pour water around both sides of the island.

At the foot of the hill, you come to a third footbridge, this time crossing Second Creek. The trail takes you a short distance through a pine stand, up a rise, and over some rocks, with the sound of the falls growing louder with each step. Suddenly you see the dark-colored water, so typical of the Adirondack area, rushing through boulders and tumbling over a rocky ledge into a large pool below. On the far side is the flat face of a huge boulder. At the end of the pool, the water picks up speed as it rushes downhill through a rock garden of boulders.

This is Gleasmans Falls. Stay a while and enjoy it. The yellow-marked trail, however, continues eastward along the Independence River. If you have the endurance and time, about 10 miles more of hiking would bring you to a wide, level area called Balsam Flats, one of the few still-water sections of the river, where the water is tame. The area around the river here is also one of the important deer wintering yards in the western Adirondacks.

50

Otter Creek State Forest

Total distance: 17⅛ miles (2 days)

Hiking time: 9 hours

Vertical rise: 386 feet

Maps: USGS 7½' Brantingham; State Horse Trail Map

Compared to the size of other state tracts in this region, Otter Creek State Forest is relatively small, only 1206 acres. Still, it returns a nice dividend for the time you invest hiking its lanes, truck trails, dirt roads, and horse trails.

For one thing, it gives you Otter Creek, a broad, scenic stream that runs the entire length of the state forest, tumbling over rock ledges to make a series of attractive falls. It's here that people come to swim, slide down smooth rock slabs, and engage in tube races over small falls.

For another, Otter Creek State Forest allows free camping at the river's edge. However, you must obtain a camping permit from the regional office of the Department of Environmental Conservation (DEC) in Lowville (315-376-3521).

For yet another, the state forest adjoins the western part of the Adirondack Park's Forest Preserve, so you can hike from one to the other. If you have the time and endurance, you can continue hiking eastward until you reach the high peaks area of the Adirondacks, 80 miles away.

Finally, you have horse trails—43 miles of trails that meander throughout Otter Creek State Forest and extend northward into Independence River Forest Area (see Hike 48). Collectively, this network of trails is called the Otter Creek Horse Trail System; it makes use of old sandy roads, truck trails, and forest paths. The horse trails are well used by equestrians and this produces trails that are easy to walk; since they are all color-coded with yellow, red, or blue trail markers, they are also easy to follow.

An Assembly Area for equestrian groups is found near the intersection of Chase Lake Road and a road called Blue Jog; it contains a trailhead parking area, 72 roofed tie stalls, a water system for humans and horses, and toilet facilities.

You may obtain a map of the Otter Creek Horse Trail System by writing or calling the state's Department of Environmental Conservation office, RD 3, Box 22A, Lowville, NY 13367 (315-376-3521, weekdays 8:00 AM–4:45 PM).

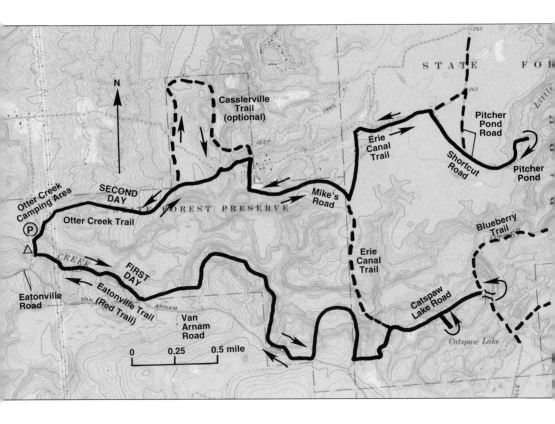

The state forest is on a sandy plain—flat terrain that is made most attractive by the dense population of graceful white pine interspersed with hardwood. This sand-plain, about 5 miles wide and 25 miles long, was produced during the last Pleistocene ice age. It was during the period of glacial retreat that the whole of the Black River Valley filled with water. As torrents of glacial waters flowed westward through Otter Creek and Independence River, they swept sand into the Black River Valley. When the flowing waters slowed, the sand was gently deposited to form today's long plain.

This plain is now deeply cleft by rivers and streams flowing out of the higher Adirondack foothills in the east. As they cut through the sand, the waterways encountered resistant rocks and boulders that today make up the riverbeds. The rounded boulders, many quite impressive in their size, were left behind by the retreating glacier.

This has produced the unusual and attractive features that characterize the state forest as well as its close neighbors in the north, Independence River State Forest and Independence River Wild Forest Area (see Hike 48). The land is flat, sandy, and gentle-looking, but the terrain is sprinkled with giant boulders, what geologists call "erratics," brought here during the glacial advance and left after its meltback. The rivers have a rugged, even wild appearance as they tumble over rock ledges and rush through boulder-strewn riverbeds.

Falls in Otter Creek State Forest

Access. The state forest can be reached from NY 12 several miles to its west in the Black River Valley. NY 12 runs from Utica through Boonville to Watertown. Fourteen miles north of Boonville, or ten miles south of Lowville, NY 12 is intersected on the east by Burdick Crossing Road. Turn onto this highway, and drive 1.6 miles to the intersection with the Pine Grove Road. Turn left here, and drive north for 2.4 miles through the hamlet of Greig to where a single-lane dirt road, Eatonville Road, intersects on your right. Turn here, and drive 1.2 miles to a fork. Take the left leg, and a short distance brings you to the camping area, where you can park.

Trail. The hiking routes found here are part of the Otter Creek Horse Trail System. There are two recommended routes in this portion of the state forest. One, hugging the forest's southern section, generally follows along the south side of Otter Creek in an eastward direction to Catspaw Lake. The other, farther north, also takes you eastward, to Pitcher Pond, but this time by several connected trails.

To allow you to take in both routes in a leisurely manner, it is recommended that you plan an overnight campout at the camping area on Otter Creek; this can serve as the starting point for each day's hike. Camping permits must be obtained from the state's Department of Environmental Conservation in Lowville.

First Day
From Otter Creek Camping Area to Catspaw Lake and back
Distance: 8⅝ miles
Hiking time: 4½ hours

From the camping area walk south for ⅛ mile on a single-lane sandy road to where you encounter a horse trail entering the woods on your right. Since it is flagged by red trail markers, we will call it the Red Trail; on the map provided by the state's Department of Environmental Conservation, it is called the Eatonville Trail. This trail actually runs on what once was a narrow, sandy jeep trail. (When trails run on old roads, they take on the names of these roads but are also identified by the color of their trail markers.)

The Eatonville or Red Trail takes you eastward through the forest and up a gradual rise. At ¼ mile you reach the top of the rise and pass beneath some power lines; the power-line right-of-way gives you a fine view to the north, overlooking Otter Creek. The trail now starts a gradual descent, taking you along the side of a small hill. On the north is Otter Creek; in the south is a forested, rolling landscape. From the ⅜-mile mark onward, the trail curves first eastward and then southward.

An additional ¾ mile brings you to the northern edge of a dirt road, Van Arnam Road. The trail follows the northern edge of Van Arnam Road for ¼ mile, where the trail turns gradually northward. The next ¾ mile takes you, first, north to where the trail curves to your right, and then south again until it intersects what was once a lane, Catspaw Lake Road.

This road continues northeastward for ⅜ mile, where the Erie Canal Trail intersects on your left. However, continue on Catspaw Lake Road for another ⅜ mile to where you encounter a path on your right; it takes you a short distance (⅛ mile) to the west shore of Catspaw Lake. This attractive, elongated lake is ¾ mile long, and from your vantage point you have a fine view of it.

Return to Catspaw Lake Road and continue walking eastward for ¼ mile to where you reach the northern edge of Catspaw Lake. A bridge takes you over an inlet stream. From here you have a scenic view of the upper part of the lake.

This is also your turnaround spot. It can serve as a rest area; you might pause for a lunch break. When you are ready, retrace your steps over the route you came until you reach your camping site.

Second Day
From Otter Creek Camping Area to Pitcher Pond and back
Distance: 8½ miles
Hiking time: 4–5 hours

After leaving the camping area, walk north on the dirt road. This is the route of the red-marked horse trail as it heads north over Otter Creek. Once over the creek, the horse trail, called the Otter Creek Trail, bears to the right. At first it heads north for ⅛ mile, where it passes beneath some power lines and then swings eastward through Otter Creek State Forest.

From the power lines it is ¾ mile to an intersection. The red-marked trail turns sharply left and heads north to eventually form a 1½-mile loop called the Casslerville Trail. You, however, continue straight ahead on a horse trail with yellow trail markings. This trail runs eastward for ½ mile, where it intersects the red-marked Casslerville Trail, completing its loop. The red-marked trail now turns eastward to follow a lane called Mike's Road.

Mike's Road, in turn, hugs the northern boundary of the state forest for ⅝ mile, where it intersects the north-south Erie Canal Trail. Turn left (north) onto this yellow-marked trail and follow it north for ⅜ mile to where you come to a junction with an east-west trail; the route running east is called Shortcut Road and contains blue trail markers.

Take this trail and follow it over level terrain for ⅜ mile to where you encounter a fork; take the right leg, which is the continuation of Shortcut Road. Continue on Shortcut Road for ¼ mile to where the red-marked Pitcher Pond Road intersects on your left. Shortcut Road ends here and Pitcher Pond Road continues eastward; follow this route for an additional ½ mile to where you reach the western shore of Pitcher Pond. The road partially circles the pond before ending. This is your turnaround spot.

When you are ready, start your return trek. In a little over 2 hours you will be back at your camping site in the Otter Creek Camping Area.

Let Backcountry Guides Take You There

Our experienced backcountry authors will lead you to the finest trails, parks, and back roads in the following areas:

50 Hikes Series

50 Hikes in the Adirondacks
50 Hikes in Connecticut
50 Hikes in the Maine Mountains
50 Hikes in Coastal and Southern Maine
50 Hikes in Maryland
50 Hikes in Massachusetts
50 Hikes in Michigan
50 Hikes in the White Mountains
50 More Hikes in New Hampshire
50 Hikes in New Jersey
50 Hikes in the Hudson Valley
50 Hikes in Western New York
50 Hikes in the Mountains of North Carolina
50 Hikes in Ohio
50 Hikes in Eastern Pennsylvania
50 Hikes in Central Pennsylvania
50 Hikes in Western Pennsylvania
50 Hikes in the Tennessee Mountains
50 Hikes in Vermont
50 Hikes in Northern Virginia

Walks and Rambles Series

Walks and Rambles on Cape Cod and the Islands
Walks and Rambles on the Delmarva Peninsula
Walks and Rambles in the Western Hudson Valley
Walks and Rambles on Long Island
Walks and Rambles in Ohio's Western Reserve
Walks and Rambles in Rhode Island
Walks and Rambles in and around St. Louis

25 Bicycle Tours Series

25 Bicycle Tours in the Adirondacks
25 Bicycle Tours on Delmarva
25 Bicycle Tours in Coastal Georgia and the Carolina Low Country
25 Bicycle Tours in Maine
25 Bicycle Tours in Maryland
25 Bicycle Tours in the Twin Cities and Southeastern Minnesota
30 Bicycle Tours in New Jersey
30 Bicycle Tours in the Finger Lakes Region
25 Bicycle Tours in the Hudson Valley
25 Bicycle Tours in Ohio's Western Reserve
25 Bicycle Tours in the Texas Hill Country and West Texas
25 Bicycle Tours in Vermont
25 Bicycle Tours in and around Washington, D.C.
30 Bicycle Tours in Wisconsin
25 Mountain Bike Tours in the Adirondacks
25 Mountain Bike Tours in the Hudson Valley
25 Mountain Bike Tours in Massachusetts
25 Mountain Bike Tours in New Jersey
Backroad Bicycling on Cape Cod, Martha's Vineyard, and Nantucket
Backroad Bicycling in Eastern Pennsylvania
Backroad Bicycling in Connecticut

Bicycling America's National Parks Series

Bicycling America's National Parks: Arizona & New Mexico
Bicycling America's National Parks: California
Bicycling America's National Parks: Oregon & Washington
Bicycling America's National Parks: Utah & Colorado

We offer many more books on hiking, fly-fishing, travel, nature, and other subjects. Our books are available at bookstores and outdoor stores everywhere. For more information or a free catalog, please call 1-800-245-4151 or write to us at The Countryman Press, P.O. Box 748, Woodstock, Vermont 05091. You can find us on the Internet at www.countrymanpress.com.